P9-DGV-497

# The Kurdish Question in Iraq

*Contemporary Issues in the Middle East*

# the KUROish QUESTiON iN iRAQ

## EDMUND GHAREEB

WITHDRAWN

SYRACUSE UNIVERSITY PRESS    1981

Copyright © 1981 by Syracuse University Press
Syracuse, New York 13210

*First Edition*

**Library of Congress Cataloging in Publication Data**

Ghareeb, Edmund.
   The Kurdish question in Iraq.

   (Contemporary issues in the Middle East)
   Includes bibliographical references and index.
   1. Kurds — Iraq — Politics and government.
2. Iraq — Politics and government. I. Title.
II. Series.
DS70.8.K8G48     956.7'0049159     81-8897
ISBN 0-8156-0164-6            AACR2

*Manufactured in the United States of America*

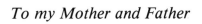

*To my Mother and Father*

Dr. Edmund Ghareeb is a specialist and consultant on Middle Eastern and press affairs. His works include *The Kurdish Nationalist Movement* and *Split Vision: Arab Portrayal in the American Media.* He has contributed numerous articles on Arab affairs to American, European and Middle Eastern journals.

# CONTENTS

# PREFACE

This work first briefly examines the history of the Kurdish question in Turkey and Iran, then concentrates on the Kurdish question in Iraq—specifically, the Iraqi Baath government's attempts since 1968 to achieve a political understanding with the Kurds concerning their status in northern Iraq. The inability to establish and implement an effective political forum acceptable to both sides contributed to a widespread Kurdish armed rebellion, encouraged by covert Iranian, American, and Israeli assistance. The rebellion faltered as conventional Iraqi military units dislodged the Kurdish irregulars and forced their retreat to peripheral border regions in Iraq's rugged mountains. When the Iraqi government consolidated its internal position and attracted significant Kurdish support, the revolt collapsed altogether.

The leaders of Iraq, some holding high positions in the ruling Arab Baath Socialist party, have tried a variety of plans to accommodate the Kurds. These leaders believed that the territorial integrity of the country should be maintained and that the primary decision-making powers should remain in Baghdad. They were willing, however, to grant the Kurds limited powers of self-rule and cultural expression.

Attempts to reconcile the Kurdish leadership with the central government foundered on a number of differences, exacerbated by unrest and armed clashes that neither side was able to control during the repeated efforts at negotiation. The underlying conflict was between a central government anxious to solidify its authority and to preserve Iraq's territorial integrity and an entrenched Kurdish leadership whose desire for self-expression was exploited by foreign interests, which sought to promote the instability—if not the destruction—of the Baath regime in Baghdad. As Iraq's forces gained the upper hand over the Kurds, these foreign powers, notably Iran and the United States, began to recognize that the Iraqi war with the Kurds also threatened their own economic interests in the oil-rich Middle East, and not just the Baath government alone.

The demise of the Kurdish revolt and the granting of limited autonomy to the Kurds in Iraq can be viewed as a victory for the Baath government and a step toward intraregional accommodation and stability. It is also an indication of Iraq's growing strength, of the country's consolidation of power, and of the need for foreign powers to refrain from exploiting minority problems for their own interests.

The principal sources for this study include, in addition to documents and statements issued by both sides, the author's interviews with pro- and anti-Iraqi government Kurdish leaders, Iraqi government and Baath party leaders, Iraqi Communist leaders, United States government officials, and other informed figures. The study also draws on numerous Arab and Western newspaper and magazine articles as well as on secondary works dealing with this subject.

Finally, I would like to express my sincere appreciation to all my friends and colleagues, too numerous to mention by name, for all their suggestions, comments, and help in arranging some of the interviews cited in this work. Through their help and encouragement they made the realization of this project possible.

# THE KURDISH QUESTION
# IN IRAQ

TURKEY

Zakho
Duhok
Rawanduz
Rania
Arbil
Koisanjaq
Mosul
Kirkuk
Sulaimaniyya
Halabja
Qasr – i – Shirin
Baiji
Khanaqin

SYRIA

Haditha

BAGHDAD

IRAQ

IRAN

Tigris

JORDAN

Euphrates

SAUDI ARABIA

KUWAIT

# 1

# ORIGINS OF THE
# KURDISH QUESTION IN IRAQ

Iraq was occupied by the Ottoman Turks in the sixteenth century. For almost four centuries it served as a buffer zone between the Ottoman and Persian empires. Persian and Turkish armies fought over the land, while the people of Iraq tried to rid themselves of foreign invaders. The violence and instability of those years destroyed much of Iraq's commerce and industry and contributed in no small measure to the deterioration of the country's political system, which still suffers from the after-effects to the present day.

When Iraq achieved its independence in 1932, it inherited the legacy of the Ottoman regime as well as problems resulting from the rise of nationalist sentiment among Arabs and Kurds, internal dissension, social and economic unrest, and foreign pressures and interventions. The British tried to form a state, which necessarily included many ethnic groups and religious minorities, each with competing demands and expectations from the new country. In a memorandum submitted to his government in the early 1930s, Faisal, the first king of Iraq, summed up Iraq's major problems as follows:

> This government rules over a Kurdish group most of which is ignorant and which includes persons with personal ambitions who call upon this group to abandon the government because it is not of their race. [It also] rules a Shia plurality which belongs to the same ethnic group as the government. But as a result of the discriminations which the Shiis incurred under Ottoman rule which did not allow them to participate in the affairs of government, a wide breach developed between these two sects. Unfortunately, all of this has led the Shiis . . . to abandon a government which they consider to be very bad. . . .
>
> I discussed these great masses of the people without mentioning the

other minorities, including Christian, which were encouraged to demand different rights. There are also other huge blocks of tribes . . . who want to reject everything related to the government because of their interests and the ambitions of their shaikhs, whose powers recede if a government exists. . . .

I say with my heart full of sadness that there is not yet in Iraq an Iraqi people.[1]

The intellectual, tribal, ethnic, and sectarian differences referred to in King Faisal's memorandum reflect the complexity of the problems that have confronted the Iraqi state since its inception in 1921. Most Iraqis seem to have been in favor of a modern national state, since the conclusion of the debate over the creation of a traditional Islamic state. Some advocated a Pan-Arab nationalist regime united with other Arab countries. They argued that the structure of the Iraqi state was an artificial creation by the colonial powers to serve their own interests, and that the only natural structure would be a larger, unified Arab state. Others favored the perpetuation of an independent Iraqi state for fear that a change in Iraq's structure might lead to internal conflict and possibly to secession and territorial rearrangements. Advocates of this view were concerned about potential Shia and Kurdish opposition to Arab unity. The Shia majority, which had suffered discrimination under Ottoman Sunni control, were concerned they might become a minority again in a larger Sunni Arab state.

The Kurds were even more outspoken in their support for a separate Iraqi state, and made it clear that any attempt to unite Iraq with other Arab states "must necessarily lead to the creation of a separate Kurdish entity, either within or outside the Arab superstructure."[2]

The inability of the Iraqi government to create a new national identity with which the majority of Iraqi Arabs and Kurds could identify contributed greatly to the emergence of the Kurdish problem, which became exceedingly difficult to resolve. The Arab Shiis were concerned that the Kurds, the majority of whom are Sunni, would merge with the Sunni Arabs. The rise of Arab nationalism following World War I encouraged the Sunni Arabs to seek a wider Arab union. The failure to create a new Iraqi identity, the emphasis on Arab nationalist positions by the government following World War I, the imposition of restrictions on Kurdish political activities, and external influences as well—all contributed to the growth of Kurdish nationalist activity among Iraq's Kurds. The Kurdish question remained the most serious problem confronting the Iraqi government until the return of the Baath party to power and its attempt to create a new framework with which all Iraqis could identify.

The Baath party recognized the need to resolve the question of ethnic and religious minorities. These minorities form a substantial percentage of the population, not only in Iraq but also in Syria, and they have legitimate aspirations and demands that must be taken seriously. The secular nationalism advocated by the Baath party offers an alternative to the sectarian and religious differences that hurt Arab interests. The question of ethnic minorities presented a real challenge to the Baath leaders. Because of their preoccupation with Arab issues, they did not begin to formulate a coherent approach to the problem of ethnic minorities until after the fall of the Iraqi Baath government in 1963. The return of the Baath leaders to power in 1968 gave them an opportunity to reconsider the question and to make an effort to resolve it under the March 1970 Manifesto. Through this manifesto the Baath leadership sought to deal with the question as a whole, within the framework of the Baath ideology, by recognizing the national and cultural rights of the Kurds within Iraqi unity and securing their participation in the country's social, economic, and political institutions.

## THE KURDS BEFORE WORLD WAR I

The Kurds are spread in varying concentrations throughout a crescent-shaped region in the Middle East that comprises a large part of the mountainous region between the Black Sea and the steppes of Iraq on one side, and the Anti-Taurus Mountains and the Iranian plateau on the other. Kurdistan may be defined as that area where a homogeneous group of Kurds predominates; so defined, Kurdistan is currently divided among Turkey, Iraq, and Iran.[3]

There are also Kurds in Syria, Lebanon, the Soviet Union, and Afghanistan, mingled with other small ethnic groups (such as the Assyrians, Armenians, Turkomans, Chaldeans, and Arabs) who are scattered throughout the Kurdish areas. In Iraq the Kurds inhabit an area to the north of the Hamrin Mountains.

The Kurdish language belongs to the Iranian group of the Indo-European language family. Figures on the number of Kurds vary from one source to another, since there are no accurate figures, especially in the countries where Kurds are not recognized as a separate ethnic group. Some claim that the Kurds number fewer than 7 million people, while others believe that their numbers exceed 12 million.[4]

The Kurdish historian Muhammad Amin Zaki estimated the number of Kurds in the 1930s to be scarcely 4.5 million, some 600,000 of whom were living in Iraq. In 1970, Abd al-Rahman Qasimlu estimated the number at 4.6 million in Turkey; 3.3 million in Iran; 400,000 in Iraq; 400,000 in Syria; 200,000 in Afghanistan; and 100,000 in the USSR, making a total of 10 million. The Kurdish nationalist leader Jalal Talibani upgraded Qasimlu's figures to a total of 14 million. He estimated that there were about 2 million Kurds in Iraq and about 6 million in Turkey. He also held that Qasimlu did not consider the Lurs of Iran to be Kurds and did not take into account the Kurds of the Caucasus and Lebanon; Talibani also adjusted the figures to reflect the population increases that have taken place since Qasimlu published his book.[5]

From antiquity, the inhabitants of this area have been portrayed as tough, proud, and resistant to foreign rule. To this day the Kurds remain separate and distinct from the people of the countries they inhabit. Several factors contribute to the Kurds' isolation: the mountainous terrain that formed a geographic and cultural barrier between them and their neighbors; their ferocity in defending their own territory; and their largely self-sufficient economy, which reduces their dependence on outsiders. The fact that most Kurdish areas are remote and inaccessible has fostered the independence of even the small villages. The scarcity of arable land and pastoral range lands increases the struggle for water and pasture. The isolation of the villagers in their tribe-oriented and class-ridden society has remained very strong, despite modern influences.

The Kurds today live in a variety of settings as urban dwellers, rural villagers, peasants, and nomadic and seminomadic tribesmen, but the vast majority continue to live in small villages. The number of nomads and seminomads has steadily decreased, although that way of life still exists. Small working-class and middle-class groups have begun to emerge in the cities, but in most rural areas the basic form of social and political organization is still based on descent, clans, and ownership of land. In the villages the leadership is divided between the *mir* or *beg,* who leads the tribe (or the *agha* who leads one of the clans that form a tribe), and the shaikhs or mullas, who are the religious leaders.[6] The peasants are roughly divided into two groups. Those who are traditionally related to the tribal leaders enjoy greater status and a higher standard of living and tend to follow their leaders into rebellions or local wars more quickly than do the lower-class peasants, those without kinship ties to the tribal leaders. The peasants are downtrodden and rarely take part willingly in rebellions against the regime, because they regard their Kurdish landlords, not the central authorities, as the real power controlling their day-to-day lives.

The Kurds have never formed an independent political entity; throughout their history they have been ruled by outsiders, including the Armenians, the Persians, the Byzantines, and later the Turks and Arabs. From the sixteenth century the Kurds were divided between the Ottoman and the Persian empires. The Ottomans were able to attract the Kurds to their side since most of the Kurds were Sunnis, while the Persians were Shias. In return the Kurds were able to preserve a degree of autonomy under their tribal chiefs. Kurdistan was at the center of the sharp struggle between the two empires.

The situation was further complicated in the nineteenth century by British and Russian designs to extend their influence into the area.[7] A number of Kurdish uprisings against both the Turks and the Persians were put down harshly, and the Ottomans destroyed the autonomous principalities and imposed direct rule. In the revolt of 1880–81, led by Shaikh Ubaidullah al-Nahri, the Kurds were declared to be a nation separate from the Ottomans and the Persians.[8]

The spread of nationalism among the Kurds before World War I stems from many factors: the placing of the Kurds under direct Ottoman rule in the nineteenth century and the reaction of feudal forces to the central authority, the social and economic development that promoted a sense of ethnic identity, the emergence of closer ties among the Kurdish areas as a result of their coming under one central administration, the emergence of nationalist movements among other subject nations of the Ottomans (Arabs, Armenians, Bulgars, Albanians, and Greeks) and the influence of Turkish, Russian, and Iranian reformers seeking constitutional regimes.[9]

At first, the Kurdish nationalists tried to cooperate with Turkish reformers and Persian constitutionalists in the hope of gaining some form of self-rule for Kurdistan. In 1908 a group of Ottoman Kurdish tribal leaders, officers, intellectuals, and students formed a society called *Al-Taali wa al-Taraqi* and published a newspaper entitled *Kurdistan*. Other Kurds founded a number of magazines and schools, but the war gave the government an excuse to shut these down. Furthermore, the Young Turks were not sympathetic to the nationalistic aspirations of ethnic groups within the Turkish empire and pursued a repressive policy toward them. As a result, the Kurds moved their operations outside Turkey. After World War I, the Kurdish leaders tried to have the Kurdish people placed under direct British supervision. Later they demanded full independence.[11]

## THE POSTWAR SETTLEMENTS

The second stage of Kurdish nationalism was influenced by the overthrow of the Russian, Austro-Hungarian, and Ottoman empires and the concurrent spread of revolutionary ideas. No less influential was the rise of nationalism among Arabs and Armenians and the power vacuum created by the collapse of the Ottoman Empire. This stage began in 1918, when the Kurdish Committees were formed in Cairo and Istanbul. Meanwhile, the Allies were considering the establishment of an independent Armenian state; the Kurds felt that if such a state were established it would be at their expense. To avoid conflict, the Kurds cooperated with the Armenians and presented a joint memorandum to the Peace Conference at Paris in 1919 in which they outlined their demands.[12]

The Kurds and the Armenians were rewarded when the Allies, in the Treaty of Sèvres recognized in Articles 62, 63, and 64 the rights of both people to form independent states. Article 62, perhaps the most important part of the treaty for the Kurds, states:

> A commission existing at Constantinople and composed of three members appointed by the British, French, and Italian governments respectively, shall draft within six months from the coming to force of the present Treaty a scheme of local autonomy for the predominately Kurdish areas lying east of the Euphrates, south of the southern boundary of Armenia as it may be hereafter determined, and north of the frontier of Turkey with Syria and Mesopotamia.[13]

Articles 63 and 64 made it incumbent on the Turkish government to execute and accept the decisions of the commission. If the majority of the population in the Kurdish area indicated a desire for independence and if the Council of the League of Nations deemed the Kurds capable of such independence, Turkey was obligated to agree to execute a recommendation for autonomy and renounce all rights and title over the area. The treaty further stipulated that if Turkey were to give up this area, the Allies would not be opposed to a voluntary union between the Kurdish state and that part of the Mosul region where the Kurds formed a majority. But the emergence of Mustafa Kemal Ataturk and the defeat of the Greeks led to the signing of the Lausanne Treaty in 1923, which put an end to Kurdish aspirations.

The Sèvres-Lausanne period presents what might be called a tragic incident in the Kurdish struggle. The recurring and unfulfilled promises led many Kurds to feel — as they have many times since — that they were expendable tools in the hands of the great powers. Moreover, after Sèvres, the creation of new national boundaries, which distributed the Kurds among several countries — Turkey, Iran, and Iraq — further complicated Kurdish plans.

## THE KURDISH QUESTION IN TURKEY

Before we discuss the Kurdish question in Iraq under the Baath, it is necessary to deal briefly with the position of the Kurds in Turkey and Iran. Turkey's official position was one of warmth in 1919, for in the name of Muslim brotherhood Turks and Kurds fought a war against the Armenian Republic and the Greeks. Afterward, when the Kemalists adopted a policy of Turkification and assimilation, their relations with the Kurds began to deteriorate. The use of the Kurdish language was forbidden, because the Turkish government considered the Kurds to be mountain Turks.

A revolt broke out in Turkey in 1925, led by Shaikh Said of Piran, who sought the formation of "an independent Kurdistan under the protection of the Sultan Caliph." This revolt was crushed without much difficulty.[14] Another revolt took place in 1930, which ended with the Turkish government's deportation of the Kurdish population in certain zones to the Western provinces for "health, material, cultural, political, strategic, and disciplinary reasons."[15] This action struck at the heart of the Kurdish movement, for it separated many Kurds in Turkey from the Kurds in Iraq.

Another revolt, this under Sayyid Reza, began in 1937 against the government's proclamation of martial law, but it was put down quickly and the leaders were executed. In the meantime, the Turkish, Iraqi, Iranian, and Afghan governments signed the Pact of Saad Abad to safeguard each other's national boundaries. Cooperation with their neighbors demonstrated that the Turks despaired of solving the Kurdish problem alone.[16] After Ataturk's death, the Turkish government relaxed its policy toward the Kurds only slightly, maintaining that the Kurds and the Turks were racial brothers and arresting anyone suspected of Kurdish nationalist views.

Kurdish nationalist activities in Turkey were almost nonexistent for the following three decades. During the late 1950s, however, particularly after Iraqi Kurdish nationalist Mulla Mustafa al-Barzani's return from the USSR and his subsequent conflict with the Qasim government, in Iraq some Kurdish activity began to surface. A small number of Kurdish intellectuals in Istanbul and Ankara began to organize cultural associations, and Kurdish tribes near the Iraqi border were reported to have given limited aid to Barzani by smuggling some arms and material to his forces. The government reacted with the arrest and imprisonment of fifty Kurdish intellectuals, who were accused of separatist activities. These figures were released following the 1960 military coup d'etat, when a slightly freer atmosphere prevailed, and the Kurds were allowed to engage in publishing and folklore activities.

During the late 1960s and the 1970s, however, the government's policy toward the Kurds was characterized by a crackdown on cultural and political activities. The bilingual Kurdish-Turkish journals and publications that had appeared during the mid-1960s were prohibited by decree of the Demirel government in January 1967, and their editors and authors, notably Moussa Anter and Mehmet Amine Bozarslan, were arrested. In June 1967 an article entitled "The Cries of the Red Kurds" appeared in the journal *Otuken,* urging the Kurds that "if they want to create a state of their own and continue their publications, let them go elsewhere! . . . Let them go where they want, to Iran, to Pakistan, to India, to Barzani! Let them ask the United Nations to find them a homeland in Africa."[17] In reaction, Kurdish student groups called for a mass demonstration, which took place August 3, 1967. More than 10,000 people turned out in Silvan, and over 25,000 in Diarbakr—the first time the Kurds of Turkey had dared publicly show their anger toward the authorities in thirty years. More oppression followed.

During 1970, the Demirel government began a series of "commando operations" against the Kurds in the cities of Silvan, Bengal, Batman, and Tatvan, using special troops and police to ransack homes and abuse the inhabitants. The government also continued its arrest of leading intellectuals and detention of political leaders.

The Turkish Kurds carried out their political activities through three organizations. The Democratic party of Turkish Kurdistan regrouped certain intellectuals, craftsmen, and others, and had a purely nationalistic focus. The Communist party, or Turkish Workers' party, attracted many left-wing Kurds despite its initial refusal to recognize the issue of Kurdish rights. In this climate, the Kurdish members formed their own organizations within the party known as Revolutionary Cultural Centers of the East, or DDKO, which eventually split from the party completely to become a new center of leftist political activity.

At its Fourth Congress in October 1970, the Turkish Workers' party officially changed its stand on the Kurdish question, becoming the first legal party to recognize the Kurds' struggle within the context of its own

ideology and goals. Although it did not go so far as to mention the Kurds'
right to self-government, the party's manifesto did publicize the government's treatment of the Kurds, stating that "the fascist regime of the ruling classes has followed, with respect to the Kurdish people, a policy of
oppression, terror, and assimilation, which has often been carried out in
the form of bloody operations."[18]

In the spring of 1971, the Turkish government declared martial law in
eleven eastern provinces, claiming the threat of a Kurdish uprising in Turkey, supported by Mulla Mustafa al-Barzani, who had reached agreement
with the Iraqi government on autonomy status for Iraqi Kurds a year
earlier. While it may be true that the government feared the possibility of
an uprising in the eastern provinces, the fact remained that the rise of a
strong leftist student movement in Turkey, the wave of guerrilla acts by
the Turkish People's Liberation Army (TPLA) and the clashes between
rightist and leftist students contributed to the fall of the Demirel government. The TPLA was reported to have been influenced by the Dev Genc,
the Revolutionary Youth Federation, which was seeking to transform
Turkey from a pro-American capitalist society to a socialist one. Dev
Genc's leadership included Kurdish members who favored granting a limited autonomy for the Kurds in socialist Turkey.[19]

Following the Iranian Revolution and the rebellion in the Kurdish
areas of Iran, Turkish Kurds began to increase their demands for recognition of their ethnic and cultural heritage. Some groups, such as the KDP,
which operates underground, and the Democratic Revolutionary Movement also stepped up their activity. These groups are nationalistic in the
sense that they are seeking an independent Kurdistan transformed along
radical and Marxist lines.[20]

The Turkish Communist party (TCP) also continued to be active
among Turkish Kurds, expressing its line in statements over its clandestine
radio station, VOTCP: "in the defense of the constitutional and democratic right of the Kurdish people and against the policy of assimilation
and mass massacre directed against the Kurds." The TCP, however, continued to attack the KDP for its "Kurdish bourgeois nationalism," and
"its appeals for the separation of Turkish Kurdistan." It also accused the
KDP of cooperating with the Barzani faction of the Iraqi KDP, which it
charged had become "a tool of imperialism and anti-Sovietism in the region." In another broadcast, VOTCP defended the actions of the supporters of Jalal Talibani, the Iraqi Kurdish leader, in their clashes with the
pro-Barzani Kurdish forces in the Hakkari mountains in the spring of
1978, when Talibani's forces were defeated.[21]

In the summer and fall of 1979 there were reports that Kurdish areas had been seized by armed Kurdish fighters (Pesh Merga) and declared "liberated zones". President Fahri Kotuturk warned that no separatist tendencies would be tolerated and that "there is no room for liberated regions and activities aimed at language, racial, class, or sectarian differences in our homeland. The government will defeat the disease and some heads will be crushed." In September 1979 the Turkish newspaper *Hurriyet* reported that 5000 Kurdish Turks had been recruited to fight alongside Iranian Kurds. The report was denied by the government, but the minister of the interior and the army's chief of staff toured the eastern area and promised a closer watch over the frontier across in the wake of interception by the army on August 29 of a convoy of arms believed to have been destined for Iran near the town of Dogu Bayazit.[22]

The prime minister's office had issued a statement in August 1979 denying cooperation with the Iranian government against the Kurds. The TCP charged that even the wording of the denial, which merely referred to an "ethnic minority," continued to show the government's "chauvinistic and erroneous" stand on the Kurdish question by avoiding the use of the words Kurds and Kurdish people.[23]

On January 2, 1980, the Turkish armed forces issued a warning to Turkish politicians to end their bickering and reach a consensus on measures to combat guerrilla activity and economic chaos. In a clear reference to the Kurdish political and military activity, the armed forces statement charged the political parties with having "failed to prevent anarchy and secessionism from [reaching] proportions threatening the country's integrity."[24] In the winter and spring of 1980, the government intensified its campaign. In June 1980, a government delegation visited the Eastern provinces and reported progress in the struggle against "illegal organizations" accused of causing people to flee from the region.[25] This term refers to some ten to fifteen Kurdish groups operating in the region.

The increasing boldness of Kurdish groups in Turkey has been influenced by the apparent inability of the government to put an end to the leftist-rightist violence plaguing the country or to find a solution to Turkey's serious economic and political problems. The unwillingness of the Turkish government to recognize even the existence of the Kurds as a people has also contributed to Kurdish unrest in Turkey, for they can see progress being made elsewhere: Iraqi Kurds have achieved a limited but nevertheless significant measure of autonomy, and the Iranian Kurds are fighting to achieve autonomy.

Without a major upheaval in Turkey, however, it is unlikely that the tempo of Kurdish activity will approach that of Iran's Kurds. The strength of the Turkish armed forces and the personal, regional, and ideological differences among the various Kurdish organizations at present prevent a major Kurdish rebellion. It is very likely that Kurdish political and guerrilla actions will intensify in the coming years, however, if the central government, authority continues to decline, and it fails to recognize and deal with Kurdish grievances. The situation in Turkey today was summed up by Oktay Eksi, a leading columnist for *Hurriyet,* who said, "We don't have an open problem with the Kurds yet, but when the time comes and they start fighting against us openly, I believe it will be a guerrilla form of fight. And I expect they will do it. The Soviets are definitely backing the Kurds now, with weapons smuggling. And the Syrians say they are transferring arms to Iran through Southeastern Turkey, but in reality they are going to the Kurds, too."[26]

## THE KURDISH QUESTION IN IRAN

The relations between the Kurds and the government of Iran have not been much better than those with Turkey. Despite attempts by both central governments to subdue the Kurds, Turkey's efforts have proved more successful because of significant differences between the two countries. Turkey is far more homogeneous than Iran, which has substantial Turkic, Arab, and Baluchi minorities in addition to the Kurds. Furthermore, while Ataturk enjoyed genuine public support in Turkey and was not dependent on foreign support, Reza Khan was dependent on foreign backing and, therefore, subject to foreign pressures, particularly from the British.

Several revolts broke out in Iran when Reza Khan sought to subdue the various tribal communities and bring them under government control. Two Kurdish rebellions were led by Ismail Simku of the Shikak tribe. Simku, like his counterparts in Iraq, Shaikh Ahmad and Shaikh Mahmud, was motivated by personal ambition as well as nationalism to block the central authority's control over his region. He was ambushed and killed by government forces in 1930.[27]

Shaikh Tafar of the Hamadan tribe attempted another revolt in 1931, but it failed. In the 1920s and 1930s Reza Khan harshly suppressed all local and tribal interests, and he followed a policy of repression and forced assimilation of the Kurds.

During World War II, the Russians occupied northern Iran, and the British occupied the south. In 1942, Kurdish nationalists formed a nationalist party, Kumala Jiwanin Kurd, to fill the political vacuum in Kurdistan, which had become a no-man's land. In 1945, however, it merged with a recently founded leftist party, Hiwa, and with a group of Kurdish communists. Under the influential religious leader Qazi Muhammad the alliance came to be known as the Kurdish Democratic Party (KDP). On January 22, 1946, Qazi Muhammad proclaimed the Kurdish Republic of Mahabad in the heart of the recently established Autonomous Republic of Azerbaijan, with the backing of Russian troops. Under the Republic of Mahabad, schools and hospitals were opened, Kurdish newspapers published, and the government tried to promote the development of commerce, industry, and agriculture, aided by Mulla Mustafa al-Barzani, who had escaped from Iraq into Iran with some 3,000 tribesmen and their families.[28] When the Mahabad Republic was established, Mulla Mustafa placed himself and his men at the service of the Mahabad Republic. In March 1946 he was made one of the Republic's four generals and was entrusted with its defense. The arrival of Barzani and his troops strengthened the Kurdish nationalist movement. A meeting of Kurdish representatives from surrounding countries was held to support a greater Kurdistan.

The Soviet Union played an important role in the recent history of Iranian Kurdistan. While later the Russian concern was for oil concessions, the Soviet leaders were not particularly interested in Kurdish nationalist aspirations. Their principal objectives in the occupation of northern Iran in 1941 were first to expel Axis agents and then to obtain an oil concession in the Azerbaijan area.[29] Had the Russians sympathized with Kurdish aspirations for autonomy, the history of the Iranian Kurds might have been different. However, as it became clear to the Russians that their security problems were becoming involved with a strong nationalistic force and realizing that they must also preserve the trappings of Iranian sovereignty, they encouraged the Kurdish separatist movement in northern Iran. But with the withdrawal of Russian troops and the collapse of the Azerbaijan regime, the government of Mahabad was overthrown by the central government, and its leaders were executed in 1947.

After the fall of Mahabad, the Kurdish nationalist movement went underground in Iran. The Kurdish language was prohibited and the Kurds' printing presses were destroyed. One motivation for Iran to participate in the Baghdad Pact of 1955 was to cooperate with Iraq in suppressing the Kurdish nationalist movement. The Iranian KDP met underground in 1956 and adopted a leftist program. Following the Iraqi revolution and the return of Barzani to Iraq, the Iranian KDP witnessed both an increase in activity as well as an increase in government harassment. Contacts between Iranian Kurdish leaders and Barzani were made in 1958. Barzani, stressing the need for concerted action, proposed the creation of a single Kurdish party, declaring, "For me the borders do not exist," and he suggested the appointment of an Iranian Kurd as Secretary General of the party. When an Iranian Kurd said: "I am Iranian," Barzani reiterated: "You are a Kurd."[30]

The Iranian authorities began to monitor KDP activities closely. In 1958, Ghani Bolurian and Aziz Yusufi, members of the KDP Central Committee, were arrested and remained in jail until the outbreak of the Iranian Revolution in 1979. In 1959, about 250 KDP activists were arrested, including Chari Atti, a member of the Central Committee. The arrests of some KDP leftist leaders and the escape of others to Baghdad had a demoralizing effect on the party. Mulla Mustafa al-Barzani's influence also contributed to the emergence of a more conservative leadership of the Iranian KDP (IKDP) under Abdullah Ishaqi. Ishaqi called for a conference in 1964 in Iraqi Kurdistan at which some members were forcibly prevented from attending and leftist members were accused of deviation. Some KDP cadres, under the name of the Revolutionary Committee, led by Abdullah and Sulaiman Muini (sons of the Interior Minister of the Mahabad Republic), Mustafa Muhammad Amini Rowand, and Abd al-Rahman Qasimlu (then in Europe) initiated limited guerrilla activity against the Iranian regime, which responded with harsh repression. Barzani is said to have warned this group to stay in Baghdad, or to move to Iranian Kurdistan and put an end to all contacts with him. About one hundred men moved into Iranian Kurdistan and began their operations. Barzani, who was receiving aid from the Shah, blocked any contact between this group and Iranian Kurdistan. He later arrested and executed Sulaiman Muini on his return from a trip to Europe.[31]

The Second KDP Conference, held in 1969, decided to move the party back to the left. The conference ousted Ishaqi, after Barzani declined to support him, and invalidated the results of the previous conference.

The March 11, 1970, agreement between Barzani and the Iraqi government revived Baghdad's centrality for Iranian Kurds. Many of the KDP leaders exiled in Lebanon, Syria, or Europe went to Iraq, where a temporary Central Committee was formed to prepare a new program and an agenda for a new conference. Kurdish leaders found a willing backer in the Baghdad regime. The Baathists and the Iranian KDP adopted progressive and anti-imperialist positions and declared their opposition to the Shah's regime. Iraq allowed the Iranian KDP to establish an office in Iraq and provided it with limited amounts of arms and money. Barzani, however, was receiving larger amounts of aid from the Shah.[32]

The Third Conference was held in June 1971 and elected a Central

Committee and a Politburo. It also elected Abd al-Rahman Qasimlu, a socialist intellectual who had taught at the Sorbonne, secretary general. The new leftist trend of the party was manifested in the Third Party Congress held in September 1973, which called for "armed struggle" and cooperation with all revolutionary Iranian parties fighting against the Shah's regime.

Following the resumption of fighting between Barzani's forces and the Iraqi government, however, Iranian KDP leaders refused to denounce Barzani publicly. The Iraqi government therefore suspended its aid, and the KDP leaders had to leave Iraq.[33]

According to a pro-Talibani leader, the Iranian aid to Barzani during the fighting against the Iraqi government improved the Shah's image among Iranian Kurds, but his agreement with the Iraqi government in 1975 at Barzani's expense revived Kurdish antagonism toward the Shah. Furthermore, the leadership of the Iranian KDP differed markedly from that of the Iraqi KDP. While the Barzani leadership rested on tribal loyalty, the Iranian leadership depended on intellectuals and enjoyed the backing of urban dwellers and peasants.[34] This leadership accounts for the emergence of a strong Kurdish movement in Iranian Kurdistan following the collapse of the Shah's regime in 1979.

The Iranian Revolution and the disintegration of state institutions offered a new opportunity for Iran's Kurds to demand regional autonomy. The victory of the Iranian Revolution nourished Kurdish hopes for an autonomous region, and they began pressing the new and weak central government in this direction. To back their demands, the Kurdish groups, like others in Iran, took over the arms stored in police and army barracks following the collapse of the Shah's government.

It was obvious from the beginning, however, that Kurdish demands would not be welcomed by the Islamic government for ideological as well as political reasons. The revolutionary regime advocated the unity of the Muslim umma (nation) and consequently was not willing to recognize the question of ethnic minorities outside an Islamic framework. The only minorities recognized in the new Islamic Constitution were the religious minorities.[35]

Ibrahim Yazdi, one of Khumaini's closest aides, who was to become Iran's Foreign Minister, told *Al-Hawadith* magazine a few weeks before the collapse of the Bakhtiar government that "There is no Kurdish problem in Iran. The Islamic Republic will respect all religious and national minorities in Iran and will give them the freedom to live, exist, and work within the regime of the new Islamic Republic."[36]

The new regime deemed it essential to the protection of Iran's econ-

omy and political stability that it maintain a centralized government.
Centralization means that power should be in the hands of the regime's
leaders and that economic development should continue. The Iranian
leaders were also fearful that granting autonomy to the Kurds would lead
to similar demands by other minorities and, consequently, to the disintegration of the country. Although the KDP stated during the last days of
the Bakhtiar regime that the Kurds had no separatist intentions, this assurance was found unsatisfactory to the Iranian authorities.[37]

Before the escalation of events in the Kurdish region, Iran's new
Chief of Staff warned that the military would never allow part of the
country to secede. On February 21, 1979, Deputy Prime Minister Abbas
Amir Intizam announced in a press conference that the Mahabad army
barracks had fallen to the people, and that "There has been unrest in Kurdistan and it has gotten worse during the revolution. There are hands at
work to provoke the people but the government will ruthlessly crush those
behind the unrest." His statement followed the wounding of an army general on the western frontier. The general blamed the attack on followers
of Jalal Talibani, leader of the Patriotic Union of Kurdistan. This group
was responsible for attacks on police posts in the western parts of the
country in January 1979. Talibani's attack was probably aimed at captur-
ing arms from the police posts.[38] Despite these attacks, both Talibani and
his rivals in the Provisional Command of the Iraqi KDP—the remnants
of Mulla Mustafa al-Barzani's forces under the leadership of his sons
Massud and Idris—came out in support of the revolution, each faction
accusing the other of collaboration with the Shah's regime.[39]

The new Iranian authorities were angered by the takeover of the army
camp in Mahabad after the troops fled their barracks, and by the threats
to other army barracks near the Iraqi border when Kurdish militants prevented army reinforcements from reaching them.[40]

These actions prompted the government to send Labor Minister Dariush Furuhar, a Kurd, as head of a mission to investigate the situation.
The mission was met by a hastily chosen delegation representing Kurdish
towns under the leadership of Shaikh Izz al-Din Husaini, a prominent
Kurdish religious leader and a Kurdish nationalist. Husaini, supported by
the KDP and the Maoist oriented Komeleh party, submitted an eight-
point program. The program demanded:

1. Official recognition of Kurdish autonomy and reference to it in
the new Iranian constitution.

2. The autonomous Kurdish region to include the four provinces of
Ilam, Kermanshah, Kurdistan, and West Azerbaijan.

3. The election of a Kurdish assembly by secret ballot. The council to

select a local government to administer economic, social, cultural, and internal security affairs for the Kurdish region.

4. Kurdish to be considered an official language in schools and in official correspondence; Persian to be taught in the Kurdish elementary schools after the fourth grade.

5. The allocation of a portion of the budget to develop the region.

6. Kurdish representatives to be given important positions in the central government.

7. The central government to have control over the army, foreign policy, national economy, and long-term economic planning.

8. The guarantee of freedom of the press, of expression, and of political and religious organization.[41]

The Kurdish representatives were also reported to have demanded a crackdown on the political and military activities of the supporters of Barzani.

Furuhar said that the extreme demands, especially for self-determination, would have to be discussed by the new Iranian assembly when it was formed. Shaikh Husaini stressed that the Kurds were not separatists and would use peaceful means to achieve their goals, but that "the Baluchis, Arabs, Azerbaijanis, and Kurds all want limited autonomy." KDP leader Qasimlu asserted that "It is important for us not only to have Kurdish schools and economic development, but most important, the Kurdish people must feel that they govern themselves."[42]

There was, it seems, no formal reply to the Kurdish demands. The situation deteriorated on March 18, 1979, when heavy fighting broke out in Sanandaj between Kurdish guerrillas and the Revolutionary Guards (Pasdaran). The clashes came in the wake of daily incidents between the Pasdaran and Kurdish peasants, backed by the radical Revolutionary Organization of the Kurdish Workers (Komeleh) and the Kurdish branch of the Fedayin Khalq in the areas around Sanandaj and Marivan. The peasants, at the urging of these groups, had begun to seize lands owned by feudal landlords following the revolution. The Komeleh party charged that the government was using the Pasdaran, the "reactionary" Kurdish forces led by Ayatullah Safdari, and feudal landlords backed by the forces of Massud Barzani's Provisional Command against the Kurdish peasants.[43]

These two Kurdish groups adopted Marxist-Leninist slogans and called for radical economic and social transformation in Kurdistan, and their approach toward the government was more confrontational than the KDP's. On March 19, however, Ayatullah Khumaini issued a call to the citizens of Kurdistan, saying that a "group of people has created chaos in our dear Kurdistan and does not wish the Muslims to live in peace. This group is acting contrary to Islamic principles." He also warned that "any attack on the army and gendarmerie post is rejected by us. We have no dispute with our Sunni brothers. We are all members of a single Koran. If anyone attacks them he is not a part of the Muslim people, (but) is an agent of the foreigner."[44]

Following heavy fighting in Sanandaj, the government sent Ayatullah Mahmud Taliqani, a prominent religious leader known for his liberal views and respected by the Left, to mediate the conflict in Kurdistan. Following his visit, the government released the remaining Kurdish prisoners taken in the Sanandaj fighting and named Ibrahim Yunisi, a Kurd, governor general of Kurdistan province.

The situation deteriorated further in April 1979, however, as clashes erupted in the town of Naghadeh in the province of Azerbaijan. Gunmen opened fire on a meeting of the KDP and fighting broke out between Turkish and Kurdish minorities.[45] The Kurds accused the government of inciting the conflict and of complicity with the Turks.

Kurdish missions continued throughout the spring to travel between Mahabad and Tehran without much success. More demoralized police posts and army barracks were occupied in the Kurdish region, and their garrisons disarmed and told to leave the region, and a de facto Kurdish autonomy was established in large parts of Kurdistan.

Concerned about the decline of governmental authority in Kurdistan and the failure of some military officers to heed government orders to move against the rebels, the government accepted in late July the resignation of Major General Nasir Farbod, the army's chief of staff, and replaced him with Brigadier General Husain Shakir, a hardliner.[46]

The appointment of Shakir was accompanied by a determined media campaign against the KDP. It was accused of collaboration with foreigners and of planning to secede from the Islamic Republic.[47] For its part, the KDP's Central Committee sent an open letter to Ayatullah Khumaini on August 5, 1979, denying these charges and appealing for a peaceful solution to the conflict. The letter said that the "long struggle" of the Kurdish people had two aims: The overthrow of the "corrupt Shahnshahi regime; and the establishment of a democratic regime in Iran that would guarantee the Kurdish people its rights of "self-rule or federal union."[48]

The KDP and Komeleh charged that the government allowed officers loyal to the Shah to be in control of the army in Kurdistan, and that it had placed anti-Kurdish elements in the Revolutionary Committees and sought to stir up intercommunal fighting between the Turkic and Kurdish peoples in Naghadeh and Urumiyah.

The letter went on to add that despite the assurances given by Khumaini and Bazargan that all Iranians would reap the fruits of the revolution and that "national discrimination" would be eradicated, these promises remained unfulfilled. The letter also charged the government with
failure to select Kurdish officials for the revolutionary committees even in
cities where Kurds formed a substantial percentage of the population,
such as Urumiyah and Silmas. It also accused the government of placing
anti-Kurdish officers and government officials in charge in Kurdistan,
and that officials responsible for the events in Sanandaj were promoted
and rewarded, while their innocent victims continued to languish in jails.

The Central Committee denied government charges accusing the
KDP of treason against Iran and the Iranian people. It stressed that "our
party has stated many times before and we state it again that there are no
separatists in Kurdistan. And it would be unreasonable and unjust if the
Kurdish people were suppressed under the banner of separatism while it is
only demanding its national rights of self-rule. It is obvious that such actions and methods were used by the Shah's regime. A revolutionary regime is not supposed to behave in a similar manner and ought to reject
such tactics." The letter concluded by saying that "five million Kurds are
impatiently awaiting your response and initiative. And we are certain, as
has been your custom in the past to respond with clarity and determination to our requests and to quickly implement them."

The Ayatullah Khumaini did not, as far as is known, respond to the
letter. Instead, the two sides continued to escalate their activities. On July
22, one of the first major clashes occurred as the government sought to
reoccupy a police post near the Turkish border. Another major clash
erupted when the government sought to take over the town of Marivan.
On August 16, Kurdish guerrillas occupied the town of Paveh. Two days
later, Ayatullah Khumaini gave a direct order to government forces to
move into Paveh.

In addition, on August 19, Khumaini proclaimed himself Commander in Chief of the armed forces and threatened officers who did not
achieve immediate results with "revolutionary justice" and called for a
"feast of blood" to crush what he described as a "Kurdish rebellion" in Sanandaj.[49] Kurdistan's governor general, Muhammad Rashid Shakiba
said, however, that a Kurdish revolt did not exist in the town. Khumaini
also described the KDP's leadership as "corrupt and satanic agents" and
called for their arrest. Furthermore, the Revolutionary Council declared
the election of Qasimlu to the Council of Elders null and void. The Iranian army, using tanks, artillery, helicopter gunships, and phantom jets,
attacked and occupied Paveh, Sanandaj, and Saqqiz, and prepared to at-

tack the Kurdish capital of Mahabad. The fall of Saqqiz and Paveh was followed by Ayatullah Sudiq Khalkhali's "revolutionary courts, which executed more than seventy people, including a few soldiers who had refused to fight."[50]

In the meantime, Khumaini ordered that a day's oil revenues be put at the disposal of Kurdistan province while Shaikh Husaini charged that the government was "moving toward a new dictatorship."[51]

The army held off from its assault on Mahabad as a Kurdish delegation went to Tehran to try to negotiate at the request of the Bazargan government. The peace mission failed in its objective, however. Speaking on behalf of Khumaini, Abu al-Hasan Bani Sadr, the revolution's lay ideologue and Iran's future president, squelched any idea of a negotiated settlement when he said that the rebellion must be stamped out.[52] Following this development, Kurdish leaders and forces withdrew to the mountains without a major battle, and on September 4 and 5, the government forces occupied Mahabad and Sardasht. Qasimlu appealed to the government to end the "massacre against the Kurds," while Shaikh Husaini continued to insist that the Kurds "were not secessionists and only wanted to run their affairs within the framework of a united Iran."[53]

However, the following months showed that the government had failed to achieve a decisive victory. In fact, the situation reached a stalemate with the government in control of most Kurdish towns while guerrillas continued to roam freely in the mountains and the countryside.

The KDP's tactics of surrendering the cities without a fight were explained to a *Le Monde* correspondent by the KDP's secretary general in early October. Qasimlu stated: "We do not intend to repeat Barzani's mistake by waging positional warfare. We have light weapons and munitions for at least five years of wars. The material recovered from the military lease in Mahabad is considerable. Already we have dispersed it into caches. If the government wants war, it will get it, but not the kind of war it wants. At first, losses will be heavy. The Iranian Kurds are not experienced in war. They will learn. We will never defend the cities, they do not interest us. They are traps." Qasimlu said that in addition to the arms seized during the fighting, cargoes of smuggled weapons were coming in from Turkey, Iraq, and the Gulf countries.[54]

The KDP's secretary general also hinted that some differences existed between the KDP and some of the Marxist-Leninist Kurdish groups that had emerged during this strange revolution. These latter were competing with each other and countering the KDP's "cautious attitude" with their "revolutionary spontaneity." Qasimlu said that these groups charged that the KDP was a party of the old feudal system and the liberal bourgeoisie;

that it was restraining the peasants from fighting against the feudal system; that it favored the Soviet Union and the Iraqi Baath party; and that it was inclined to compromise with Barzani's old party.

But he insisted that the KDP was in control of Kurdistan on "both the military and the political planes." Qasimlu again emphasized the differences between the Iraqi and Iranian experiences when he stated that, "while the Iraqi Kurds were led by a prestigious but old-fashioned man — General Barzani — the leadership of the IKDP is controlled by a western-educated cadre, most of whom owe their training to the exile into which they were forced by the Shah."

In the meantime, government officials were speaking of the need to begin a "development and construction crusade after the great military victory."[55] On September 11, the Islamic Gendarmerie called on the Muslim people of Kurdistan to cooperate with government forces, and on everyone to: "Counter the provocations by the enemies of Islam aiming at sowing religious discord. . . . Counter the provocations by the enemies of Iran who are sowing discord under the guise of autonomy. . . . Counter the creation of discord in the rural area between the farmers and the landlords or former landlords."[56]

Government claims of victory notwithstanding, Kurdish guerrillas began to strike again at government posts. On October 11, Kurdish guerrillas attacked a frontier post and on October 12, they attacked the Pasdaran post in Mahabad, killing several of the guards and the police chief.

On October 12, Ayatullah Khumaini commented on these and similar incidents over Tehran radio by saying that they demonstrated Kurdish weakness and that "unfortunately, the Kurds neither understand Islam nor care about the oppressed. . . . Rest assured that they cannot accomplish anything fundamental. They have suffered a great defeat. Their leaders have escaped; the remainder are like thieves who suddenly strike. The remainder will be destroyed, too."

In another speech on October 14, Khumaini called on the Kurds to "wake up" and report the KDP elements whose "ties with the foreigners, the Zionists, the United States, and with the former regime have been proved." Khumaini added that the government did not want "to act with excessive harshness and strength so that, God forbid, our Kurdish brothers are trampled underfoot. Otherwise, it would not be difficult for us to put an end to the rebellion in one or two days."

In the meantime, Minister of State Dariush Furuhar urged the government to refrain from launching a crusade against Kurdistan if it wanted the problem to be solved "especially as it is now clear that the

Baathist government of Iraq has been chiefly responsible for the crisis in the western part of the country."[57]

These statements reflected the government's growing concern over developments in the region as the Kurdish guerrillas worked their way back into effective control of much of the Kurdish region as the government became preoccupied with other problems.

By the end of October, spurred on by the poor showing of the Pasdaran and the army, the government reversed itself and authorized negotiations with the Kurds on their autonomy demands. On October 27, Tehran Radio announced that the cabinet, in order to solve the problems of the country's "deprived provinces," including the border and Kurdish inhabited regions, had set up a special four-man mission and delegated to it powers in connection with development, cultural, military, welfare, and budgetary affairs of the Kurdish inhabited regions.[58] The delegation included Defense Minister Mustafa Shamran, Minister of Planning Izzatullah Sahabi, Minister of the Interior Hashim Sabbaghian and Kurdish Minister of State Dariush Furuhar.

In order to facilitate the mission's task, Khumaini agreed to Kurdish demands to withdraw the hated Revolutionary Guards (Pasdaran) from Kurdistan and to abolish the revolutionary courts in the troubled province.[59]

The team arrived in Mahabad on November 2, where they were met by a crowd of several thousand, including armed Pesh Merga, chanting their support for the KDP and carrying pictures of Husaini. In a speech to the crowd, Furuhar declared that the government intended to meet their "legitimate demands," and that the government had always favored granting "self-administration" over the internal affairs of the region, and favored the preservation of its cultural characteristics, and asserted that, "Iran's Islamic Republic is capable of granting individual and social freedoms for Muslim Sunnis and Shiis and for national minorities." He also said that his group was ready to negotiate with Shaikh Husaini and Qasimlu.[60]

Despite continued clashes between government forces and the Kurdish guerrillas in Sanandaj, Javanrud, and Saqqiz, relations between the two sides improved dramatically following the first phase of negotiations. The takeover of the United States embassy and the holding of its employees as hostages and the consequent rise in anti-imperialist themes and calls for national unity by the government helped to reduce tensions. Khumaini contributed to this trend when he sent an uncharacteristically conciliatory message to the Kurdish guerrillas on November 17, calling for a continuation of the negotiations. Referring to his age, Khumaini said that he was expressing his "humble desire as a servitor of the nation who is passing his last days of life."[61] He added, "Those who have accused you of conspiring against the Islamic Republic commit a calumny. I hold out my hand to you humbly, and I beg you to safeguard our unity . . . all divisions will only benefit American imperialism. . . . Are you going to reject the prayers of an old man who sees his last days?"[62]

In a speech on November 20, Qasimlu hailed Khumaini's message by saying, "We appreciate the good will of the Imam. We only hope that his representatives are equally well disposed toward us."

Similarly, the anti-American fervor sweeping Iran served as a convenient vehicle for two radical Kurdish groups to join the negotiation as silent partners. The Marxist-Leninist Fedayin Khalq and the Maoist Komeleh were previously willing to accept only what they demanded, but at this time agreed to form a single delegation with the KDP and allow Shaikh Husaini to speak for them.

Qasimlu said that the aim of the negotiations was to transform the cease-fire into an armistice. He added that this could only be achieved if the government "accepts two preconditions we consider essential — to remove the Pasdaran who still camp on the outskirts of the cities, and to freeze the number of army troops in Kurdistan and their freedom of movement within the region." Qasimlu also expressed optimism that once the armistice was reached the government and the KDP would submit their proposals for a solution to the negotiations.

However, less than a week later, on November 23, a high-ranking Iranian leader, Ayatullah Muntaziri, asked the Kurds not to back Qasimlu and Husaini "who do not wish you well. . . . And you should stand up to these people who back communism, the U.S., Zionism, the Shah's agents, the Izz al-Din Husaini, whose SAVAK dossier is now public knowledge."[63]

Khumaini, however, after meeting with the peace mission, told the Kurds in a broadcast that he accepted their demands but offered no specific definition of autonomy.[64] Qasimlu, for his part, insisted that the new Islamic constitution include specific guarantees of Kurdish autonomy despite the fact that the constitution referred only in general terms to the rights of Iran's ethnic groups.

After weeks of negotiations the government submitted a four-page proposal to the Kurdish leaders on December 16 entitled "Rights and responsibilities of the self-governing regions of the Islamic Republic of Iran." The proposals, described in general terms what the recognized rights of ethnic minorities would be in the following fourteen points:

1. The Provincial Council would administer the affairs of the population in other areas than those exclusively under the competence of the central government. These are: national defense, foreign policy, the monetary system, long-term planning, the large industrial firms, telecommunications, the railroads, and the principal roadways.

2. The higher-ranking civil servants — notably the governor, the commanders in chief of the police force and the gendarmerie of the region would be named by the central government on the basis of proposals submitted by the Provincial Council. The latter would designate directly those responsible for security in the towns and villages.

3. The judicial system of the province would function autonomously but would be subordinated to the control of the Supreme Court of the Republic, which will be headquartered in Tehran.

4. Maintenance of order and security would be the resort of the provincial leadership.

5. The Provincial Council alone would have the capacity to legislate in those areas regarding personal status, religion, social customs, and the traditions of those whom it governed.

6. The religion of the majority of the inhabitants of the province would be considered the official religion, in the same way that Shiite Islam is the state religion.

7. The provincial budget would be funded from two sources: from subsidies accorded by the central government and the taxes which would be raised directly by the provincial authorities.

8. The central government would commit itself to seeing that underdeveloped provinces had the right to higher subsidies than would be justified by the size of the population.

9. The self-governing regions would be responsible for assuring the freedom of speech, organization, and action of all political formations, professional, religious, and cultural associations, as stipulated by the Constitution of the Islamic Republic.

10. The freedom of language instruction — in Kurdish, Baluchi, Azeri (the dialect of Azerbaijan), Armenian, Assyrian, Hebrew, Arabic, and Turkish — would be guaranteed to all citizens. The principal languages — Kurdish, Baluchi, and Azeri — could be taught from primary school onwards, on an equal status with Persian, the official and common language of all the ethnic peoples. However, at the university level, subjects other than the language and literature of the minorities would be taught in Persian.

11. The provincial administration would have recourse to the local

language for its internal documents; however, only Persian would be used mandatorily in exchanges between the provincial authorities and the central government.

12. Each province would be provided with its own university, or at least with institutions for advanced studies. Moreover, the University of Tehran would create colleges dedicated to teaching minority languages.

13. Each province would have its own radio and television stations, which would broadcast regional programs in the local language several hours a day. Freedom of the press would be guaranteed to newspapers and publications in languages other than Persian.

14. The Provincial Council would determine, in proportion to the size of the population administered, the number of candidates to the national schools in charge of educating the officers of the army, the police, and the gendarmerie.

Qasimlu stated that while it was not acceptable in its original form, the government program was not without merit. However, he faulted the program because it appeared to recognize the Kurds not as a people (khalq) but rather viewed them as a tribal group (qawm), and only offered them a form of "decentralized administration" (khod gardani) in place of the autonomy (khod mokhtari) they were seeking.[65]

Negotiations between the two sides continued, as did the fighting around Sanandaj and a number of other areas. On January 1, 1980, a ceasefire was reached in Sanandaj. On the same day, Ayatullah Muntaziri, one of Iran's highest religious leaders, called on the government to negotiate with "all (Kurdish) groups," particularly religious groups, not only with Qasimlu, Husaini, and the Fedayin Khalq whose aim is separation.[66] The growing tensions between the two sides led the governor general of Kurdistan, Husain Shahwaysi, to resign and join the demonstration in Sanandaj because the government refused to honor its pledge to withdraw the Pasdaran from the city.[67]

However, on January 16, Shaikh Husaini also spoke of progress in the negotiations and said that an understanding had been reached with the government delegation concerning the withdrawal of the Pasdaran from Sanandaj. The government delegation announced after its return to Tehran that future negotiations would be based on the Kurdish proposals for autonomy, but that the government view concerning a decentralized administration would have to be taken into account.[68]

These understandings proved to be short-lived. The differences went beyond the question of Pasdaran replacements. The KDP charged the government was negotiating in bad faith by playing "hide and seek" with the issues and by addressing the public in one language and the negotiators in another. Qasimlu said that while agreement had been reached on matters concerning the use of the Kurdish language and local security, other issues remained unresolved. One issue was the government's insistence on naming the police commanders in Kurdistan. Another was the rejection of Kurdish territorial demands. The Kurdish negotiators wanted the Kurdish area to include, in addition to the province of Kurdistan, the Kurdish districts of West Azerbaijan, Ilam, and Kermanshah. The government maintained that West Azerbaijan was inhabited mainly by Azeri Turks, and that Ilam and Kermanshah were inhabited by Shia Kurds. Qasimlu rejected this argument, saying, "we are not talking about religion, but about nationality." The government also rejected proposals for the use of the term autonomy, and insisted on using self-administration instead, charging that Kurdish demands would lead to separation. Qasimlu denied these charges by saying that "there is no force in Iranian Kurdistan for separation. We are against any kind of separation."[69]

Each side's insistence on pursuing its own demands led inevitably to renewed fighting. In late January and early February fighting took place around Kamyran and Paveh. These clashes were followed by a lull as both sides sat out the severity of winter. In mid-February, newly elected President Abu al-Hasan Bani-Sadr said at an Islamic conference that what the Kurds were demanding was not autonomy but virtually an independent state financed by Tehran.[70]

Qasimlu reacted by asking Bani-Sadr if he would receive a KDP mission to explain the party's position. Bani-Sadr accepted, and a KDP mission arrived in the capital with a six-point plan to restore peace in the region.

The Kurdish six-point plan was studied by the government and presented to the president with comments and recommendations. Hashim Sabbaghian, a member of the government mission, said that the plan proposed by the KDP was an "autonomy plan," which the delegation requested to be inserted as a supplement to the constitution.[71] The proposal included: the right of autonomy for an Iranian Kurdistan and that this autonomy be recognized officially in the Constitution; the recognition of Iranian Kurdistan as a "geographical unit to include all Kurdish inhabited regions to be established on the basis of a majority vote; apart from four issues of foreign relations, the army, national defense, long-term economic planning, all other issues relating to Kurdistan should be run by the local people; election of an executive committee which would administer the region as an autonomous unit; internal security of the region, police, and gendarmerie, would be in the hands of autonomous authorities; and the recognition of Kurdish as an official language. This plan differed in some respects from the earlier plan of the Kurdish representatives, and Bani Sadr accepted the proposal orally. The plan also asked for a general amnesty for those engaged in the conflict, the payment of allowances for the families of persons killed in incidents, and assistance to those adversely affected in the disturbances.

This plan was rejected without explanation by the government. In response, Qasimlu announced in late March that the Kurds would not lay down their arms until they had achieved autonomy. Bani Sadr countered by saying that no further negotiations would be held until the various political groups lay down their arms.[72]

Clashes erupted between the two sides near the Oshnoviyeh district in early April. Confronted by skirmishing between Iraqi and Iranian forces along the border, Tehran ordered an army column to march through Sanandaj to the border area. The column's advance was halted by Kurdish groups who suspected that the aim of this deployment was to take over Sanandaj in violation of previous agreements. The column was attacked by Fedayin Khalq and Komeleh partisans as it skirted around Sanandaj and headed toward Saqqiz. The government responded harshly by attacking Kurdish urban strongholds with gunships, leading Shaikh Husaini to charge that the army had begun a war against the Kurdish people.[73]

Heavy fighting broke out in May as government forces attacked Sanandaj and Mahabad. President Bani Sadr announced that he would accept the Kurds' six-point plan but that they must lay down their arms first.[74] The demand for disarmament was rejected.

Bani Sadr outlined his view of the conflict in a speech in Tehran on May 16. He stated that, "In Kurdistan, liberty, freedom, and Islam were faced and are faced with paganism, dependence, and dictatorship," and called on soldiers "to pursue the struggle with all their might until victory has been achieved." On the same day, Colonel Sadri, Commander of the army forces in Kurdistan told Ayatullah Khumaini, "By the grace of the Imam, we the soldiers of Islam cleansed Sanandaj from the filth of the infidels."[75] The government, in the meantime, intensified its attacks on other areas and imposed an economic blockade on the Kurdish region. Ayatullahs Khumaini and Muntaziri announced that they planned to establish an Islamic University in Kurdistan.

The fall of Sanandaj did not bring an end to the fighting, however. Ayatullah Khumaini and President Bani Sadr met on May 22 to discuss the Kurdish problem and to try to end the "Kurdish gangrene" as quickly as possible and by whatever means necessary. Ayatullah Shirazi said that any negotiation with the KDP and its allies could "only be described as hypocrisy and betrayal of Islam." In the meantime, the Kurds withdrew to the mountains and began a guerrilla campaign against the government forces as these gained control of most of Kurdistan's cities.

By the summer of 1980 the situation seemed to have reached a stalemate, with government forces in control of most Kurdish towns but with Kurdish guerrillas still roaming the mountains and the countryside. Neither the government nor the Kurds exercise much leverage with the other. Continued conflict can be expected with periods of rest until the Kurds are well armed and able to rid themselves completely of a weak central government, or until a stronger government imposes its authority over them. A negotiated settlement appears to be unlikely as long as both sides refuse to compromise and negotiate from extreme positions. The weakness of Iran's central government after the revolution and its bitter conflict with Iraq offers the capable but disunited Kurdish leadership an opportunity to continue to fight as it negotiates.

In the absence of fruitful negotiations between the Kurdish leadership in Iran and the Khumaini regime and failing government recognition of the Kurds as a national minority deserving autonomy, it is likely that the conflict might take the form of a prolonged guerrilla war. The Kurds have a less charismatic leadership than Barzani but one that is more aware of the complexities of the world it is facing. The Kurds also appear to have captured huge amounts of weapons from the Shah's military arsenals following the revolution. There are reports that some Kurdish groups are receiving aid from Iraq and that arms and ammunition are also smuggled from Turkey.

The Iranian government has at different times charged that Iraq, Israel, the United States, and the USSR are aiding the Kurds. It is unlikely that contacts with the United States and Israel exist. The leftist ideology of many Kurdish leaders and Barzani's experience with the Shah, the United States, and Israel does not encourage the growth of a similar relationship. There is no firm evidence of Soviet support for the Kurds, although the Tudeh party, through its clandestine radio broadcasts from the Soviet Union, has constantly called for peaceful resolution to the problems of national minorities, which should "enjoy the rights of administrative and cultural autonomy within the framework of a united Iran."[76]

Iraqi President Saddam Husain has called on Iran to recognize the "national rights" of its minorities and to follow Iraq's example.[77] Iraq has welcomed several thousand Iranian Kurds fleeing from the fighting of the spring of 1980![78] Iranian leadership, the Iraqi Communist party, and Massud Barzani's faction of the Iraqi KDP have charged that Iraq is seeking to overthrow the Khumaini regime by providing aid to various Iranian Kurdish rebel groups.[79]

The Barzani group, which is backed by the Iranian government, has claimed that Iraqi aid was being given to the Komeleh, to Shaikh Jalal Husaini (Shaikh Izz al-Din Husaini's brother), and to other individuals and groups.[80] The Iraqi Communist party has claimed that Iraqi military and financial aid as well as training were being given to the Herki tribes through Muhyi al-Din Herki, an adviser to the Iraqi minister for northern affairs, and Shaikh Uthman Bayara of the Shaikh Uthman family, and through a former colonel in the Iranian army, Ali and several others. Qasimlu has, however, denied receiving any aid from Iraq and described the KDP's relations with Iraq as "cool."[81] Furthermore, the Marxist Fedayin Khalq announced in a statement to the *Keyhan* newspaper on January 29, 1980, that two leaders of the Javanrud tribe had crossed into Iraq and returned with three cars of arms and ammunition, which were later seized by KDP elements and which would "not be returned until their origin and destination have been determined."[82] The statement said that while the organization was not opposed to the establishment of "no-strings relationships with progressive governments," it condemned receiving arms from Iraq, which has a "record of crushing Arab and Kurdish workers and masses," and because it leads to increased dependence on foreign powers.

# 2

# ᴛʜᴇ ɪʀᴀǫɪ ᴋᴜʀᴅɪsʜ ǫᴜᴇsᴛɪᴏɴ BEFORE ᴛʜᴇ ᴀᴄᴄᴇssɪᴏɴ OF ᴛʜᴇ BAAᴛʜ PARᴛy

In 1914 a British Expeditionary Force occupied Southern Iraq in order to protect the route to India and British interests in the Gulf and Iran.[1] In 1918 the British forces also occupied the Mosul province, which was still in the hands of the Turks at the time of the armistice. Britain was interested in Mosul for its vast oil reserves and was able to incorporate it into Iraq under the provisions of the Sykes-Picot Agreement of 1916. In 1920, Britain was formally entrusted with the mandate over Iraq. The Arabs of Iraq reacted with mass protests, which developed into a full-scale revolt.[2] To meet the country's demands, the British government declared its intention to form an independent Arab government under British mandate. They also responded to Iraqi popular feeling by proposing the Amir Faisal, son of the Sharif Husain and leader of the Arab revolt of 1916, as king of Iraq. In a referendum, the Iraqi people voted for Faisal to be king of Iraq, although the two provinces inhabited mainly by the Kurds were opposed; in Kirkuk the majority of the population voted against Faisal and in Sulaymaniyya the election was boycotted.[3] Faisal was proclaimed king on August 12, 1921.

Britain, Iraqi leaders maintain, used the threat of establishing a separate Kurdish state in the north of Iraq to strengthen her position and to gain control over the country's oil resources, particularly in Mosul, which was still contested by Turkey.[4] The Mosul Vilayet was very important to Iraq, because the vilayets of Basra and Baghdad alone "could never for economic and strategic reasons be built to a viable state."[5]

British plans for Mosul, which had a large Kurdish population, were to set up one or several semiautonomous Kurdish provinces to be loosely attached to whatever regular administration was developed in the rest of Iraq.[6] The threat posed by disgruntled Turkey and the effort to set up a viable regime in Kurdish Sulaymaniyya induced the British to allow Shaikh Mahmud to become governor of that province. Shaikh Mahmud had already enjoyed a widespread support in Sulaymaniyya as the descendant of a prominent religious leader, Shaikh Kaka Ahmad. No sooner than he had become governor in 1919, Shaikh Mahmud proclaimed himself king and declared the establishment of a Kurdish state in Iraq. His methods were tribal and ineffective, and he was opposed by some of the Kurdish tribes from Kirkuk and Kufri who enjoyed friendly relations with the Iraqi government.[7] He was soon removed and exiled to India.

In 1922, when Shaikh Qadir, brother cf Shaikh Mahmud, cooperated with the Turks and occupied Imadiyya and Koisanjaq, Shaikh Mahmud was allowed to return from exile. He again declared himself king of Kurdistan and threatened Kirkuk.[8] Because of his corrupt and oppressive regime, the business community complained to the Iraqi government of the lack of security in Sulaymaniyya and appealed for help.[9] An Iraqi force was sent to occupy Sulaymaniyya. Shaikh Mahmud fled, escaping across the Iranian border.

During the negotiations of the Treaty of Lausanne (signed in 1923), a few Kurdish leaders sent petitions to the British government demanding the establishment of a separate Kurdish state in Iraqi Kurdistan, though rival Kurdish leaders friendly to the Iraqi government countered with petitions pledging their loyalty to the Iraqi government.[10] The Treaty of Lausanne, however, did not resolve the dispute over Mosul (including the fate of the Kurdish area), which was later put before the League of Nations. The Council of the League decided, upon the recommendation of a commission that went to Mosul to investigate, that the province should be included within Iraq. Turkey agreed to cede the province in a treaty signed in 1926 with Iraq and Britain. The League's commission also recommended that Iraq should recognize the Kurds' expressed desire to speak their own language and use it in their schools as well as to have Kurdish officials administer the area. The Iraqi government agreed to honor the recommendations of the League of Nations and accorded the Kurds a generous share in the administration of the country.

In 1930, when a treaty was signed between Iraq and Britain to terminate the British mandate over Iraq, relations between the Kurds and the Iraqi government began to deteriorate as the new arrangement cleared the way for further transfer of power in the north to the Iraqi government. This induced Shaikh Mahmud to revolt again and demand from the British government a united Kurdistan. Meanwhile, other Kurdish leaders demanded more moderate Kurdish safeguards. A group of Kurdish notables at Geneva asked for a League-supervised Kurdish government. Six

Kurdish deputies worked in the Baghdad government to get unified Kurdish administration for the Kurdish provinces, but the Iraqi government rejected these demands even though it had earlier granted the Kurds other rights in accordance with the League of Nations recommendations.[11]

Shaikh Mahmud, with his demand for independence ignored by both Britain and Iraq, resorted to violence.[12] Strikes and demonstrations erupted in Sulaymaniyya in September 1930 in response to genuine Kurdish nationalist feeling. Some Kurdish historians see the demonstrations and strikes in Sulaymaniyya as a new turning point in the history of the Kurdish nationalist movement, revealed in a change in its outlook and leadership.[13] Jalal Talibani holds that this uprising was a movement by the Kurdish "salary earners, students, workers, and merchants" and a transfer of the political base of the Kurdish nationalist movement from the countryside to the cities, and a change in the leadership from the religious and tribal chiefs to the urban petty bourgeoisie.[14] While it is true that the intelligentsia and urban dwellers might have played a significant role, the majority of Kurds, living in the stronghold of feudalism in northern Iraq, continued to be led by religious-tribal leaders like Shaikh Ahmad and his brother Mulla Mustafa al-Barzani.

## THE BARZANI CLAN

The rise of the Barzanis to leadership roles in the Kurdish insurrections — whether on the strength of sheer tribal loyalty, as under Shaikh Ahmad or of tribal-national appeal, as under Mulla Mustafa — exemplifies the power of a "shaikhly establishment" to rally tribal forces to a religious, feudal, and charismatic leadership.[15]

The Barzanis lived in the village of Barzan, in a remote and almost inaccessible area in the mountains of northeastern Iraq. The poverty and ruggedness of the terrain left their marks on its people. Livelihood often depended on attacking and pillaging neighboring villages, a practice indulged in by the region's nomadic and seminomadic tribes since the earliest recorded history. As a result, it was long a center of tribal warfare and lawlessness.

The Barzani leadership, though outwardly nationalistic, was essentially tribal and religious. Muhammad, grandfather of Mulla Mustafa and first of the Barzanis to attract a large following, was a prominent religious leader of the Naqshabandiyya order. His piety and fame attracted a number of followers to his cause, and he and his descendants became the temporal and spiritual leaders of the area.

For more than forty years running, there were repeated clashes with the Turkish and Iraqi authorities, who strove to limit the power of the Barzanis. This pattern of a tribal leadership developing control over an area and refusing to recognize the central government was to be repeated again and again in Kurdish history. The central government—be it Turkish, British, or Iraqi—would send in troops, which usually failed to root out the Kurds from their mountain homelands. A temporary, unsatisfactory equilibrium was achieved until the next round began.

This pattern was often played out between Mulla Mustafa, grandson of Shaikh Muhammad, and the Iraqi government. Mulla Mustafa first came to the attention of the authorities in the 1930s: following clashes between the Barzanis and rival Kurdish tribes; later the Barzanis came into conflict with the Iraqi government. Relations between the Barzanis, led by Mulla Mustafa's older brother, Shaikh Ahmad, and the Iraqi government deteriorated in 1932 following the signing of the revised Anglo-Iraqi treaty that ended the Mosul mandate and cleared the way for a transfer of power in the north to the Iraqi government. With this transfer of power, the government tried to install its own police force in the Barzan region and to collect tribal taxes that the British had allowed to lapse. These actions led to violent clashes with the forces of Shaikh Ahmad, who considered the police force an intrusion into his affairs. The clashes lasted until June 22, 1932, when the government surrounded Ahmad near the Turkish border, where he was forced to surrender to Turkish border police.[16]

The Turks resettled Ahmad in Erzerum, while his brothers Mulla Mustafa and Muhammad Sadiq remained in Turkey near the Iraqi border. They were occasionally able to return clandestinely to their former region; they were granted amnesty on May 13, 1933. On June 29, Mulla Mustafa and his followers surrendered to the Iraqis and were later followed by Shaikh Ahmad. The government allowed the Barzani tribesmen to return to their villages, but the three Barzani brothers were settled in other parts of Iraq and given monthly allowances by the government.

The Barzanis blamed the British for their conflict with the Iraqi government and for the failure of the Iraqi government to keep its promises.[17] The Iraqi government asked the governor of Mosul to secure the support of Shaikh Ahmad for the Iraqi state. Shaikh Ahmad replied that he would support the king (since he was a descendant of the Prophet) instead of Britain and would also send 18,000 young Kurds to join the army.[18] He also told the governor that he had the capability to oust the

British army from his region and have it replaced by an Iraqi division. Ubaidullah al-Barzani suspected that the British interpreter who was at the meeting must have reported the matter to his supervisors. Consequently, the British encouraged a rival Kurdish leader, Shaikh Rashid of the Shirwani tribes, to move against the Barzanis. The British may have also undermined Shaikh Ahmad's position by rumors about his unorthodox religious views. The question of his religious beliefs aggravated tribal strife.[19]

By 1936 Mulla Mustafa had agreed to live in Sulaymaniyya, where he remained until World War II broke out. In July 1943 he escaped to Barzan and resumed his conflict with the government. In his escape, he was assisted by the Hiwa party, because the Barzani leaders had shown a nationalist outlook in their activities.[20] This was borne out by Barzani's contacts with Kurdish military officers who had expressed nationalist feelings. With the help of Hiwa, Barzani rebelled in 1943. Observers seem to agree that this uprising was the first in which Mulla Mustafa expressed nationalist demands.[21]

Nuri al-Said, prime minister in the postwar Iraqi government, wrote a report in 1944, immediately after his resignation from the cabinet because of the unsolved Kurdish problem, in which he briefly analyzed the Kurdish question. His reflections on the situation in Kurdistan were as follows:

> The Iraqi Kurds are divided in three groups: (1) The tribal leaders live a life closer to feudalism than to civilization. They do not have a specific political goal. Their main concern is to maintain the power and influence they have inherited over their own tribes and geographical areas. (2) The merchants demand government control for security and order necessary to increase their trade and protect their interests. (3) The educated class is constantly on the increase. Their desires are no different from those of other educated Iraqis. They demand an increase in schools and the spread of education and development, such as construction and health projects, in their areas. They also want to have local administration in their hands and to destroy the influence of the tribal leaders. As to their political goal of achieving an independent Greater Kurdistan, the moderates among them don't believe that this is possible without the help of the great powers, since more than 90 percent of the Kurdish areas are outside Iraq. . . . If we look closely at the events and developments up to this destructive war, we can see signs that some of the great powers want to exploit the Kurdish problem for their own interests.[22]

Nuri al-Said goes on to warn that Iraq must be cautious in its treatment of the Kurds, particularly because of the instability in Iran, the conciliatory attitude of Tehran toward the Kurdish tribal leaders, the formation of Kurdish councils in areas under Russian control, the mobilization of the Turkish army on the border between Iran and Iraq, and the cooperation among Kurds in all of these countries.

With the resignation of al-Said, the government took a less conciliatory attitude toward the Kurds. The success of Barzani in repelling government attacks, and the support he enjoyed from Kurdish nationalists strengthened his resolve and imbued him with a new sense of mission. His growing power and prestige led him by 1945 to act as the real ruler of the area under his control. According to a report by the London *Times,* he arrogated to himself the power to intervene in intertribal disputes, intervene in government distribution of supplies, maintain armed followers, and prevent the construction of police posts, roads, and hospitals, so that the area was out of government control.[23]

Barzani's position seems to have been further stiffened because he believed he had British backing, a situation which would reoccur in the 1960s and 1970s with Soviet, American, Iranian, and Israeli aid. It is not known what the private stand of the British actually was. Publicly they urged Barzani to submit to the government. Al-Said, in his report, hinted at outside aid to the Kurds; he may have been referring to British as well as Russian aid. Government forces moved against Barzani and fierce battles erupted in the summer and fall of 1945. The Kurdish leader retreated and later fled to Iran.

Many of the neighboring tribes that opposed the Barzanis did so not for ideological reasons, but because they "welcomed the chance to repay old scores and be subsidized for doing it."[24]

Barzani's reputation as a leader in the 1943 and 1945 revolts, in addition to his having his own army, made him welcome in Mahabad, where, with Soviet support, a Kurdish government was established in Iran. He was granted the rank of general of the army at Mahabad. The newly established Kurdistan Democratic party (KDP) adopted a seven-point program for autonomy in Iranian Kurdistan. But the republic collapsed when the Soviets, under pressure from the Americans and the British, allowed the Iranian army to move against it.[25]

Barzani refused to surrender and was driven back to Iraq, where he was met by government forces, then to Turkey, and back to Iran, each country forcibly evicting him. With some 500 men, after a dramatic march, Barzani finally reached the Soviet Union, where he lived in exile until 1958, when he was allowed to return to Iraq.

## KURDISH POLITICAL PARTIES

There were other groups active in Kurdish politics besides Barzani's followers, including the Hiwa party, founded in 1936 and composed mainly of professionals and officers. Hiwa was in touch with Kurdish organizations in Iran and Syria and with the Iraqi Communist party. Essentially a nationalist coalition, Hiwa began to weaken after 1940 when its leadership became tribal and its membership embraced rightist and militarist supporters who alienated the leftist intelligentsia, a major element in the nationalist movement. This led to a split in 1944. The rightist faction was unable to survive by itself and the party collapsed.[26]

In the fall of 1945 a Kurdish Communist party (Shurish) was formed under the leadership of Salih Haidari. Shurish later split over the attempt to attract pro-Barzani tribal leaders, and the more radical elements under Haidari joined the Iraqi Communist party (ICP) instead. In the meantime, Shurish helped found Razgari Kurd (the Kurdish Liberation Front) which became a Kurdish nationalist front. It was under the influence of Shurish and Razgari Kurd that the Kurdish intelligentsia became attracted to Marxist-Leninist ideas and began to rely on Soviet aid.[27] The Soviet presence in Iranian Kurdistan triggered this trend.

The formation under Soviet influence of the Kurdistan Democratic party in 1945 in Mahabad encouraged Barzani and the leaders of the Razgari Kurd and the Shurish party to form a rival KDP in Iraq. A group under the leadership of Mulla Mustafa al-Barzani and Hamza Abdallah called for the formation of this new vanguard group. However, the Mahabad KDP already had a branch in Iraq under the leadership of Ibrahim Ahmad, who refused to join the new group without permission from Qazi Muhammad, the head of the Mahabad KDP.[28] This problem was resolved; but later, further differences emerged over entrusting the party's leadership to two feudal leaders. Salih Haidari, leader of the Shurish group, opposed their admission, while Hamza Abdallah, the representative of Mulla Mustafa, favored it. A conference was held in August 1946 and the majority voted to allow the two to become members. Opposed to tribal leadership, Ahmad and Haidari, among others, withdrew from the conference and joined the ICP.[29] Barzani was elected president of the KDP Central Committee. The Politburo was also formed, mainly from the leftist urban elements. The conflict between leftist and Marxist Kurdish elements on the one hand, and the more conservative and traditional wing of the Kurdish movement on the other, began at the founding conference of the KDP and has continued ever since to have an impact on the developments of the party and its attitude toward the Iraqi government.

In the KDP the Kurds had, for the first time, a vanguard party that sought to lead the Kurdish nationalist movement and define its goals. The party sought to achieve the Kurdish national aspirations within the framework of Iraqi national unity. It also stressed the brotherhood between Kurds and Arabs. It called for a joint struggle by the Arabs and Kurds against domination of the region by the Western powers, achievement of full independence and the formation of a truly parliamentary system. The program also advocated reform of the political and social structure, nationalization of heavy industries and the banks, and the elimination of illiteracy, including the establishment of a Kurdish university and making Kurdish the official language in the schools and government offices in the north of Iraq.

Some of the leftist Kurdish elements criticized the party for aligning itself with the tribal leaders and its failure to deal with the basic social and economic problems such as agrarian reform and the rights of the peasants.[30] The party was bound to do so because the tribal leadership was the main force which bore the burden of fighting against the Iraqi government. Another factor was the belief by some intellectual leaders, such as the party's general secretary, Hamza Abdallah, that national cohesion was the answer to achieving Kurdish unity and the key to his idea of a spontaneous nationalistic revolution. Hamza also believed that the national liberation movement would very soon start in Iraq and would be led by the tribal leaders loyal to Kurdish nationalism, since they were the driving force of the Kurdish revolution. Another Kurdish leader held that the Kurdish bourgeoisie was too weak to arouse the countryside without the tribal leaders, and so it was "stamped with a rightist tinge."[31] For these reasons, the KDP gave up the idea of building a truly popular political organization and refrained from including social reform proposals in the party program.[32]

Major changes were made in the KDP's program, however, beginning with the Third Party Conference in Kirkuk in 1953. The name of the party changed at that time from the Kurdish Democratic party to the Kurdistan Democratic Party of Iraq. The party under the leadership of Ibrahim Ahmad adopted a program clearly to the left of its earlier positions. It advocated agrarian reform, opposition to feudalism and tribalism, and supported the rights of peasants by helping to organize secret organizations, establishing cooperatives and generally agitating. Among the goals adopted at this conference were: support of the socialist camp against the imperialist camp; rejection of neutralism; abrogation of the treaties with

Britain and the ouster of British forces; ending the monarchy and establishing a popular democratic regime in Iraq; and self-rule for the Kurds within Iraq.

The trends manifested in the third conference program reflected the need for joint Arab-Kurdish cooperation and the opposition to secession or chauvinism as well as the need to link the Kurdish national movement with other liberation movements throughout the world. As a result, a number of leaders who had left the KDP and joined the Kurdish branch of the ICP returned to it. However, the Kurds maintained on the whole their normal characteristics, described by Stephen Longrigg as "their restlessness in a minority status, their antipathy to an Arab government, their uneasy leadership by feudal Aghas or intellectual townsmen toward a non-Iraqi nationalism or communism."[33]

To sum up, there have been two outstanding leaders who dominated the Kurdish nationalist movement: Shaikh Mahmud and Mulla Mustafa al-Barzani. Mulla Mustafa considered himself the man who carried the national banner after Shaikh Mahmud.[34] But the same factors that defeated Shaikh Mahmud in the 1930s led to the downfall of Mulla Mustafa in the 1970s. These included the lack of a clear national goal and the predominance of tribal elements and tribal loyalties that often frustrated nationalist activities. Modern concepts of nationalism and socialism were confined to a small number of educated young men in the cities and their ideas rarely penetrated to the masses in the rural areas. Often the Kurdish revolts were motivated as much by concepts of honor and pride, possibilities of financial gain, and a desire to struggle against the encroaching authority of the government as by nationalist goals.


## THE 1958 IRAQI REVOLUTION


After the death of King Faisal I in 1933, the monarchy rapidly lost its hold on the country. Faisal's successors lacked his intelligence, ability to work, and popularity. Moreover, the regime's close ties to the British and its failure to introduce reforms led to disaffection among intellectuals, students, army officers, and religious leaders. Moreover, the political parties failed to compensate for the lack of a strong monarchy.

The internal situation remained relatively quiet until 1948, when suddenly disturbances began anew. The immediate cause was Britain's attempt to perpetuate its influence over the country after the war. Early in the 1950s there were further difficulties over the renewal of the concessions to the Iraq Petroleum Company; and in the mid-fifties, over the Baghdad Pact. The situation continued to deteriorate until July 14, 1958, when under the leadership of generals Abd al-Karim Qasim and Abd al-Salam Arif a military group calling themselves Free Officers overthrew the monarchy.

The major reasons for the revolt were the impatience of a young generation with the slowness of reforms, the disenchantment with the way the country was governed, the growth of Arab nationalism as a radical ideology, which reached a high point after the merging of Syria and Egypt into the United Arab Republic, and the opposition to the Arab Union of Jordan and Iraq, which was seen as a deterrent to Arab nationalism.[35]

The ruling officers were more tolerant of minorities than the monarchy and sought to meet Kurdish demands for self-administration within a decentralized autonomy, although they did not approve of full autonomy because they felt it might lead to separation. The Kurdish nationalists welcomed the revolution because of its seemingly tolerant outlook.

Internal struggle between Qasim and Arif on the one hand, and some of the other Free Officers, who advocated union with the UAR, led Qasim at first to seek support from the Kurds and the communists. On July 27 the Provisional Constitution was announced. Article twenty-three stated that "The Kurds and the Arabs are partners within this nation. The Constitution guarantees their rights within the framework of the Iraqi Republic."[36] Many Kurds were appointed to high offices, and Mulla Mustafa al-Barzani was welcomed back to Iraq as a hero by Kurds and Arabs alike.

Kurdish activities suddenly increased under Qasim. Kurdish publications were freely circulated and many Kurdish intellectuals joined the ICP or cooperated with it. For this reason, the Kurds supported the Qasim regime. Qasim, faced by opposition from pro-monarchist tribal leaders and Arab nationalists such as Rashid Al Arif and the Baath, armed the Kurds and used them to terrorize opposition groups. The pro-Barzani Kurds took part in the massacre following al-Shawwaf's abortive revolt in Mosul on March 8, 1959. Similarly, the Kurds in Kirkuk attacked the Turkomans because of social grievances and historical enmity with the Turkomans, and in the hope that Qasim would in return grant them self-rule. Perhaps one might add that the Kurds aspired to replace the Turkomans as the largest single ethnic group in the oil-rich city of Kirkuk.[37]

The alliance between Mulla Mustafa al-Barzani and the communists, and the government's harsh action against the landowners frightened the chiefs of other Kurdish tribes, especially the Bardosts, who had helped the Iraqi government in the 1930s and 1940s against Barzani. As they began to move against the government, Barzani seized the opportunity to settle old scores.

Barzani's principal aims seem to have been to gain power over his opponents and to unify Kurdish forces under his control as the future representative of government authority in the northern area. By 1961 he was well on his way to achieving all of them.

Politically, Barzani was seeking control of the Kurdistan Democratic party, which had come under Marxist influence during his exile. Because of his reputation and increasing prestige, his control over the party was almost complete by the time the Fourth Party Conference was held in October 1959. On January 9, 1969, Barzani and nine others applied to the minister of the interior for a license to operate the KDP, which had been an underground group until that time. Their proposed program showed clearly the influence of the leftist intellectuals in the party, and the probable Soviet influence on Barzani stemming from his stay in the Soviet Union.[38]

A marriage of convenience, albeit with suspicion on both sides, seems to have been struck between the KDP intellectuals and Barzani. They needed a strong figure who had popular appeal and military strength, and he needed a structure through which to act and receive advice — although neither side wanted its territory encroached upon.

While Barzani's power within the KDP increased, relations between Qasim and the Kurds began to deteriorate. Neither Qasim nor his government were willing to give the Kurds the administrative self-rule they aspired to. The Kurds were led to believe that the reference to Arab-Kurdish partnership in the Constitution meant they would receive larger economic, social, and cultural roles in the country. But Qasim seems to have become suspicious of the Barzani leadership, particularly after the growth of its influence in the north.

In July 1961 Barzani submitted a memorandum to the government, demanding a substantial degree of autonomy for the Kurdish region. The government, afraid that such a plan might induce the Shiis to demand a similar status, rejected it, and the relations with the Barzanis worsened.[39] Qasim adopted a hard line against the Kurds and began to play off one faction against the other. Suspicion bred conflict, and very soon the war started between the central government and the Kurds.

At first the Barzanis fought alone against the government and the Kurdish tribal coalition. But in 1962 the KDP joined the Barzani faction. This change took place largely because Kurdish nationalist feeling had increased, but also partly through communist influence and partly in reaction to Arab nationalist agitation. In addition, Barzani gained supporters when Qasim alienated some traditional Kurdish leaders by pushing for agrarian reform and increasing taxes on tobacco, liquor, and gasoline. The fighting continued until January 1963, when a truce was declared.[40] The Barzanis had done rather well in the fighting, partly because they adopted guerrilla tactics and partly because Qasim was unwilling to press the fighting.[41]

In February 1963 Qasim was overthrown by members of the Baath party, who were in turn ousted by Abd al-Salam Arif in November of that same year. In November Barzani, who needed a breathing spell from the vigorous campaign waged against him by the Baath, sent a message to Arif that he was willing to accept government demands. The new government also needed some time to consolidate its authority, so a truce with the Kurds was arranged on February 10, 1964. Barzani's announcement of the cease-fire without prior consultation with the KDP created friction between him and his party.

Arif thought that a cease-fire and an attempt to rehabilitate the north would solve the Kurdish problem. Instead, tensions increased when Kurdish leaders objected to the deployment of Iraqi troops "within a few kilometers of the area occupied by the Kurdish army."[42] The government warned that the rebel activity had created a dangerous situation in the north and called for the disbanding of the Kurdish forces (Pesh Merga).

The situation further deteriorated when the government published the new Provisional Constitution, which declared that "The Iraqi people are a part of the Arab people, whose aim is total Arab unity."[43] Despite a guarantee of Kurdish national rights, the Kurds felt that they were offered less than in the 1958 Constitution, which had declared Arabs and Kurds to be partners in Iraq.

Barzani's acceptance of the cease-fire had led to a sharp split between him and the KDP. The KDP Politburo, headed by Ibrahim Ahmad, Jalal Talibani, Nuri Taha, and Umar Mustafa, opposed the proposals Barzani had negotiated without approval of the party. These leaders submitted new demands to the government and passed a resolution criticizing Barzani.[44] Barzani in turn held his own congress of the KDP and renewed contacts with the government. After acrimonious disputes, there were armed clashes, which ended with the Politburo faction being forced to flee temporarily into Iran, pursued by Barzani's forces.

The rift between the Politburo and Barzani was deeper than disagreement over the cease-fire. Conflict between the urban bourgeoisie and the tribal-feudal leaders had plagued the Kurds throughout the twentieth century, hindering their endeavors to achieve self-rule. By 1964, Barzani controlled major areas of Iraqi Kurdistan and had larger forces than did the Politburo. He held sway over the northern mountainous area, while the KDP under the Politburo was strongest in the southern, more urban plain. The Politburo's program of political education, establishing village councils, combatting illiteracy, and collecting taxes frightened and angered the feudal leaders, who already saw the KDP as an enemy. Barzani, on the other hand, criticized the KDP on the strength of tribal loyalty and his family's religious standing which he had long enjoyed. A temporary patching up of the differences between Barzani and the KDP did not last long. In 1967 the Politburo charged Barzani with betraying the party and its goals, and it rejected his leadership.[45]

Clashes between the Kurds and the government had also been going on during the Barzani–KDP struggle. In October 1964 Barzani resumed the negotiations with Arif, demanding the right of the Kurdish people to self-rule within the constitutional framework of the Iraqi republic.[46] The government made counter-demands, and the fighting continued until the death of President Arif in a plane crash on April 13, 1966.

General Abd al-Rahman Arif succeeded his brother as president. The new president declared that the Kurds would be granted self-rule guaranteeing their national identity, traditions, and language. Barzani suggested a truce to allow the government to show that it was genuinely interested in granting autonomy to the Kurds. Needless to say, both Barzani and the government needed a breathing spell from the fighting. Moreover, Barzani was hoping to undercut Talibani, who was also trying to negotiate with the government. On July 12, 1966, Premier Abd al-Rahman al-Bazzaz offered a twelve-point program, which Barzani accepted. While it did not grant all Kurdish demands, it went a long way toward meeting them. Barzani accepted the program, but the Bazzaz government fell before it could implement the program. Bazzaz's successor, Naji Talib, felt that Barzani did not represent a majority of the Kurds, and declared, "We do not want to turn Iraq into a second Lebanon."[47] President Arif toured the north and promised to implement several points of the Bazzaz program. This helped to calm the situation, but the hardliners in Talib's government were irritated when Barzani established his own de facto authority and undertook measures on behalf of the Kurds as part of carrying out the Bazzaz program, though it seemed "to be more than their due by virtue of their number in the country."[48] An uneasy truce with minor clashes prevailed during the remaining period of the Arif government's control, until the return of the Baath to power in 1968.

## KURDISH RELATIONS WITH FOREIGN POWERS

*The Soviet Union.* In the wake of the Russian Revolution some of the czarist junior officers and soldiers stationed at Khanaqin to fight the Turks revolted against their officers, sought contacts with the Kurds, and discussed with them the new ideas spread by the October Revolution. In 1919 Shaikh Mahmud sent a letter to the Bolshevik government seeking aid, without much response due to the communist government's problems at home.[49]

The Communist party has favored self-determination for the Kurds and Soviet influence was paramount during the establishment of the Mahabad Republic. Its influence spread to Kurdish areas in Iraq. Kurdish Iraqi officers who were sent to Mahabad by Barzani also contacted Soviet Colonel Jaafarov, of Kurdish origin, while they were there. Barzani ultimately found refuge in the Soviet Union in 1947.

Under Qasim the Soviet Union supported the government during the early months because of Qasim's reliance on the Iraqi Communists and because of his opposition to Jamal Abd al-Nasir, who often criticized the Soviet Union. The Soviets supported the Kurds because they saw in the Kurdish revolt the seeds of trouble for the Turkish and Iranian governments, which had become members of CENTO, but they did not want to alienate the Arabs. However, when relations cooled between Qasim and the communists in early 1962, East European radio stations began to criticize the Iraqi regime for its undemocratic and oppressive methods.[50] Nevertheless, the Soviet government continued to support Qasim because "Despite the Qasim government's undemocratic practices at home, the foreign policy of Iraq is generally anti-imperialistic thanks to the constant popular struggle. This is a bitter pill for the imperialists and their agents."[51]

Under the Arif regime, the Soviets granted aid to the Kurds, leading the Iraqi government to protest its action.

*Turkey.* Having suppressed its own Kurds after a number of revolts, Turkey was understandably opposed to Kurdish uprisings in Iraq. Earlier the Turks tried to use Shaikh Mahmud and his brother to revolt against the Iraqis and the British, hoping to reclaim Mosul. Mukarrum Talibani told this writer that the Turks were in contact with the Barzanis during the 1930s and promised them self-rule if they would help the Turks to take over Mosul.[52] After the fall of the monarchy, the Turks adopted a neutral position but did not close their borders to the Kurds. On the one hand, they favored the revolt because it created difficulties for the Qasim regime—a regime which had close ties with the Soviets. On the other hand, the Turks were cautious lest the Kurdish uprisings spread to their country.

Turkey was irritated by Iraqi military operations near her border but did not take action until August 15, 1962, when an Iraqi plane bombed a Turkish frontier post by mistake. On the following day, Turkish jets shot down an Iraqi plane which they claimed violated their air space, although the Iraqi government claimed the plane was miles inside its own border.[53] Though Turkish-Iraqi relations deteriorated and Turkish diplomats were withdrawn from Iraq, relations were improved later following the kidnappings by Kurdish rebels of Turkish peasants who had informed authorities about the gun-smuggling operations by the Kurds from Iran.[54] However, no significant change in the relations between Turkey and the Kurds had taken place during the Baath and Arif regimes.

*Iran.* After the overthrow of the Iraqi monarchy and the spread of socialist and Arab nationalist ideas among the Iraqi Arabs, Iran followed a friendlier policy toward the Iraqi Kurds. Iran kept its borders open and extended modest amounts of aid to the rebels. In 1963, Iran adopted an even more favorable policy, encouraging the Kurds to hold out because of her concern that the Kurds and the Baath might reach an accord. A transmitter was set up in Kermanshah to broadcast three hours daily in Kurdish, and a land reform law was instituted in the Kurdish area of Iran.[55]

After the fall of Qasim, the Iraqi chief of staff pointed out that fighting with the Kurds "proved Iranian borders are still open to the rebels and are still the main sources for staging, financing, and training them. . . . The Kurds were armed with Iranian and CENTO weapons."[56] And while Turkey's neutrality was praised, Iran's policy of supporting the rebels was often criticized by Iraqi officials. Iraq officially protested in early 1966.[57] In December 1970 a Kurdish leader, Kamuran Badr-Khan, told this writer that the Kurds received over 20 percent of their aid from Iran. Other sources believe it was much higher.[58]

In 1966 Iran and Barzani reportedly signed an agreement that granted Barzani substantial military and economic aid on the condition that he would not let Iraqi Kurdistan be used as a base for the Iranian Kurdish movement, and that he would side with the Iranian government against the Iranian Kurds.[59]

*Great Britain and the United States.* Qasim accused the "oil imperialists" of initiating the war against the government to put pressure on Iraq in two areas: the oil negotiations then in progress, and Iraq's claim to Kuwait. Two British civilians working with the IPC were arrested on charges of inciting the Kurds to revolt.[60] While Barzani and the KDP may not have needed an instigator, Britain and the United States were suspected of opposing a regime that had adopted anti-Western stands. The oil companies, particularly the IPC, were rumored to have given financial aid to the Barzanis in 1961. A Kurdish leader who represented the Kurdish revolution in Europe told this writer that "KDP threats to bomb oil installations were not taken seriously until the KDP bombed a pipeline. I was then contacted by a high official of the IPC, and I told him 'We will not stop attacks against IPC installations until you freeze Iraq's assets or give us aid.' He rejected this, and I warned him that we were serious. However, I believe that Barzani was getting money directly from them and this is the reason no serious attacks were mounted against the oil installations at that time, although such attacks would not have proven difficult."[61]

Barzani appealed to the United States for aid in 1962 when he told the *New York Times* correspondent Dana Adams Schmidt, who was the first American journalist to visit him, "Let the Americans give us military aid, openly or secretly, so that we can become truly autonomous, and we will become your loyal partners in the Middle East."[62] The United States may have responded at that time by giving Barzani aid through Iran, but it was not until a later period that the Americans became directly involved in giving aid to Barzani.

# 3

# Che BAACh PARCy FROM
# iCs ORiGiNs Chrough 1963

On February 8, 1963, the Iraqi branch of Hizb al-Baath al-Arabi al-Ishtiraki (Arab Renaissance Socialist party) overthrew the government of Abd al-Karim Qasim and brought to power in Iraq one of the most unusual political parties to emerge in the history of the Arab world. This seizure of power ushered the party onto center stage in the Arab world. The Baath party was able to stay in control for only nine months before it was ousted from power. However, it was to return five years later, and it remains in power until this day.[1]

Baath historian Kamel Abu Jaber stated accurately that regardless of its position, "left, right, or center, whether in power or out of power, the Baath party has left an impression on the entire political thinking of the Arab world, and perhaps its influence extends beyond these boundaries."[2]

## THE HISTORY AND IDEOLOGY OF THE BAATH PARTY

The Baath party was founded in 1940 in Damascus by Michel Aflaq, a Syrian Orthodox Christian intellectual, in collaboration with a Sunni Muslim Syrian intellectual, Salah al-Din al-Baitar. Both Aflaq and Baitar were sons of middle-class Syrian families. Both men had studied at the Sorbonne in the 1930s, where they came in contact with Marxist, Hegelian, and nationalist ideologies and philosophies. After graduation, Aflaq and Baitar taught in government schools during the French rule in Syria. Aflaq and to a lesser extent Baitar had established reputations as intellectuals and writers. Aflaq had written for *Al-Tariq al-Shuyuiyya,* a Communist publication, and the newspaper *Al-Ayyam*.[3] He also began to attract followers, mainly students, and to exert an influence which continued as his students went on to higher education or professional life as teachers, where they began to attract other students in other parts of Syria and, later, in Jordan, Lebanon, and Iraq.

In 1940, with a handful of supporters, Aflaq and Baitar founded the Harakat al-Baath al-Arabi (the Movement of the Arab Baath). The word *hizb* (party) was not used until 1944–45.[4] There are very few figures available on Baath membership, but Shibli al-Aysami claims that in 1941 there were twenty-five students who were members, divided into several cells.[5]

On April 7, 1947, the First Party Congress was held, attended by about two hundred Baathist youth primarily from Syria, with some also from Lebanon, Jordan, and Iraq. The constitution was approved at this congress, making it the official date for the founding of the party. The name of the party itself is worthy of close scrutiny. The literal translation of the word Baath means resurrection from the dead. The word also means to rise, to excite, to put in motion. This came to be very useful for a party that aspired to be dynamic, activist, and revolutionary.[6]

The party's influence grew as a number of its adherents entered the civil service and the army. By the early 1950s the party could count among its supporters a number of civil servants and army officers. While it never became a mass party, its influence began to grow in Syria because of the sensitive positions its adherents held in the government and the army. This influence was to spread to Jordan and Iraq as college graduates and intellectuals began to embrace the principles of the party.

The Baath party was unusual not only for its level of organization and the fact that its leaders did not come from the traditional sectors of Arab society, but also because it formed an ideology of its own. It is one of the few political parties with a comprehensive ideology and political doctrine to emerge in the Arab world.[7] It is the only party to call for pan-Arab unity, stressing the Arabs' need to overcome the boundaries and other artificial restraints imposed in the Middle East by the colonial powers.

The party's position on Arab unity is tied to its attitude toward the concept of nationalism itself. When the Baath party was born the world was witnessing the military and ideological struggle against fascism. This struggle was reflected in their ideas. Consequently, Baathist ideology contains a reaction to the communist view that nationalism is merely "a stage which had been bypassed by socialism, an accumulation of backward influences that form hurdles in the party of class consciousness and of human liberation."[8] On the contrary, Aflaq declared, "Nationalism is not a step in the ladder of rational but superficial logic of growth and development, nor is there a barrier between it and full humanitarianism. Rather it is the breeding ground for humanitarianism. It is not a social or political condition which can be realized materially in history, but is a spirit, direction, and set of values which contribute to the formation of peoples."[9]

The Baathists adopted the slogan of "one Arab nation with an eternal message." The Baathists hold the view that the Arab nation extends from the Atlantic Ocean in the West to the Arab Gulf in the East, and that centuries of Ottoman and Western control led to decline, division, and confusion. Theoretically, the Baathists preached nationalism as open to all inhabitants of the Arab nation regardless of religion, sect, or ethnic origin. In his writings, Aflaq said that the message must be understood as "willingness, readiness, and movement, rather than as a specific goal."[10] He added that "this nation has expressed itself and its attitude and life differently and variedly in the laws of Hammurabi, the poetry of Jahiliyya, the religion of Muhammad, and the culture of al-Ma'mun. It has a common feeling awakening it at different times and has one goal despite the periods of interruption or deviation." The present day message is for Arabs "to live in the present with its tragedies and pains" and to "respond to its call and necessities." One of the main conditions for the Arabs to do this is to be "honest in treating their illness in a courageous and serious manner . . . and as a result of sensing the diseases and corruption in their society, to admit them and to save themselves by their own efforts, without depending on foreign aid or on magical solutions."

Aflaq called for a revitalization of Arab society by taking the path of *al-inqilab,* which could be translated *revolution* or *transformation* of the people and the system. Aflaq said that "before being a political and social program, (the revolution) is that primary propelling power, that powerful psychic current, that mandatory struggle, without which the reawakening of the nation cannot be understood."[11]

The Baath party was seen by its members as a revolutionary party which believes that "its chief aims of resurrecting Arab nationalism and building socialism can only be achieved by revolution and struggle. . . . Hence the party decides in favor of transforming the present rotten situation into a revolution which is to include all sectors of life—intellectual, economic, social, and political."[12]

## THE BAATH PARTY IN IRAQ

Published material concerning the time and manner in which the Baath party entered Iraq is scarce. Baath party sources refer to two pamphlets which appeared in Iraq in 1948 under the titles *Ahadith al-Baath al-Arabi* and *Al-Siyassa al-Arabiyya.* The second pamphlet is said to have been widely distributed with significant impact on the intelligentsia and students.[13]

The only earlier reference to the party in Iraq is the attendance by some Iraqi university students of the founding conference in Damascus in 1947.[14] It becomes apparent, however, that the party spread to Iraq through two main routes: the recruitment into the Baath of a number of Iraqi students studying in Damascus and Beirut;[15] and the arrival in Iraq of a number of students from Iskandarun who carried with them the seeds of Baathist ideas.[16] Due to their youth and low standing in the Baath these students carried confused ideas of the party, but they were able nevertheless to put forward some ideas and expressions which left their impact on nationalist groups in Iraq. Some of the expressions were "the struggling Arab people has one common cause, struggle, and destiny"; "rejection of compromise," and "radical solutions." Some of the later arrivals also brought slogans about class and "popular classes."

By 1949 and 1950 Baathist ideas had spread farther among Iraqis, particularly among students and to a lesser extent among teachers and lawyers. Prior to 1952, the small number of the members did not allow for more than discussion, painting of slogans on the walls of Iraqi cities, and proselytizing among other students. But by 1952, Baath members were able to play a significant role in the nationalist strikes and demonstrations against the government's policies in October and November of that year.

This was due to two factors: the increase in party membership and enhanced party organization. Consequently, the leadership decided to take a more active role in the country's strikes and demonstrations.

The Baathists benefited greatly from this experience and were to excel in organizing strikes and demonstrations, challenging the regime, and working underground. They were to benefit further from the immobility of the ICP following the arrest of its top organizer and leader, Baha al-Shaikh Nuri, and the takeover by a more radical figure who contributed to the split of the ICP. This left the Baath as the main mover and organizer of nationalist activity during the last five years of the monarchy.

In 1953, the party published for the first time an underground newspaper, *Al-Arabi al-Jadid,* which was to change its name after two issues to *Al-Ishtiraki (The Socialist),* in order to "emphasize the social characteristic of the party and the role of the working classes in the struggle."[17] Baath officials admit that socialism was not pushed as a goal at this time since the movement was more concerned with liberation from colonialist control and establishment of a progressive democratic government which would allow political freedom and the right to organize labor. However, this did not prevent the paper from raising labor issues and emphasizing struggle as a principle for achieving workers' rights. Although the paper was published irregularly, and often printed on old mimeograph machines, it provided the party with an organ, maintained the spirit of the organization and brought it closer to the people.

The party during the 1950–56 period benefited from and contributed to the increasing nationalist tide in Iraq and in the Arab world as a whole. The party in Iraq began to realize the importance of organizing against Western designs in the Middle East and against the Iraqi groups sympathetic to the West. Through demonstrations and strikes in Iraq the party supported Egypt during the Anglo-French-Israeli attack which led the government to take strong repressive measures against the demonstrators, leaving many dead and wounded. Deciding that unified action was essential, in July–August 1956, the party issued a call in its newspaper *Al-Ishtiraki* for reviving the National Union Front. The call was renewed in early October 1956.[18]

The main problem was bringing in the Communist party, although Baathist literature had accused it of "hallucinatory leftism," of "sick leftism," and of betraying the nationalist movement during various stages.[19] The task was to convince the communists that individual action would not be sufficient to combat the government and cooperation was necessary. The efforts made by the Baath and other groups bore fruit when the National Union Front was reestablished in 1956.

The party continued its opposition to Nuri al-Said's government, especially to his reference in London to a permanent solution of the Palestine question by advocating Arab-Israeli negotiations in 1956. It also organized a successful strike in support of the Algerian war of independence in 1955.[20] As soon as the government reopened the schools following the pro-Egypt demonstrations in 1956, the party again organized strikes against the Al-Said government and the Baghdad Pact and called for the release of political prisoners. Clashes resulted and hundreds were arrested.

In the meantime, the party held its Fourth Regional Meeting in mid-November 1957, in which the main issue to be discussed was the party's role in the National Union Front. The Baath party also opposed the formation of an Arab Union between Jordan and Iraq as a response to the Syrian-Egyptian Union in the UAR.

Meanwhile, the party was gaining in numbers. Paradoxically, it was helped by a law passed by Nuri al-Said which provided military training for students who were considered troublemakers or who had taken a prominent part in demonstrations. He hoped that putting students in the army, which he considered loyal to the government, would change their ideas. Fuad Rikabi, the party's regional secretary, and Ali Salih al-Sadi, who was later to play an important party role, were among the Baathist activists to be sent to training camps in the north.[21] These two leaders not only managed to convert their fellow students to their ideas, but also officers, including the camp's commanding officer Major Salih Mahdi Ammash, who were to form the nucleus of party organization in the army.

The Baath party played only a small role in the July 1958 revolution against the monarchy. None of the 14 major Free Officers was a Baath party member, and of the 150 officers who knew about the planned revolt and associated themselves with it, only a few were Baathists. However, Abd al-Salam Arif, although he was not a member of the Baath, had family ties to Rikabi and supported the Baathist view of Arab unity and of unity with the UAR.

The party welcomed the revolution and urged its members to support it. In a party circular distributed in late August 1959 the party declared that it was confident that "the revolution and the government possess many of the elements which lead it in the progressive Arab direction."[22] It further urged support for the government and said that by getting popular support for the government it would be serving the goals of the party. Aflaq visited Baghdad in late July 1958 to add his voice to those of other party members urging that Iraq join the UAR.[23]

The period of the honeymoon did not last long. The break between Qasim and Arif and the ouster of Arif from his position in the government also brought an end to Rikabi's position as minister and to the Baathist role in the government. Qasim also began to rely more and more on the communists, which raised the ire of nationalist groups, including the Baath.

The party faced a number of setbacks and crises between 1959 and 1962. Some of these difficulties were internal and others external. In its efforts to combat the well organized communists, who were gaining strength and seeking to dominate labor and peasant organizations, the student unions, and civil defense groups,[24] the party sought to increase its numbers. It was able to make major gains in this area, particularly following the collapse of the Shawwaf revolt and the Kirkuk incidents when the government, with the Communist party, waged a harsh campaign against Baathists and Pan-Arabists, leading to an anti-communist reaction. This increase in numbers, however, was achieved at the expense of lowering the stiff membership standards. Many people were admitted simply because they had pan-Arab sympathies, which was to cause the party a number of problems including lack of control over its members and the appearance of internal party enemies.[25]

Externally, the Baathists and Pan-Arabists were a primary target of the regime. Many Baathists were killed and imprisoned, following the Regional Command's plot to assassinate Qasim, a move supported by the leaders of the UAR but not by the Baath's National Command. On October 7, 1959, a group of six Baathists (including Saddam Husain, now president of Iraq and chairman of the Revolutionary Command Council and assistant secretary general of the National Command of the Baath party) intercepted Qasim's car, wounding him and killing his driver. Baath Secretary General Fuad Rikabi escaped to Syria, while a number of leading Baathists were arrested and brought before the Courts.

The attempt on Qasim's life caused the government to strike further at the Baath and other pan-Arab elements, which greatly weakened the party apparatus in Iraq. The party's leaders criticized the attempt on Qasim's life and expelled Rikabi for planning it, because at that time the party still opposed assassination as a means of overthrowing the government and because the regional leadership under Rikabi had independently decided on the plan when it lacked a wide-ranging and detailed schedule to change the government.[26]

One of the problems of the sprawling Baath organization, as this incident shows, is that regional leaders acted without direction from the National Command, often cooperating with the UAR. This assassination plot is an excellent example, as was Jordanian Secretary General Abdullah Rimawi's advocacy of the supremacy of regional leadership in the party.

The defections of Rimawi, Rikabi, and others, the conflict with the leaders of the UAR, and the repressive acts of the Iraqi government left the party in Iraq, as well as outside, battered and weakened. The National Command, which was criticized because of its decision to dissolve the party in Syria when the UAR was formed, was nevertheless able to hold its ground during the Third National Congress and to preserve its legitimacy, although with a great loss in power, prestige, and members. The lower ranks of the party had to function on their own for a while in Iraq.[27]

The National Command set up a provisional Regional Command in Iraq with Talib Shabib replacing Rikabi as secretary general, and Ali Salih al-Sadi and Faisal Habib Khaizaran as members of the Regional Command.[28] This new leadership was able to restore party strength because of the following factors:

• The public reaction against Qasim and the communists, who had used brutal methods in suppressing the opposition;

• The fearlessness of the Baathist prisoners before the Mahdawi court. Some of them declared that they did what they believed was right and would do it again.

• The organizational skills of the new leadership and its ability to work underground.

• The withdrawal or expulsion of party members who were not strict partisans, leaving a tough, disciplined, and well-organized corps.[29]

Under the new leadership, the party issued an important circular in early October 1961, calling for united front action against Qasim.[30]

In a regional conference in May 1962 a permanent Regional Command was set up with al-Sadi as secretary-general. The party began to work to oust the communists from the labor unions and the teacher, student, and peasant organizations. The Baathists were able to score important gains in these organizations, where they accounted for two-thirds of the leadership.[31] The party was able to resume publication of its underground newspapers, and even when its offices were discovered it was able to continue publication from other places.

The organizational efforts were also paying off in another area. The party, despite its small number of actual members, was able to gain hundreds if not thousands of supporters and candidates for membership, and to train these people into a para-military organization called "al-Haras al-Qawmi" (National Guard). The party was further able to gain some support inside the army, despite the repression of the government and the opposition of the communists, because many nationalist officers saw the party as the only force capable of checking communist and regionalist tendencies. In addition, some supported it because they were opposed to Qasim. Although some of the Baathist army officers such as Ahmad Hasan al-Bakr and Mustafa Nasrat were discharged by the government, they were able to maintain their contacts with the military officers.[32]

In the meantime, Qasim's government was beginning to show signs of weakness and disintegration. The war against the Kurds was not conclusive and Qasim was becoming concerned over the activities of the opposition. Security forces began to tighten their control over the opposition and anyone whose loyalty to the regime was suspect.[33] Anti-government activity continued to rise, particularly among Baathists, who were preparing to seize power. The Regional Command had earlier informed the National Command, in the latter part of 1962, that it was ready to seize power, but the National Command was opposed to seizing power by a military coup except in special circumstances.[34]

The opportunity for the party arose when a student strike in Baghdad grew into a general strike with the help of the Baath. The strike grew out of a small incident between the son of Fadil Abbas al-Mahdawi, Qasim's cousin, and another student. When the school tried to punish both students, al-Mahdawi intervened on behalf of his son. This led to a strike against favoritism, which grew into an anti-regime rallying point, used by the Baathists to major advantage.[35]

The strike benefited the Baath party in two ways. It was able to mobilize large sectors of the people to support the party and to show them the weakness of the regime. It also enabled the party to advance its plans for seizing power. After the arrest of the party's regional secretary, Ahmad Hasan al-Bakr gave orders that the date of the revolt be moved ahead before Qasim could move against other Baath leaders.

On February 8, 1963, a group of well-armed National Guard members attacked the house of Jalal Awqati, the commander of the air force, and killed him. A second group attacked the Defense Ministry, where Qasim resided, and another group moved to the Rashid Army Camp to prevent troops from supporting Qasim. Still a fourth group took over the radio transmitter. The party then announced its coup, promising "to respect the rights of minorities and enable them to participate in national life."[36]

The outcome of the revolution was for a time uncertain, as the communists and some army officials rallied to Qasim's side. Heavy fighting continued for two days. On the second day Qasim surrendered and was sentenced to death by a court martial appointed by the new National Council of the Revolutionary Command (NCRC). The NCRC appointed Abd al-Salem Arif, who had helped organize the July 1958 Revolution, president of the republic, and Ahmad Hasan al-Bakr, the party's regional secretary, as premier.

## THE BAATH AND THE KURDS

A close study of Baathist ideology prior to 1963 shows that the Baath did not discuss in depth the question of minorities, including the Kurds, in the Arab world. But the party's background and ideas did reflect and express certain ideas about this question. Party literature declares that the development of the party in an environment of national suppression, division, backwardness, and Western domination led Baath leaders to dedicate the party to the liberation of the Arab nation by advocating progressive Arab nationalist ideas.

Zayd Haydar, a former member of the Baath National Command

and chairman of the party's foreign relations department, admits a tendency in the Baath party toward Arab chauvinism, in reaction to the oppression the Arabs had suffered. But he insists that this trend was not manifested in the writings of the Baath, whose struggle was aimed against the oppressors, not the oppressed nationalities.[37]

In 1955 Michel Aflaq gave the most detailed view of the Baath's stand on the question of national and religious minorities in the Arab world during a meeting with students from the Arab Maghrib. One of the students had raised the question of Berber identity in the Maghrib, and how to reconcile it with Arab nationalism.[38]

Aflaq explained that often the problem resulted from an incorrect understanding of Arabism:

> We need a new concept of Arabism to present to the world, to civilization, and to human thought. Closed, bigoted nationalism is more a danger to us because it fosters division instead of overcoming it. There were always hundreds of people in the Arab homeland who, due to ignorance, adopted the Nazi view even prior to the emergence of Nazism. There were always those who pictured Arabism as being limited to a specific group of people, and others who understood it as boastfulness and supremacy over others. Consequently there was a reaction to this fanatic nationalism among the Kurds, the Assyrians, and the Armenians.

Aflaq contended that the Baathist definition of Arab nationalism, by stressing flexibility, openness and dedication to fundamental human aspirations, provided protection for minorities in the Arab world:

> Defining Arabism alone is not sufficient, but the main issue in this question is that we have explained our nationalism through socialism and the idea of freedom. These are the real guarantees: socialism accompanied by nationalism and nationalism accompanied by socialism. When we call for economic equality and the offering of equal opportunity, we mean that we have delivered the nation's cause to its true owners, the people. And they are in fact one with no distinction between Muslim and Christian, Arab or Kurd or Berber.

To Aflaq, socialism and freedom, linked to nationalism, were the answer. He said, "It is inconceivable that nationalism be socialist and at the same time be bigoted, because socialism's philosophy is the erasing of all discrimination, exploitation, and the control of one group by another."

Concerning the Kurds and other ethnic minorities Aflaq asked:

> Why do ethnic minorities, like the Kurds or some amongst them, fear Arab nationalism? Most of this fear is a result of new imperialist propaganda that goes back fifty years, to when the British and the French en-

tered the Arab East. The Kurds lived side by side with the Arabs for hundreds of years and fought courageously to defend the Arab lands. What does the Kurdish sector of the people want, and to what do they aspire (except for some of the leaders who have feudal interests) other than to live a happy and dignified life where they receive what others receive and give what others give. These individuals do not want more than what the Arabs want for themselves.

Aflaq uses socialist analysis to overcome the conflicts between ethnic minorities:

> Now there are no oppressed minorities or sects, but there is an oppressed majority of the people which is the Arab people, and there is an oppressing minority of those conspiring with imperialism. The Arab, the Kurd, the Assyrian, the Moslem, the Christian, the Druze—individuals who form 90 percent of the Arab nation are oppressed and deprived by a minority which exploits the corrupt situation and benefits from the presence of foreigners.

To Aflaq the problem was one of class structure. There were exploiting classes "conspiring against the interests of the people, and the way to solve the problem is through ending this exploitation in order to eradicate the distinction among citizens."

Aflaq went on to say that "no one will prevent the Kurds from learning their language as long as they submit to the laws of the state and do not become a threat to it."

In another speech on Arab nationalism, given in Cairo in 1957, Aflaq again emphasized: "The Arabs today do not wish their nationalism to be racist. This desire springs from their nationalist experience. They have experienced racism. They have experienced oppression."[39]

Despite Aflaq's views, Article 11 of the Iraqi Constitution has caused the Baath some embarrassment and led to mistrust on the part of ethnic minorities, particularly the Kurds. This article was used by enemies of the Baath as an example of Baathist chauvinism and anti-Kurdish attitudes. The article reads as follows:

> To be excluded from the Arab fatherland: whoever has fought for or has belonged to a factious anti-Arab association; whoever has lent himself inside the Arab fatherland to colonial ends.[40]

The Baathists were concerned over this issue. Their response to the charge of chauvinism was:

> Enemies of the Arab cause seek to stir up ethnic minorities in this or that minority of the Arab homeland and make it believe that it is the group in-

tended in Article 11 of the Constitution. The condition is clear in this article: it is concerned with the formation of an anti-Arab bloc. Does the
Kurdish nationality or (do) other nationalities and minorities fall under
this category? And the answer here is clear because Arab-Kurdish brotherhood . . . and the relation between Arab nationalism with the nationalities and minorities with whom it lives in one homeland was always on
the level of affection, friendship, and common struggle.[41]

The Baath sought through occasional meetings with Kurds before the
1958 Revolution to explain this issue. These meetings were rare and not on
a high level. The most important one, however, occurred a few days after
the July Revolution, between Aflaq and a Kurdish delegation headed by
the leftist KDP Secretary General Ibrahim Ahmad.[42]

While the meeting did not detail the Baathist attitude on how to deal
with the Kurdish question, it served to erase some Kurdish suspicions,
creating a mood of trust between Ahmad and Aflaq. In fact Aflaq is rumored to have played a major role in getting Ahmad and the KDP to
agree not to oppose Baathist attempts at seizing power[43] and contributed
to the KDP decision to join the United Front, of which the Baath was a
member.[44]

Yet the Baathist call for Arab unity continued to alienate Kurdish
leaders. The Baath accused the ICP of "distorting the position of the nationalist movements among the minorities and particularly among the
Kurds"[45] and later admitted the partial success of attempts to portray
Arab unity as being aimed against national minorities.[46] The seriousness
of these charges was manifested in the party's efforts to explain its stand.
An article published on September 5, 1958, in the Baath newspaper, *Al-
Jumhuriyya,* expressed the party's point of view, declaring that, "Kurds
and Arabs are partners in Iraq," and that "The brotherhood is formed
and sustained by time, common interests, and a common goal: achieving
freedom and a better standard of living." The article sought to explain
that Arab nationalism:

> cannot be aggressive or bigoted. It cannot deny others what it seeks for
> itself. Kurdish-Arab brotherhood is something precious, and the Arab
> liberation movement is seeking to prevent its disruption. . . . Arab na-
> tionalism does not deny anyone his legitimate rights or lessen his role in
> society. Iraq's being a part of the Arab homeland and the Kurds being
> partners with the Arabs in this country are genuine and basic facts. . . .
> The Kurds and the Arabs are brothers, not because we want this today,
> but because it is a historical fact. Brotherhood includes rights and status
> to all the partners.

This statement is perhaps the most significant the Baath party ever made on the subject: there was a hint in it of the Kurdish rights to self-determination and unity, since it said the Arab nationalist movement would not deny to others what it sought for itself. However, it spoke only of rights and partnership — nothing more.

Following the initiation of the Provisional Constitution, which declared that the Kurds and the Arabs were partners in Iraq, the party newspaper, *Al-Jumhuriyya* (October 10, 1958), stated that "the existence of the Kurds in this region does not need proof, because our existence as Arabs and Kurds in Iraq indicates that there is a common homeland for us. Arab-Kurdish brotherhood never was something that had to be put down on paper, because it is not a commercial agreement or a temporary treaty between two groups seeking to move closer to each other. Rather, it is the tie of past, present, and future life."

The Baath, however, condemned the Kurdish uprising of 1961. Baathists said that this stand was not taken against the Kurdish cause as such but against the political position taken by some Kurdish factions, which had opposed Qasim without taking into account the movement of the Iraqi people against the Iraqi government.[47] The Baath also accused Qasim of fostering trouble among the Kurds by stirring up tribal tensions and by arming the Kurds with military supplies, until "the north became a great armed camp threatening the security of the country."[48]

But regardless of its criticism of the leadership of the Kurdish movement and its allies, the party's underground newspaper, *Al-Ishtiraki,* declared:

"Kurdish aspirations cannot receive the aid and support of all of our people in Iraq unless the Kurdish movements are aware of the Arab liberation struggle and its demands, and cooperate and support the progressive Arab movements. . . . The [proper] Kurdish movement, which could embody and fulfill the Kurdish cause, is the one that ties itself to the Arab nation's cause and which sees in Arab unity and its victory support and not a threat. . . . The movement that thinks the Arabs are its enemies is an enemy to the Kurdish people."[49]

Baathists are reported to have made contacts with the Kurdish rebels as early as February 1962. Dana Adams Schmidt reports that Colonel Tahir Yahya had contacted Ibrahim Ahmad of the KDP to discover the conditions under which the Kurds were prepared to support the revolt and that the Kurds demanded autonomy as the condition for their support.[50] Other sources speak of contacts between General Ahmad Hasan al-Bakr and Colonel Abdallah al-Shamzini, a Kurdish officer and leader of the KDP.[51] These sources also report rumors that Aflaq may have had a role in the negotiations but cannot confirm it. Furthermore, they claim that the KDP leaders were aware of the time and plan of the Baath revolt and did support it. Uriel Dann, however, states that the Baath revolt was undertaken without the Kurds being informed.[52] Dann also reports that Baath leader Ali Salih al-Sadi and KDP leader Salih al-Yusufi met and agreed on autonomy for the Kurds. Devlin, however, doubts that any meaningful contacts or discussions took place.[53]

While most sources agree that contacts did take place, there is no evidence from the Baath side that they had made any agreement concerning autonomy other than promising to study the issue.[54] It is unlikely that the Baath officials had given sufficient thought at the time to this question to have promised the Kurds anything beyond recognition of Kurdish civil rights within an Iraqi national framework.

## THE BAATH GOVERNMENT AND THE KURDS

The Kurdish issue was one of the questions mentioned in the National Revolutionary Command Council's (NRCC) statement on the morning of February 8, 1963, when the Baath came to power in a coup. This statement declared that one of the new government's goals was to achieve national unity by "the strengthening of Kurdish-Arab brotherhood in a manner that would guarantee the national interest, strengthen the common struggle against imperialism, and [express] respect for the rights of minorities by allowing them to participate in the national life."[55]

Immediately after the pronouncement of the revolt, Barzani sent a telegram to the new government expressing his support and demanding self-rule for the Kurds. He also ordered his followers to cease armed activities against government forces. On its side, the government issued orders to the Iraqi forces to cease firing, released Kurdish prisoners, and allowed former government officials who had joined the rebels to return to work. Two Kurdish leaders who had not taken part in the rebellion were appointed to the cabinet.[56]

These gestures of good will on both sides contributed to a better atmosphere for negotiations and encouraged the belief that a peaceful solution to the Kurdish question was possible.[57] On March 1, 1963, the NRCC issued a statement on the Kurdish question, declaring: "The revolution is determined to eliminate the traces of the hated Qasim regime, and to erase them by working to achieve participation of all citizens in the one homeland by guaranteeing the rights of our Kurdish brothers."[58]

A meeting between government representatives and Barzani took place shortly thereafter, on March 5, 1963. The Iraqi delegation was headed by General Tahir Yahya, the Iraqi chief of staff; Fuad Arif, a Kurdish minister in the government; and Ali Haidar Sulaiman, a Kurd who was serving as the Iraqi ambassador to Washington. During the meetings Barzani presented his views concerning Kurdish self-rule, giving it a broader interpretation than previously, and warned that unless his views were accepted within three days he would resume the fighting.[59] However, he is also reported to have told the delegation that his demands represented a position paper and that he was not insisting on any specific points.[60]

The government delegation returned to Baghdad to discuss his sweeping demands with the NRCC, which decided to form a delegation to negotiate further with Barzani. The delegation, headed by Muhammad Rida al-Shabibi, head of the Popular Front party, was composed of well-known leaders of political parties as well as leading Iraqi and Kurdish personalities.[61]

The delegation met with Barzani on March 7 and was able to reach a preliminary agreement. However, this agreement had to be accepted by Barzani's followers and by the government before it could go into effect. The agreement included the following points: general amnesty for all Kurdish rebels; the purging of Iraqi officials guilty of misconduct in the north; the immediate lifting of the economic blockade of the Kurdish areas under Barzani's control; general amnesty for all participants in the Kurdish revolt; and withdrawal of Iraqi military units from Kurdistan. The most important section of the agreement, however, was the first article, which referred to "Recognition of the national rights of the Kurdish people on the basis of self-administration (this item to be incorporated into the provisional and forthcoming permanent constitution), and establishing a joint committee which would begin immediately to clarify the way to execute [the above-mentioned item]."[62]

On March 8, the delegation held its second meeting with Barzani, only to discover that he was reluctant to accept the agreement reached on the previous day and was now making additional demands. Barzani's attitude may have been influenced by the news that the Syrian Baathists had seized power in Damascus. Iraqi government sources, however, question whether the news was released in time to change Barzani's attitude. They believe that Barzani was not negotiating seriously. In spite of Barzani's reluctance, the delegation was able to persuade him to accept Kurdish self-administration in principle after assuring him that his views would be discussed in detail during future negotiations. Barzani was also promised that the government would issue an immediate declaration concerning its acceptance of the agreement.[63]

Following the delegation's return to Baghdad, therefore, the government announced the lifting of the economic blockade of the north on March 9, 1963, and on March 10 the National Revolutionary Command Council declared amnesty for the Kurdish rebels. The NRCC followed that declaration with a major statement outlining the government's policy toward the Kurds. This announcement declared the government's recognition of the national rights of the Kurdish people on the basis of decentralization.

The NRCC announcement added that the principle of decentralization "shall be inserted into the Provisional Constitution and into the permanent one when it is legislated."[64]

Along the same lines, Baathist leader Ali Salih al-Sadi stated on March 16 that "Granting the Kurds a decentralized system of government is acknowledging a principle recognized in all modern states. . . . This does not, in any way, mean secession, nor does it mean delegation of power on foreign, economic, or internal political matters, for these are all within the competence of the central government."[65]

It is important to note that autonomy, or self-rule, was not mentioned at this stage, although "decentralization" was understood and accepted by both sides as the recognition of the rights of the Kurds to self-administration.[66]

Prime Minister Ahmad Hasan al-Bakr announced on March 15 the text of the provisional program of the revolution, which emphasized "The revolution views with consideration the aspirations of the Kurdish nationality to increase its participation in developing the country, to develop and oversee its culture and language, and to assist in realizing the system of decentralization which allows for greater flourishing of the whole people."[67]

These declarations and statements, however, failed to satisfy some Kurdish leaders who were critical of the government's decision to negotiate with Barzani, claiming that Barzani did not represent all of the Kurds.[68] Barzani responded to this criticism by holding a KDP conference on March 17–19 in Koisanjaq in order to consult with Kurdish representatives on the agreement reached with the Baghdad delegation. The conference was attended by about 2,000 people, of whom 168 were official delegates, including leftist factions of the KDP, representatives of the Kurdish armed forces, and representatives of Kurdish tribes and minorities.[69]

A committee of 35 members was formed to prepare a new set of demands. Another committee, formed of fourteen Kurdish figures, including seven as advisers and headed by Jalal Talibani, was selected to continue negotiations with the government.[70]

The committee arrived in Baghdad on March 30 to meet with an official government delegation, but the government was preoccupied with its negotiations with Syria and the UAR concerning the formation of a unified Arab state. These talks held in Cairo alarmed the Kurds, who were concerned about their status in a larger Arab state. Jalal Talibani was allowed to join the Iraqi popular delegation which went with the official delegation to Cairo where he met with President Nasir.[71]

On April 8, Talibani presented a note to the Iraqi delegation in Cairo on behalf of the Kurdish committee, indicating the Kurdish attitude toward the proposed federation. The memorandum, copies of which were sent to members of the Syrian and Egyptian delegations, consisted of the following three points: The Kurds demanded the right to be represented at the conference, because whatever decisions were taken would affect the Kurdish people and their rights in Iraq, including decentralization; The Kurds would at no time stand in the way of the Arab people's will and the type of relationship they established among their regions and governments; In order to avoid any future conflict between the decisions adopted at the Cairo conference and the Kurdish people's national rights in Iraq, the delegates should be made aware of the Kurdish people's views concerning relations with the Arab people: if Iraq remained completely independent, the Kurdish people asked only that their national rights be respected on the basis of decentralization, as had been agreed upon; if Iraq joined a federation, the Kurdish people must be granted wide autonomy in the classic meaning of the term; if Iraq were fused in complete union with one or more Arab states, the Kurdish people would form a region in this state in a way which would fully preserve their existence, and at the same time remove suspicion of possible secession.[72]

On April 10, after Talibani had been unable to meet with an official government delegation to present his demands, the KDP distributed a circular which included the party's proposals concerning the concept of "decentralization."[73] Some of these proposals bordered on secession. This circular required the election of a Kurdish vice president of Iraq who would be elected only by Kurds and the establishment of a separate vilayet of Kurdistan, which would have its own constitution, government, and national council. It also demanded the establishment in the vilayet of Kurdish ministries of education, interior, health, labor, settlement, transportation, justice, agricultural reform, agriculture and social affairs, and economic affairs. (This last ministry was to be in charge of industrial, planning, and oil affairs in the Kurdish areas.) These ministries would carry out in Kurdistan the functions performed by the national ministries for all of Iraq. The ministry of education of the Kurdish area was to have the right to send students abroad and to give scholarships without having to consult with the national ministry of education.

While the KDP circular provided that foreign affairs and defense would be the responsibility of the national government, the section on defense raised Baathist fears because it required that the under-secretary of the ministry of defense as well as the vice chief of staff, be Kurds. Moreover, should the Iraqi army change its name and become part of the proposed Arab Union's forces, the part of it placed in Kurdistan would then be called a Kurdish army. This army would be composed of soldiers and officers from the Kurdish area. Additionally, the central government was denied the right to send additional troops to the Kurdish area except in the case of a foreign invasion or the threat of foreign aggression on the borders of the republic. Even that could not be done without the approval of the government of the decentralized area or its National Council. The circular added that the content of this section was not intended to hamper the Iraqi army in its normal maneuvers or training, which could be carried out after informing the authorities of the decentralized area of the time and place of these activities.

The circular also demanded that the commander of the Kurdish forces be nominated by the Kurdish government and that the National Council have veto power over his appointment. Furthermore, the army within Kurdistan would not be mobilized or moved internally without the approval of the Kurdish government and its National Council. A proportionate number of Kurds in the population was to be taken into national military institutions (in amended proposals this referred specifically to the police, army, air force, and other military services) until similar institutions were set up in the Kurdish areas. This provision implied that the Kurds were planning to set up their own separate military services.

The revenues for the Kurdish areas would come from the taxes levied inside Kurdistan and from its share in oil revenues and customs duties. This share was defined as half of the income from the oil revenue in Kurdistan and a percentage, in proportion to the population of the Kurdish area, of Iraq's customs duties and other taxes. Two other alternatives for revenue were offered: half of Iraq's oil revenues, or a share of all taxes and income in proportion to the population figures.

The April 10 KDP circular also called for the appointment of a Kurdish under-secretary in each of the central ministries and stated that the number of Kurdish officials in these ministries must be in proportion to the number of Kurds in the general population. The circular also demanded that the new National Council be responsible for administration and legislation of all internal affairs of the region. The plan promised that Kurdish authorities would guarantee the social, economic, and cultural status of national minorities such as Assyrians, Turkomans, and Armenians.

Consequently, on April 13 a ministerial delegation headed by Sadi met with the Kurdish delegation, which officially submitted these proposals for decentralized administration. The proposals were rejected by the government.

An amended set of proposals was submitted to the government one week later, following the signing of a federal charter between the governments of Syria, Iraq, and Egypt on April 17.[74] This plan did not differ greatly from the previous Kurdish proposal. Some of the changes, however, were significant. The earlier KDP circular called for the Kurdish area's ministry of education to act as if it were the ministry of an independent country, initiating actions with foreign governments and sending students abroad without the approval of the central government. This section was deleted in the amended proposal. The demand for the appointment of a Kurd as vice-chief of staff of the armed forces was also deleted. And while it still demanded that a proportionate share of all revenues of Iraq be given to the Kurdish area, the new proposal stated that this share should be computed after the central government had deducted its expenses for matters remaining under its jurisdiction.

The amended proposal, however, also demanded a share of the loans and nonmilitary aid received by the government. It required appointment of a Kurdish assistant chief of staff and appointment of other Kurds according to their number in Iraq's population in every central government ministry, not just specified departments. But the proposal which most angered the Baathist government was the one concerning the delineation of the Kurdish area. Article Six of the Kurdish proposal declared that "The Kurdish area includes the provinces of Sulaymaniyya, Kirkuk, Arbil, and the districts inhabited by a Kurdish majority in the provinces of Mosul and Diala." Differences between the government and the Kurdish delegation immediately arose over the borders of the Kurdish area. The Kurds insisted that Kirkuk must be a part of the Kurdish area, while the government said that Kirkuk, with the exception of the Chimchimal district, which would be allowed to become a part of the Kurdish region, was inhabited by a Turkoman-Arab majority. The fact that Kirkuk was the center of an oil-rich area may have figured in this argument.

The government went on to appoint a five-man ministerial committee, joined with five members of the delegation that had met with Barzani on March 7, and assigned to the group the authority to negotiate with the Kurdish delegation and to prepare the self-administration program for Iraq. This government team was composed of General Salih Madhi Ammash, the minister of defense; Mahmud Khattab, the minister of municipalities; Naji Talib, the minister of industry; Hazim Jawad, the acting interior minister; and Mahdi al-Dawlai, the minister of justice. The five nongovernment figures included Shaikh Muhammad Shabibi, Husain Jamil, Aziz al-Duri, and Ali Haidar Sulaiman.[75]

In accordance with the declaration the NRCC had made on March 15, 1963, the ten men prepared a proposal called the Decentralized Administration Project.[76] Iraq was to be a unified country composed of Arabs and Kurds each enjoying equal rights. To achieve this, the plan proposed the formation of six provinces in Iraq, one of which, the Sulaymaniyya governorate, was to be the Kurdish region. The new Sulaymaniyya governorate would be composed of Arbil Province, the new Duhok Province (which would include five districts of oil-rich Mosul province), and Sulaymaniyya province (to which would be added the Chimchimal District from Kirkuk). Kurdish and Arabic were to be the official languages in this province. The language of education in the elementary and secondary schools, however, would be Kurdish, while Arabic would be taught as a second language.

Each of the six governorates, including Sulaymaniyya, was to have control over the following areas: education, municipal affairs, development, housing, transportation, trade and provisions, health, labor, irrigation, and agriculture. The governorates would be run by a governor who would direct two regulatory councils with a mix of officials elected by popular ballot and appointed by Baghdad. One would have council authority to legislate local regulations, approve annual budgets for local administration, and make suggestions concerning development projects in the governorate. The other council would be charged with carrying out all the decisions of the governorate council and the laws and regulations of the Iraqi government.

The revenue for the governorate would be collected from half of the national government's income from property taxes; half of the taxes on gasoline; special grants from the central government; tolls from bridges and other passways; any share of government revenues assigned by the central government by law; loans from the government; revenues allocated in the general budget to local administration; and other additional taxes within the provinces.

This plan was undoubtedly a step forward on the part of the government, although it fell far short of the Kurdish demands. Nevertheless, the ideas it put forth and the rights it granted to the Kurds were more than any government had been willing to grant to the Kurds previously. A form of self-administration was offered allowing the Kurds to participate in running their own educational, economic, and social affairs. The plan, however, retained for the central government a significant share of power by allowing it to appoint the governors and some other leading provincial officials and denying the local authorities power to act on sensitive issues without the approval of the appropriate ministry in Baghdad.

Barzani and the KDP, however, rejected this plan, primarily because it did not grant them the oil-producing province of Kirkuk and because they feared that implementation of the proposal would significantly weaken their authority in the Kurdish areas. The government, for its part, was fearful that acceding further to Barzani's demands would mean the disintegration of the country.

The situation became tense, as the government increased its pressure and added restrictions on the Kurdish delegation; the government also re-imposed the economic blockade on the north. Barzani continued to reorganize his forces and train new recruits. He extended his control over new areas, attacked Kurdish opponents and set up a radio transmitter in the Kurdish area.[77]

The situation quickly deteriorated. Barzani's forces began kidnapping government officials and members of the National Guard in the Kurdish areas, attacked army units, burned villages of Barzani's traditional Kurdish opponents who refused to side with him, and set up their own courts in Koisanjaq. On June 8, one week after the government's offer of self-administration, Kurdish partisans attacked a military convoy on routine maneuvers in Sibilik, killing one officer and a number of other soldiers. The Iraqi army commander in the region called on Barzani to surrender the attackers, and Barzani responded in a telegram that, "They are free in their own country."[78]

Two days later, on the direction of the Iraqi cabinet, the NRCC accused Barzani and his collaborators of committing a number of crimes: aiding and sheltering communists and criminals; cutting telephone lines between cities and villages; attacking Iraqi forces; kidnapping local officials and national guardsmen; disarming pro-government Kurdish villages; ordering citizens in the northern region to ignore the central authorities and treating Barzani's forces and representatives as the real authority; extorting money from citizens; searching cars and buses within the Kurdish regions; and attacking anti-Barzani Kurdish leaders and clans and burning their villages.[79]

The statement further ordered Barzani and his followers to lay down their arms and support the government in order to save the region from the woes of war. The government called on the public to help liquidate "this traitorous gang" and its supporters.

Sadi held a press conference that same day (June 19, 1963) saying that negotiations had continued from June 6 through 8[80] despite the incidents mentioned above, but that Barzani had refused the government's proposals and sent Jalal Talibani abroad to publish a series of antigovernment statements.[81] Talibani had gone to Cairo where he was received sympathetically because of the growing differences between Nasir and the Baathists.

## RESUMPTION OF THE FIGHTING

On June 10, four Iraqi divisions were moved to the north, as well as the cavalry of Khalid ibn al-Walid (Arab irregulars) and the Salah al-Din cavalry (recruited from anti-Barzani Kurdish tribes).[82] The fighting proved fierce and difficult, but the Iraqi forces were able to advance during the summer months and occupy a number of important towns and strategic positions previously held by the Kurds. On June 14 Jabl Sir Aqrah fell; on June 19 Mount Pierce was taken; and on June 22 the Baathists captured Koisanjaq, the spiritual capital of Kurdish nationalists. By July 7 the government forces had occupied the Raniyah District, and the next day Bikhair Mountain in the Zakho area near the Syrian-Turkish border was taken. On July 23 the second capitol of the Barzanis, Sir Piran, fell and was followed on August 13 by the town of Barzan itself, and on September 14 by Shirwan.

The retreating Kurds left much of Iraqi Kurdistan controlled by the government forces, but the Kurds refused to surrender. The Iraqi army's quick successes were based on its ability to move into areas where roads and communications allowed it to get logistical support. But their advance was blocked when they reached the more remote mountainous areas, where Barzani's experience and the Kurds' ability to carry on mountain guerrilla warfare told heavily in their favor.

The army also benefited from the use of its generally unopposed small air force.[83] In addition the army had superior firepower and benefited greatly from the support of Kurdish irregulars. Many of these came from traditionally anti-Barzani tribes such as the Zibaris, Harkis, Brifkanis, Lulanis, Baradosts, and Sharafis.[84]

The Iraqi army also benefited from the establishment of a military union between Iraq and Syria, which followed the announcement on September 30 of a proposed Syrian-Iraqi federation.[85] General Ammash, Iraq's Minister of Defense and a long-time Baathist, was appointed commander of the joint Syrian-Iraqi forces. One division of the Syrian army under the command of Colonel Fahd al-Shair joined the fight against the Kurds near the Syrian-Turkish border on October 28, and Shair announced that Syrian-Iraqi forces "had mopped up the regions of Fish Khabur and Bikhair in the Zakho area."[86]

Nevertheless, the Kurdish forces were able to hold the remote mountainous areas near the Iranian and Turkish borders. The lack of good roads, the coming of winter, and Kurdish expertise in mountain warfare were able to block the army, which had been close to crushing the Kurdish revolt. The Kurdish position was further strengthened by serious conflicts within the Baath party and between the Baathists and the rightist military officers who were their partners in power.

On November 18, 1963, the Baathist government was overthrown by a coalition of rightist and Nasirist officers led by President Arif. Their forces marched on Baghdad and ousted the government following brief clashes with the pro-Sadi national guard. With the collapse of the Baath government, the army's drive against the Kurds also collapsed.

The Kurdish revolt did not fail to have wide repercussions within and beyond the Arab world. Most Arab countries backed the Iraqi government with varying degrees of enthusiasm, with the notable exception of Egypt, which actively opposed Baghdad. Nasir was undoubtedly motivated by his rivalry with the Baath and his concern over the possibility of the Baathists' achieving a successful union between Syria and Iraq. The success of this union would have challenged Nasir's leadership of the Arab world. Nasir himself received Kurdish leader Jalal Talibani in June, 1963.[87] *Al-Muharrir,* a Nasirist newspaper published in Beirut, summarized Egypt's stand as follows: "Cairo rejects any Kurdish secession, and stands opposed to their demand for a Kurdish division within the Iraqi army. These points aside, Cairo believes it possible to solve the Kurdish question on the basis of granting autonomy to the Kurds.[88]

As relations deteriorated further between Nasir and the Baathists, Nasir's confidant and the editor of *Al-Ahram* newspaper, Muhammad Hasanayn Haykal, waged a campaign against the Baathists, whom he charged with seeking Iranian, Turkish, and Western support against the Kurds.[89]

In the West the Kurdish cause received sympathetic hearing, but there was no public support for the Kurds from Western governments.

The Soviet Union adopted a hostile attitude toward the Baathist government because of its repression of communists. On June 10, Soviet Foreign Minister Andrei Gromyko sent official notes to the Iraqi, Iranian, Syrian, and Turkish governments in which he charged Iraq, Iran, and Syria of intervening militarily in northern Iraq. The note added that such activity would concern other countries besides Iraq, since the entry into the area of any forces linked to military blocs would have political repercussions threatening many states, including the USSR.[90] The three countries denied the charges.

On July 11, the U.N. Economic and Social Council refused to consider the Soviet charge that Iraq was seeking the "physical elimination of the Kurdish minority."[91] At this time the Soviets also suspended their arms shipment to Iraq. (Iraq in the meantime had signed an arms deal with Britain.) The Soviet position was made clear in a May 6 *Pravda* article, which accused the Iraqi government of following "a policy of terror and repression" and of intentionally protracting the negotiations with the Kurds.[92]

In Turkey, Kurdish leaders began to agitate for Kurdish rights in the eastern provinces where they formed a majority, and some minor clashes took place.[93] Turkish authorities reacted promptly and severely by jailing Kurdish leaders and sending troops to the Iraqi-Turkish border.[94] The Turkish paper *Millyet* declared that "Turkish and Iraqi authorities will cooperate whenever necessary."[95]

Iran, because of its conflict with Iraq, was interested in exploiting the Kurdish war for its own benefit. Most of the arms reaching the Kurds came through Iran.[96] But Iran limited its support to the Kurds for fear that the Kurds under Tehran's authority might begin agitating.

## THE BAATH'S ASSESSMENT OF THE 1963 IRAQI EXPERIENCE

The Kurdish conflict was one of the major factors behind the ouster of the Baath government in Iraq, although undoubtedly a number of other factors contributed. In his assessment of the Baath party's 1963 experience in Iraq, Gebran Majdalani, a Lebanese Baathist intellectual and a member of the National Command in 1963, said: "In Iraq, the party succeeded as a mobilizing force but failed as a governing instrument. . . . Its leaders lacked experience in government and their sudden translation from the narrow confines of jails and clandestine work to that of supreme power led some of them to adopt irresponsible attitudes and to make statements incompatible with a profound knowledge of political and economic conditions and a sound evaluation of strategic and tactical necessities."[97]

One of the major difficulties of the Baath party was the differences among the leaders. Some planned for gradual development and a policy of cooperation with other political movements in order to achieve limited objectives. Others considered moderation a betrayal of the party line and suggested a policy of exclusion and opposition toward all political movements and class enemies. They summarized their attitude with this striking statement: "We can solve all our problems by putting 200 reactionaries in jail."[98]

Aflaq and Majdalani stated that intra-party rivalries allowed the Baath's opponents to exploit the contradictions and so to overthrow the regime. Neither writer mentions the impact of the Kurdish revolt on the ouster of the regime at this stage. A report by the Eighth National Congress, held in Damascus in April 1965, however, listed the Kurdish problem as one cause for the party's defeat.[99] But neither this report nor an earlier assessment during the Emergency Congress of the National Command in February 1964 discussed the impact of the Kurdish problem on the collapse of the regime, other than in very brief sentences.

Despite the party's limited written attention at the time, the Kurdish revolt did have a major impact on the party's 1963 ouster. It weakened the party militarily and economically: several months of serious fighting could not but have a major impact on the economy. The Kurdish revolt also diverted the party's attention from implementing its transitional program of economic and social transformation, which the party needed to do, if it was to realize its slogans and show that it was different from previous regimes. Furthermore, this preoccupation gave the party's rightist military partners a chance to plot successfully against it.

# 4

# Che BAACh AnD Che
# KURDish question, 1968-70

O n July 17, 1968, the Iraqi Baath party, with the help of conservative
military officers, staged a bloodless and successful coup d'etat
against the regime of General Abd al-Rahman Arif. The Baath leaders
had hoped to gain the cooperation or at least the neutrality of the Barzani
leadership and of the Central Command faction of the Iraqi Communist
party without much success.[1] Consequently, the Baathists found themselves under pressure to ally with the military elements in order to overthrow the Arif regime. Less than two weeks later, on July 30, however, the
Baathists succeeded in ousting their military allies and began efforts to
implement the goals they had failed to achieve in 1963.

The party's ouster from power in 1963 was only the first of a number
of major crises that the party had to weather in the years that followed.
The first of these crises occurred when a number of leaders of the Iraqi
Baath challenged the National Command and began to seek support from
the party's rank and file in Iraq. This issue, however, was finally settled
during the Seventh National Congress held in Damascus in 1964, when
Saddam Husain was elected the party's regional secretary general.

The party had hardly begun to unify itself when the Arif regime waged
a campaign of repression against it in September 1964. Many Baathist
leaders and party members were arrested, and some were executed following an abortive coup.[2]

The party faced another major crisis in Syria in 1966 when a serious
internal political schism led to the ouster of the party's historic leadership
(Aflaq and Baitar) by Baathist army officers. This event caused serious
divisions within the party, leaving it with deep internal conflicts that have
persisted.

In Iraq the party was also beset with internal conflicts until a special meeting of the Regional Congress was held in September 1966 and new regional leadership was elected. The new Iraqi leadership, which had remained loyal to the historic national leadership of the party, was facing a complex and difficult situation. The leadership was forced to challenge the Arif regime, while it was fighting the ideological schisms both within the national party and with the ruling party faction in Syria.[3] As a result, the party had to operate clandestinely and with financial, political, and organizational difficulties. It was two years before it was able to hold the Ninth National Congress in Beirut in February 1968.[4]

As a result of the congress, the party decided to redouble its efforts to overthrow the Arif regime. Failing to gain the support or at least the neutrality of the Barzani Kurds and the communists, the party found itself compelled to seek the cooperation of the Presidential Guard and its commander, Ibrahim al-Dawud, despite reservations about his political leanings and personal ambitions. Al-Dawud unsuccessfully urged the party leaders to cooperate with Abd al-Razzaq al-Nayif, then the head of military intelligence. But al-Nayif, who had been informed of the plans for the coup against Arif by al-Dawud, sent a message offering his cooperation on the morning of July 16 to regional party leaders meeting in al-Bakr's house. The party leaders felt they had little choice but to make an open show of accepting the offer, but covertly they made plans to disassociate themselves from both al-Nayif and al-Dawud as soon as possible.[5]

Following the ouster of Arif and his government, al-Nayif and al-Dawud were appointed to the posts of premier and defense minister, respectively, under Baathist President Ahmad Hassan al-Bakr. But if the two officers had hoped to dominate the government, they were soon to be disillusioned. On July 30, following al-Dawud's visit to Jordan to inspect Jordanian forces, Baathist officials arrested al-Nayif in his office and made arrangements to send him to Morocco. Al-Dawud was ordered to Spain to serve as Iraq's ambassador there. A number of non-Baathist officers were also dropped from the government.

By moving quickly and decisively against their potential opponents and rivals, the Baathist leadership showed that it had learned well the lessons of 1963. They were seeking to consolidate power into their own hands in order to implement their programs without having to worry about threats from rightist army officers, as they did in 1963. Furthermore, the party heeded the counsel of the National Command to avoid any serious disruptions and gave instructions "to avoid violence except in extreme cases where the revolution and the party are exposed to danger."[6] This tactic proved useful to the party, allowing it to undertake its massive reforms peaceably and without strong opposition under very difficult circumstances. The party's goals included:

1. The consolidation of the new government's authority and of the party's control of the government;

2. The achievement of a reeducation of the masses to rid them of their "medieval mentality, which impedes their forward progress";

3. The achievement of economic transformation to "replace semi-feudal and semi-capitalist relations of production by socialist relations" in the urban and rural areas;

4. The safe-guarding of the political, economic and social aspects of the country's independence by eliminating the causes of instability and combating foreign and domestic opponents;

5. The reconciliation between the party and other progressive forces through the adoption of the united front strategy to include the Kurdish and Communist parties along with some socialist and pan-Arab nationalist elements;

6. The achievement of economic independence — a central aim of the new regime — which necessitated gaining control over the country's oil wealth through nationalization;

7. The undertaking of a well-rooted social and economic transformation within the country designed to lead it toward socialism;

8. The establishment of Iraq as a model for the Arab revolution and a leader in the efforts to bring about a people's liberation war against Israel;

9. The establishment of a foreign policy which would place Iraq on an equal footing with other developing nations, socialist states, and those Western nations respecting Iraq's sovereignty;

10. The resolution of the Kurdish question in a peaceful manner.[7]

The party's desire to resolve the Kurdish problem peacefully was manifested in its statements on July 17th and later on July 30th. In those statements, it sought to dispel Kurdish suspicions about the Baath party's stand. The statements declared that the party intended to respect the aspirations of the Kurdish people and the declaration of the al-Bazzaz twelve-point program.[8]

The decision to support the al-Bazzaz program came as a surprise to some observers because the party had originally opposed the agreement when it was made between the Arif government and Barzani. The opposition to the agreement, however was an expression of the party's opposition to the Arif regime and to the Barzani leadership rather than to the idea of attempting to reach a peaceful solution to the Kurdish question.

The party's position on the agreement is revealed in a statement issued in the Baathists' Beirut newspaper, *Al-Ahrar,* by the National Command. It declared:

> The National Command, although supporting the peaceful solution of the problem in the north of Iraq, considers any agreement which depends on the change of governments and not on foundations of princi-ples supported by the people, as a transitory attempt not reaching the level of a proper solution. . . . The Command also views every agreement that does not free itself from the spirit of maneuvering and secession as one that is bound to fail. We believe that any proposed plan, whatever its clauses and conditions, will not solve the problem radically and fundamentally unless it springs from the spirit of a progressive revolution based on historical factors which have their impact on the society, and unless it fully expresses this in spirit and unless it deals with the basic causes which created the problem.[9]

Aside from criticizing circumstances under which the agreement was made, this statement reveals an evolving attitude adopted by the party during the Seventh National Congress and in the wake of its ouster from power in 1963. The party leadership's position on the question of the "legitimate national rights of the Kurds" as stated on March 16, 1964, is abundantly clear. It could be summarized by the recognition of these rights and the fight for their realization within the framework of a unified Arab homeland and under the guidance of socialist and democratic relations.

## BARZANI'S POSITION REGARDING THE BAATH GOVERNMENT

The new government's declarations, however, did not seem to satisfy Barzani, who had initially voiced support for the new regime and later withdrew his support following the ouster of al-Nayif and al-Dawud. The Barzani leadership of the KDP had decided to participate in the new government and two pro-Barzani figures were appointed. This support did not last very long. The two ministers were withdrawn from the government on July 30.[10] Barzani's attitude toward the new government fueled Baathist suspicions. The Baathist leadership in Iraq had not forgotten Barzani's quick cooperation with and support for the Arif government in 1963, when he accepted offers from the new regime that were much less than the Baathist party had been willing to offer the Kurds at the time.[11]

For his part, Barzani had not forgotten that the 1963 Baath government had led one of the toughest campaigns against the Kurdish movement.


## THE SUPPORT OF THE TALIBANI FACTION


Another major internal factor behind the deterioration of relations between the government and the Barzani leadership of the KDP was the support given the new regime by the Talibani-Ahmad faction of the KDP, which was known as the KDP Politburo.

Barzani's dislike and enmity toward the leftist and urban KDP leadership led by Talibani and Ahmad was well known. Barzani's hostility for the two leaders was evident when he spoke with me in 1976. In reply to a question about the role of the two leaders and the reasons for his differences with them, he angrily replied, "They are agents for anyone who pays."[12]

The leftist Talibani leadership found it easy to cooperate with the Baath because "it was the first ruling Arab political party . . . to extend its hand to the Kurdish people directly, sincerely, and hopefully,"[13] and the first to "recognize the legitimate national rights of the Kurdish people." Talibani also stated that the Baath party was "making every effort to solve the problem peacefully and justly and in the spirit of brotherhood."[14]

The difference between the two Kurdish groups was manifested by their response to a government statement broadcast on Radio Baghdad confirming the government's intention to find a just and peaceful solution to the Kurdish problem and which made references to subversive agents of the West who were spreading propaganda against the government. *Al-Nur,* a daily newspaper representing the Ahmad-Talibani view, declared that the broadcast was "an important document in the history of evolving relations between Iraq's main nationalities of Arab and Kurd, and one which places them on a basis of equality in national rights and duties, of mutual respect and of brotherhood."[15]

The Barzani faction's reaction to the same speech, however, showed continuing distrust:

> The unrealistic attitude of the authorities toward the Kurdish problem and the government's reliance upon hirelings and vagabonds to crush the Kurdish revolution is a policy which is doomed to failure. . . . Such a policy is bound to create further tensions by threatening any chances for

peace and security in the Kurdish area and will thus subject the entire Iraqi population of Arabs and Kurds alike to hardship and distress once again. Whether the rulers like it or not, it is this policy which must be held responsible for the creation of the negative atmosphere which facilitates the penetration of imperialist designs into the whole area of the Middle East.[16]

The Talibani leadership was seeking to challenge Barzani in his mountainous stronghold and to expand its bases from the urban centers and the few pockets in the hills to some of the major towns in the Kurdish hinterland. This competition led to minor clashes in the fall of 1968 between the two groups.

In addition, the Talibani faction hoped the government would recognize it as the official Kurdish group to represent the Kurds in negotiations with Baghdad. The government, in turn, preferred to deal with the Talibani-Ahmad faction because it espoused a leftist policy not very different from that of the Baath party. By contrast the Baathists were wary of Barzani's "suspicious ties" to Iran and other foreign interests and therefore tended to tread cautiously in their dealings with him.[17]

In its editorials in the fall and winter of 1968, *Al-Nur* accused the Barzani faction of being "a reactionary Kurdish clique, working with imperialism and trying to block the equitable settlement of the Kurdish question."[18] In a later editorial it accused Western powers and their agents of fomenting trouble against the Iraqi government and urged "All honorable Kurds to prevent (the) war from starting again and if it did, may God forbid, they must defeat the mercenaries who trade in the name of our people."[19]

In an effort to gain support among other political forces in Iraq, Barzani declared in an interview given to *Al-Nahar* that he was not hostile to the regime even though he was withdrawing from active participation in the government. He further urged the government to implement the al-Bazzaz program and extend participation to all political forces in the country, not only to the Kurds.[20]

This theme was advanced further by the Barzani leadership in its party organ, *Khibat,* in October 1968. It called on the "democratic and patriotic forces" to form a coalition government which would restore "basic democratic rights and freedoms," implement the June 29th agreement with the Kurds, increase Iraq's oil revenues, and allocate a fair share of them, based on the population ratio, to the Kurds. It also called upon the new government to ensure the implementation of a land reform program and to establish the best possible relations among Arab governments, support national liberation movements, oppose imperialism, and aid the

Arab nation "in pursuing its natural right of national unity."[21] The latter proposal was an outright bid for the support of the Arab nationalists and an attempt to reassure them of the Kurds' desire not to secede from Iraq.

## RESUMPTION OF FIGHTING

In the meantime, throughout December 1968 and January 1969, the Barzani leadership had reactivated its clandestine radio and had begun broadcasting reports of Kurdish clashes with the pro-government Kurds and the army.[22] Barzani's envoy, Kamuran Badr-Khan, sent a memorandum to the United Nations demanding "a U.N. mediator to intervene and settle the Kurdish question."[23] On February 7, 1969, the government reiterated its wish to implement the al-Bazzaz program and to bring about a just solution to the Kurdish question.[24] There were growing reports of fighting during the month of March. The Barzani Kurds were reported to have shelled for the first time oil installations in Kirkuk. A Kurdish spokesman hinted that this might be a change in policy which showed the "growing frustration and apprehension of the Kurds" over the prospect of a new war and implied that oil revenues must be shared by the Kurds. A KDP spokesman declared that the attack on the British-owned Iraq Petroleum Company was forced on the Kurds who wanted to attack Iraq at its "most vulnerable spot."[25]

The fighting between the Talibani forces and those of Barzani proved to be unequal in the Kurdish heartland, in spite of the fact that the number of Talibani's forces was said to have reached 10,000 and they had moved into Qala Diza, Raniya, Koisanjaq, Halabja, and Duhok.[26]

Barzani's forces benefited from tribal support, experience in guerrilla and mountain warfare, as well as the historic appeal of Barzani's leadership.[27] Furthermore, Barzani's forces were estimated to have grown to 20,000 well-equipped men.[28]

The fighting escalated in the spring of 1969 with the government backing the Talibani faction and Iran backing and arming Barzani.[29]

In addition, the Iraqi Communist party (ICP), which had divided into two groups titled ICP Central Committee and ICP Central Command, backed Barzani. The first group adopted a hostile attitude toward the Baath party and refused to recognize the softer stance of the Baathists toward the communists, while the latter took a less hostile attitude but continued to oppose the government on the Kurdish issue. Relations with the

Central Committee, which supported the Soviet line, improved when the new government's relations with the Soviet Union improved. In spite of its reservations about Barzani's leadership, the ICP Central Committee opposed a military campaign against the Kurdish areas and urged the government to reach a peaceful solution to the problem by negotiating with the Barzani leadership.[30]

The fighting continued with the Kurds receiving growing support from Iran, while both the government and the Kurds claimed victories. By late 1969, the Kurds had an armory of weapons which included "over a hundred lightweight anti-aircraft guns, twenty 25-pound field guns, and a number of anti-tank guns" which the Kurds admitted they had purchased outside of Iraq.[31] Iran was already engaged in a major dispute with Iraq over the Shatt al-Arab. On May 17, 1969, President al-Bakr accused Iran of harboring designs on Iraqi territory and waters and claimed that Iranian-Kurdish military cooperation was designed to divert Iraqi troops from the Israeli front.[32]

In the meantime, both sides were angling for allies and stressing their belief in a peaceful solution, while the fighting continued on a small scale. Barzani, in a memorandum addressed to "the national parties, groups, personalities, and armed forces of Iraq," called upon the government to reassess its policies regarding the Kurdish question and to form a joint committee that would include representatives of all of the political forces in Iraq, including the Baathists, to study the Kurdish problem. He also accused the government of following a policy "detrimental to the interests of the people and the country" and called on the Iraqi people to "buckle down and protect the nation."[33]

The difficult situation in Iraq was exacerbated by the discovery of a number of conspiracies to overthrow the government. Secret trials were held and executions and stiff sentences often resulted. In December 1968 former premier al-Bazzaz and former defense minister al-Uqaili were accused of conspiring against the government and spying for foreign agencies, and both were given lengthy sentences. In the summer of 1969 former Baghdad mayor Midhat al-Hajj Sirri confessed that he had been working with the Central Intelligence Agency of the United States and that the Kurds had received weapons from the CIA.[34] Those among the remaining conspirators who confessed were executed or given long prison terms.

Other plots to overthrow the government in the summer and fall of 1969 came from al-Nayif and others supported by Iran and Barzani. The plots failed and the perpetrators were executed. On January 30, 1970, the government accused Iran of interference in Iraq's internal affairs. Iranian consulates in Baghdad, Basra, and Karbala were closed. Mass deportations of Iranians residing in Iraq began as the regime continued to deal harshly with its enemies.


## CONSOLIDATION OF AUTHORITY


Despite these problems, the party was able to solidify its authority smoothly. Saddam Husain, the party's assistant secretary general of the Regional Command, began to take a more visible role by the end of 1969, particularly with respect to the Kurdish question. He had shown himself to be quite competent, tough, and shrewd in running party affairs.

On November 9 the Revolutionary Command Council (RCC), the highest authority in the Iraqi government, expanded from five to fifteen members — all of whom were Baathists. In a move aimed at showing civilian supremacy within the party, all of the new members of the RCC were civilians. Saddam Husain became a member of the RCC and its vice-chairman.

Within a year of its seizure of power, the Baath party was able to preserve and solidify its authority and had made some progress in achieving some of the goals it had set for itself.

At this time, the government took a number of measures that improved its internal position: it freed leftist and communist prisoners and restored their jobs in cases where those persons had been dismissed for political reasons; it recognized East Germany; it began state-directed exploration for sulphur; it signed an economic agreement with the Soviet Union for a loan of 25 million dinars to explore for petroleum resources; it implemented an agrarian reform program, which limited the right of landowners to choose the land that they were allowed to keep and to receive reparations for expropriated lands.[35]

Regarding the Kurdish issue, the party continued its efforts to win over the Kurdish people by gradually granting the Kurds a number of political rights and adopting measures aimed at encouraging reconciliation. These measures included: the establishment of the Kurdish new year Nawruz as a national holiday; the teaching of the Kurdish language in all Iraqi schools and universities; the establishment of a new university in Sulaymaniyya; the establishment of Dohuk province (an old Kurdish demand for the establishment of a Kurdish province in Mosul province); the publication of Kurdish books and periodicals; the creation of an Academy for Kurdish Culture within the Ministry of Information; the elaboration of a departmental law based on the principle of decentralization; an increase in the number of Kurdish programs on Kirkuk television; the granting of amnesty to all civilians who participated in the fighting in the Kurdish area.[36]

According to the Information Minister Tariq Aziz, who has since been appointed deputy prime minister and elected to both the national and regional leadership councils of the Baath party, the government adopted these actions in order to reflect its "humanistic position and to pull the rug from under the feet" of the Kurdish elements opposing the government.[37]

In the spring and summer of 1969, the Iraqi communists (and other political factions) urged the government to end the war between the Barzani and Talibani forces because of Barzani's overwhelming superiority of strength.[38] The government then decided to open the channels of communication with Barzani, in order to solve the Kurdish problem permanently. These new efforts to have a dialogue brought about the declaration of March 11, 1970.

## EVOLUTION IN BAATH IDEOLOGY
## TOWARD THE KURDISH QUESTION

The decision of the party to implement measures guaranteeing Kurdish rights and later to seek negotiations with Barzani stemmed from two major factors: the evolution in Baathist thinking as to how to deal with the question of national minorities, particularly the Kurds; and the special conditions facing the party following its seizure of power in 1968.

Following its defeat in 1963, the Baath party began to review its policy toward the Kurds and to seek new ways in which to deal with the Kurdish question. This changing attitude was reflected in the previously mentioned statements on the Kurdish question in 1964 and 1966, during the Ninth National Congress, and following the party's assumption of power in 1969. The problem was discussed at length during the party's Seventh Regional Conference in February 1969 and the following declaration was decided upon:

> The conference has affirmed that our party, which begins its struggle and policies from a nationalistic, humanistic, socialistic, and democratic ideology, has always respected the legitimate aspirations of the Kurdish peo-

ple in their progressive and patriotic context, and has recognized their aspirations as legitimate human rights. . . . The Congress has begun to resolve the Kurdish issue on the basis of Arab-Kurdish brotherhood, and accepts the belief in the right of the Kurds to safeguard their national character and considers this the foundation on which to build unity in the struggle for (the) Arab and Kurdish nationalities.[39]

The party's efforts to formulate a rational and precise program were further advanced in a speech to party members by Michel Aflaq in June 1969. Aflaq tackled this issue by declaring that "the subject of the Kurds has two sides: one side is a matter of principle and the other is political. The party has no objection to the right of the Kurds to some kind of autonomy."[40] He went on to add that the political side is different because the Kurdish rebellion in Iraq, although based on national feelings among the Kurds, was being exploited by domestic and foreign forces. Aflaq compared the status of the Kurds in Iraq favorably with that of the Kurds in Turkey and Iran and pointed out that there had been no discrimination against the Kurds throughout Arab history. But, while Aflaq blamed the start of the Kurdish rebellion in Iraq on imperialism, he nevertheless drew attention to the fact that "whenever there are Kurdish uprisings the government is forced to confront them with force, which leads, with time, to the creation of hatred and the desire for vengeance, which are used as a basis and springboard for a new revolution which lacks justification in the first place." He added that "the duty of the revolutionary government in Iraq is to realize this fact and to defeat the imperialist plan by preventing the continuation and accumulation of these hatreds and invented justifications." He admitted that there could be "contradictions between the Kurdish national movement and the Arab revolution," but any such contradictions were fostered by Western powers or right-wing Arab regimes. Aflaq advocated a "socialist solution" to the problem of minorities within a country by a common effort to build a socialist state without class exploitations and the domination of one national group over another.

In a speech commemorating the first anniversary of the 17th of July revolution, Iraqi President Bakr declared that the party leadership had decided even prior to the revolution to "resolve the Kurdish issue in a peaceful and democratic manner and to oppose chauvinistic and separatist tendencies and to prevent the exploitation of this issue by the imperialist and reactionary forces in the region."[41]

By the end of 1969, the party organ, *Al-Thawra al-Arabiyya,* had published a major editorial entitled "How to Resolve the Kurdish Question." In this article the Baath government revealed its criteria for a solution to the problem. One of the first points was the recognition that the

Kurds were a nation divided by international boundary lines. It further declared that:

> The Kurdish question is a national one and our current era is one of oppressed and persecuted nationalities who struggle to affirm and develop their national personalities and to liberate their homelands from imperialist domination. The revolution of the oppressed and persecuted nationalities is an essential part of the world revolution, which must work against every form of exploitation and enslavement toward the building of socialism. The Kurdish question, being a national question, is a natural phenomenon in harmony with the spirit of the age and its movements. It has a liberating and progressive content.[42]

The article went on to add that the path followed by Iraqi Kurds in their struggle to affirm their national personality should be that of a united struggle with the Arab people of Iraq in order to achieve national unity. It further warned that there were forces on both sides seeking to profit from the confrontation between the Arabs and Kurds of Iraq. These forces were linked to regional rightist interests and the Western powers. The article concluded by calling for negotiations between the Kurds and Arabs.

The ideological position that was adopted by the party leadership following its assumption of power revealed that it was seeking to find a radical and permanent solution to the Kurdish problem, not merely a temporary or transitional solution, within the framework of the party's socialist and nationalist ideology.

## FACTORS BEHIND THE NEGOTIATIONS

The evolution of Baathist thinking on the Kurdish question stemmed from the closely held belief among party leaders that the humanitarian and socialist principles of the party offered a framework for solving the Kurdish problem, and that an escalation of the Kurdish conflict affected not only the Kurds but also threatened the country as a whole.[43] The leadership realized that it would be impossible to proceed with the country's economic and social program unless the Kurdish problem were resolved.

An article published in *Al-Thawra al-Arabiyya* (no. 3, 1971) pointed out a number of threats to the country that the government would face if the Kurdish conflict continued to escalate. These included:

• The deterioration of relations between the Kurdish and Arab peoples and the weakening of the ties for future struggle. This deterioration would be welcomed by imperialistic forces because it would shatter the idea of national unity among both Kurds and Arabs;

• The creation of obstacles to the revolution and the preparation of conditions that would allow hostile forces to play a destructive role in weakening Iraq, and force upon it a war of attrition that would absorb its energies and capabilities;

• The weakening of the Iraqi army in a civil war would paralyze it and prevent it from fulfilling its national role;

• An economic decline in Iraq, since the war in the north would continue to destroy farms and flocks, disrupt transportation, prevent production and increase smuggling, hoarding, and price manipulation; it would also continue to draw thousands of citizens from participation in productive activities and into military activities, in addition to which much of the (national) budget would continue to be diverted to military purposes, preventing the country from going ahead with its development projects;

• Arousing suspicion [among minorities in Iraq] that the Arab nationalist movement was racist and antagonistic to their aspirations and legitimate rights;

• Weakening Iraq and preventing it from achieving economic independence, since confronting imperialist monopoly is impossible without the establishment of a solid base that would permit confrontation;

• Isolating Iraq from the progressive countries by accusing it of oppressing the Kurds and inflicting repressive measures against them; . . . the isolation of Iraq from the progressive countries would lead it to defeat because this would place Iraq's independence at the mercy of world imperialism, Zionism, and Arab and local reaction.

These threats to Iraq as well as the new theoretical positions adopted by the party led it to call for negotiations with Barzani and the Kurdistan Democratic party.

In addition, there was still another external factor that contributed to the Baath government's decision to seek a solution to the Kurdish problem — "the most difficult and complex problem facing the party and the revolution."[44] The Baath party desired to play a major role in challenging the Israeli and Iranian threats. The Baathist position stressed there was a deliberate plan by the West, supported by Israel and Iran, to fragment the Arab homeland. The party believed Iran wanted to grab Arab land in the Gulf. The Kurdish problem, it believed, was seized upon by the West as an opportunity to sap Iraq's strength and to divert its forces from full participation in the struggle against Israel. Iraq, which considered itself a "confrontation state" in the struggle with Israel, was being criticized by the rival Baathists in Syria and other Arab groups for not contributing its share to the Eastern Arab Command.[45]

Relations with Iran deteriorated further in 1969. An Iranian request for a revision of the 1937 Shatt al-Arab treaty[46] which would extend Iran's boundaries from the bank to the median line of the river was rejected by Iraq.

Furthermore, the ideological hostility between the radical pan-Arab Iraqi regime and the conservative Iranian monarchy, eager to play the role of a major power in the Gulf region, was fueled by Iran's support for the Kurds and its collusion in the conspiracy to overthrow the Iraqi government in February 1969.[47] Minor Iraqi-Iranian clashes erupted in March 1969. One month later, on April 15, Iraq decided to enforce its territorial rights in the river — rights which had been violated by Iran in past years — and required all Iranian ships to pay entry tolls to the Iraqi port authority. Iran refused and began sending naval units to accompany its ships entering the waterway. On April 19th, Iran unilaterally abrogated the Shatt al-Arab treaty, claiming that it had been imposed on Iran against its will by the British. Iran's saber-rattling and Iraq's failure to take effective action were a source of humiliation to the Iraqis. Efforts at negotiation by Jordan's King Husain failed.[48] Iraq, however, retaliated by boycotting Iranian goods and expelled thousands of Iranians (some of whom were accused of spying for the CIA) and supported the efforts of General Bakhtiar as well as dissident leftists in Iran in their efforts to overthrow the Shah's regime.

Iran, for its part, increased its support of the Kurds and other anti-Baath Iraqis and was accused of involvement in the February 1970 attempted coup, contributing perhaps to the government's decision to seek a decisive solution to the conflict with the Kurds. Another factor which may have contributed to the effort to come to terms with the Kurds was the fact that the party was still not in full control of the armed forces, and a number of conservative officers remained in key military positions.[49] The party wanted to make sure that rightist army officers never posed a threat again, as they had in 1963. A peaceful resolution to the conflict would allow the party to assert civilian authority over the armed forces.

## THE BEGINNING OF THE NEGOTIATIONS

Informal negotiations between the Baath government and the Kurdish factions began around the end of 1969. Aziz Sharif, a Marxist intellectual and chairman of the Peace and Solidarity Committee who was respected by both sides, traveled to the Kurdish area controlled by Barzani to meet with him and to inform him of the government's interest in resuming negotiations.[50] Following that meeting, Barzani decided to send Dara Tawfiq, a leading Kurdish intellectual and member of the KDP Politburo who was closely associated with Barzani, to begin talks with the Iraqi authorities.

Dara Tawfiq met with Saddam Husain, the assistant secretary general of the party's regional command and vice chairman of the Revolutionary Command Council. According to Tariq Aziz, who played a major role in the negotiations between the Barzani faction and the government, Husain asked Dara Tawfiq to state what the Kurdish demands were. Tawfiq declared that they were: the lifting of the economic blockade of the north, the release of Kurdish prisoners and amnesty for those who participated in the Kurdish movement, along with minor requests. Husain is reported to have laughed and said, "Are these the demands you have been fighting for during the last ten years? What do you really want? Submit your real demands and your real program. We are a revolution that has come to deal decisively with the country's problems. Tell us what you want and we shall try to do whatever we actually can to respond to your demands and shall tell you of what we can not respond to."

Tawfiq replied that he did not have the authority at the time to go beyond what he said and that he would go back to Barzani for further consultations. Aziz Sharif engaged in subsequent negotiations and the Revolutionary Command Council decided to enter into official negotiations with the Barzani leadership.[51]

A government delegation under the leadership of Army Commander Hammad Shihab, and including Baathist intellectual Abd al-Khaliq al-Samarrai, Interior Minister Murtada al-Hadithi, and Regional Command members Samir Aziz Najm and Tariq Aziz, accompanied by military advisers arrived at the Kurdish town of Nawbirdan on December 31, 1969. The outcome of this expedition was that a Kurdish delegation with the authority to negotiate would bring the Kurdish demands to negotiations in Baghdad. A Kurdish delegation led by Dr. Mahmud Uthman and including KDP leaders Salih al-Yusufi Muhammad and Mahmud Abd al-Rahman subsequently met with the government delegation in Baghdad. The negotiators were also joined by Aziz Sharif, who was trusted by both sides and who acted as a mediator. A number of sessions took place.

In the meantime, the Baath party held its Tenth National Congress from March 1 to March 10, 1970. The party leadership again discussed the Kurdish question and "the legitimate aspirations of the Kurdish masses in

Iraq." The participants were informed of the results of the negotiations between the government and the leaders of the Kurdish movement. The Congress affirmed that "the declaration of a democratic and peaceful solution to the Kurdish question on the basis of self-rule and within the framework of Iraqi unity would establish the best conditions for cooperation between the Kurdish and Arab nationalities and must be in the forefront of the party's achievements."[52]

The concept of self-rule was not presented by the Kurdish negotiators from the beginning but evolved during the negotiations and, as noted previously, after the government delegation's insistence that the Kurds present their real demands.

The negotiations lasted throughout January and February and subsequently led to Saddam Husain's participation in the negotiations to avoid a potential deadlock.

The disagreements at this stage of the negotiations centered not on the question of Kurdish national rights, but on the future relations between the government and the Talibani-Ahmad faction of the KDP and between the government and the leaders of the Salah al-Din Cavalry, Kurdish irregulars composed of anti-Barzani tribal elements who fought alongside the government forces.[53]

The government considered this question a minor one in comparison to finding a final solution, and it was suggested that the government play the role of moderator between the two Kurdish groups. But the Barzani leadership insisted on disbanding the Salah al-Din forces and on ending any cooperation with the Talibani-Ahmad faction. The government finally agreed and all obstacles to announcing an agreement were removed.[54]

Husain traveled to the north where he persuaded Barzani to reach an accord with him on terms that Barzani finally approved. Husain's efforts were later verified by Barzani himself, who said that Saddam Husain offered him blank sheets of paper on which to write his demands and indicated he would not leave until they were signed by both sides.[55] Husain's approach succeeded, and the two leaders signed the agreement that led to the declaration on March 11.

# 5

# The MARCh 1970 MANiFESTO:
# iMPLEMENTATiON AND AFTERMATh

Following the signing of an agreement between Saddam Husain and Mulla Mustafa al-Barzani, President al-Bakr broadcast to the nation on March 11, 1970, an announcement that the Revolutionary Command Council had solved the Kurdish problem in accordance with the resolution of the Baath party's Seventh Regional Congress.[1] According to al-Bakr, the Congress had defined the party's ideological and theoretical position on the Kurdish problem and had delineated its solution by passing a series of resolutions. The program included the following measures:

• Recognition of Kurdish as the official language in those areas where Kurds constitute a majority. Kurdish and Arabic would be taught together in all schools.

• Participation of Kurds in government, including the appointment of Kurds to key posts in the state.

• Furtherance of Kurdish education and culture.

• Requirement that officials in the Kurdish areas speak Kurdish.

• Right to establish Kurdish student, youth, women's, and teachers' organizations.

• Economic development of the Kurdish area.

• Return of Kurds to their villages or financial compensation.

• Agrarian reform.

• Amendment of the constitution to read "the Iraqi people consist of two main nationalities: the Arab and Kurdish nationalities."

• Return of the clandestine radio stations and heavy weapons to the government.

• Appointment of a Kurdish vice-president.

• Amendment of provincial laws in accordance with this declaration.

• Formation of a Kurdish area with self-government.[2]

A list of steps taken by the Iraqi government between 1968 and 1970 to guarantee Kurdish rights was included in the Manifesto. These provisions included the recognition of Kurdish nationalism, the establishment of Sulaymaniyya University, the teaching of Kurdish in all schools, the recognition of Nawvuz (a traditional new year festival celebrated by Zagros and Iranian Plateau peoples) as a national holiday, the promulgation of a Governorates Law emphasizing decentralization, the establishment of a Duhok Governorate incorporating the Kurdish areas of the Mosul province, and general amnesty for all soldiers and civilians who had fought in the conflict in the North.

The manifesto included resolutions agreed upon by the two sides affirming the RCC's determination to take certain cultural, economic, and legal actions to allow "the Kurdish masses to fulfill their legitimate rights and actually participate in the serious effort to build the homeland and to struggle to achieve its national goals." These resolutions were intended to be the basis of a program of action to be fulfilled by both sides.

## BARZANI'S REASONS FOR ACCEPTING THE AGREEMENT

Barzani's immediate response to the proclamation was a statement addressed to Iraqi citizens in which he expressed his approval because the agreement "recognize[d] the just national rights of the Kurds, including the right to self-rule." Expressing a desire to forget the tragic events of the past, he promised his support of national unity in order to facilitate national development. At the same time, Dr. Mahmud Uthman, who had emerged during the negotiations as the foremost figure in the KDP after Barzani, declared on behalf of the Kurdish people and its leadership that the Kurds would "remain supporters and allies of the Arab nation in their common struggle and in the interest of the two sister nationalities."[3]

Behind the Barzani leadership's acceptance of the agreement lay a complex variety of factors, not the least of which was that the Kurds had become war-weary. Kurdish military forces and civilians fighting intermittently since 1961 were reported to have suffered heavy losses. The combined casualties of dead and wounded were estimated at 60,000, and over 3,000 villages had been heavily damaged. Some 13,000 Kurdish families were reported to be receiving assistance from the Kurdish RCC as compensation for their loss of breadwinners in the conflict.[4]

In addition to the Talibani-Ahmad faction (the old Politburo of the

KDP) and their supporters, the young progressive elements among the pro-Barzani factions of the KDP were anxious to reach an agreement with the Baathists, with whom they shared similar views on social and economic issues. The progressive elements hoped that an agreement would allow them to wrest leadership of the Kurdish movement from the "tribal, feudalist, and religious elements" that had previously dominated it.[5]

Babakr Mahmud al-Pishdari, a leading KDP figure and supporter of Barzani until 1970, declared that one of the reasons for Barzani's acceptance of the Agreement was the political pressure applied by the government through its adoption of measures guaranteeing the Kurds political and cultural rights.[6]

In the interview cited earlier (September 28, 1976), Mulla Mustafa al-Barzani declared, "At first they (Baathists) came to us and said, 'We will grant you self-rule.' I said this was a ruse. I knew it even before I signed the agreement. But (our) people asked me, 'How can you refuse self-rule for the Kurdish people?'"

Furthermore, Barzani and his supporters were nervous over the close ties between the government and the Talibani faction. Barzani also doubted the sincerity of Iranian support for the Kurds, which he felt was prompted more by traditional hostility to Iraq than by concern for the Kurdish cause. Another source of irritation with Iran was its financing of the small Kajik and Kumala Kurdish parties, which held chauvinistic views advocating cooperation and unity among the "Aryan nations."[7]

At the same time, the agreement fulfilled certain objectives for Barzani. By granting the Kurds a broad autonomy, the agreement offered Barzani an honorable way to settle the conflict as well as the necessary time to consolidate his authority over the Kurdish region.

## REGIONAL AND INTERNATIONAL REACTION

The agreement came as a surprise to most of the outside world, which believed that the Kurds were well endowed with outside support. It was also generally assumed that the Baathists, who had taken a tough stand against the Kurds in 1963, would never concede to Kurdish demands for self-rule.

The agreement was widely acclaimed, however, in the Arab world. Even some Arab governments that may have wished to see the conflict continue because of their opposition to or mistrust of the Baath government publicly hailed the manifesto as an end to the hostility. This outward approval appeared in statements from Arab national leaders (including President Nasir), political figures, and political parties, as well as the Palestinian resistance movement.[8]

The communist parties in Arab countries supported the agreement. The Iraqi Communist party had earlier made its position clear on this issue by calling for Kurdish autonomy.[9] The Soviet Union gave its support, and may in fact have applied pressure on both sides to come to the negotiating table. Moscow Radio described the peaceful settlement as "a blow against reactionary imperialist circles which sought to exploit the disagreements between the Arabs and the Kurds." Similar commentaries appeared in *Tass, Izvestia, Pravda,* and the press of other communist countries.[10]

As a further sign of Soviet approval of the Agreement, the Soviet Red Cross sent several shiploads of material to the Kurds through the port of Basrah in 1970 and 1971. The size and nature of the shipments were not disclosed but *Al-Taakhi* reported the arrival of some of these shipments and expressed the KDP's appreciation for the "sincere help" of the USSR, its "just support of the legitimate Kurdish national rights and of the just struggle of the Iraqi people against Zionism and imperialism."[11]

Israel, however, reacted differently. It would have preferred to see the war continued as a diversion of Iraqi forces from possible Arab-Israeli confrontations. This position was reflected in Israeli editorials commenting on the settlement of the Kurdish question in Iraq. *Maariv* was reported to have declared that the announcement of the peaceful solution to the Kurdish question would allow the Iraqi government to direct all of its military capabilities to other fronts, in particular, the Eastern Front. *Davar,* the organ of the Labor party, likewise analyzed the Agreement as a reflection of Iraq's desire to use its energies on external fronts, with reference again to the Eastern Front.[12]

Palestinian organizations, on the other hand, welcomed the agreement. A representative of the PLO, who attended the KDP Congress in Kallalah in July 1970, hailed the agreement and expressed the hope that it would lead to further action by Iraqi Kurds and Arabs against the "common enemy, Israel."[13] Dr. George Habash, leader of the Popular Front for the Liberation of Palestine (PFLP)[14] and *Al-Shararah,* the official organ of the Popular Democratic Front for the Liberation of Palestine, welcomed the agreement with similar enthusiasm.[15] As a consequence of the agreement, one thousand Iraqi Kurds were reported to have gone to Jordan to join the Iraqi army stationed there.[16]

The Iranian government, like the Israeli government, was not pleased with the agreement because it meant Iraqi forces were no longer diverted from the Iranian front by the Kurdish conflict. Iraq posed serious challenges to Iranian hegemony in the Gulf as well as being a potential source of disruption among Iran's restive Kurds and other minorities and dissidents. Consequently, both Iran and Israel began to work for the failure of the agreement.

While there was no public announcement concerning the agreement from either the United States or Great Britain, it is natural to assume that these two countries had, at this time, an ambivalent attitude toward the question. Despite the fact that the regime in Iraq was unpopular in both countries, the increased stability in Iraq, which assured them a steady supply of oil and ensured the safety of the investments of their oil companies, was a welcome development resulting from the agreement. On the other hand, these countries were worried about the greater pressures that a strong radical and nationalist Iraqi regime could apply, not only against Israel and Iran, but also against conservative Arab governments friendly to the West. The prospects of Kurdish rebellions in Turkey or Iran were also worrisome to their allies, the United States and Great Britain.

Fearing the impact among its own Kurds of a successful agreement granting self-rule to the Iraqi Kurds, Turkey's attitude was defensive. Turkey had closed its borders to the insurgents during the fighting and had taken a strong stand against some of its own Kurds who had supported Barzani. Within four months of the signing of the agreement, signs of growing Kurdish nationalist activity were emerging in Turkey. The Turkish Republican People's party issued a memorandum in July 1970 noting that Kurdish political activities were on the rise in the eastern provinces. The memorandum charged that Barzani had received aid from the USSR, Iran, and Israel, and that Israeli arms were flowing into the country from Iran. As a result, the Turkish government passed a firearms control law and conducted extensive searches in the Kurdish areas of eastern Turkey.[17]

The Syrian Baathist government, which had consistently opposed any Kurdish separatist movement, was influenced by its conflict with the Iraqi Baathists. On the day that the March 11 manifesto was announced, the Syrian government announced the trial of eleven members of the Syrian KDP, accusing them of spreading harmful propaganda and inciting racial conflict.[18] In addition, the Syrian authorities allowed the Arab Socialist Union, a Nasirist party, to publish and distribute material accusing the Iraqi government of making concessions to the Kurds tantamount, in its eyes, to the "Kurdification of Iraq."[19]

## BAATHIST PERCEPTIONS OF THE AGREEMENT

For the Baath leadership in Iraq the agreement represented a vindication of its principles and those of Arab nationalism. It was seen as consistent with Baathist attitudes toward ethnic minorities living in the Arab world. These beliefs were expressed by Baathist leaders publicly as well as privately. In a private interview, Baath leader Tariq Aziz declared: "We were sincere when we announced the March 11 Manifesto. It wasn't propaganda. I say this because I was one of those who participated in the negotiations, and I know the sincerity of the leadership."[20] Aziz added that there were two additional considerations that contributed to Baathist support of the agreement. The Baathist leadership realized it could not achieve a stable and popular government unless a correct and peaceful solution were found. The second consideration was the image of the Baath as an Arab nationalist party.

Aziz explained, "We are an Arab nationalist party, and the Palestinian question plays an important role in our thinking. Consequently, we cannot condemn Zionist racism and its racist structure and seek international support for our cause while there is a people which lives on our land and with which we have cultural, religious, and historic ties whose national problem we have not solved."

The Baathists believed that the March 11 manifesto went beyond the transitory goal of ending the fighting and laid the groundwork for a permanent solution to the Kurdish problem. This idea was developed in an article published by the government newspaper, *Al-Jumhuriyya,* one week after the signing of the manifesto. The paper declared that the historic meaning of the solution to the Kurdish problem was not limited to the solution itself, but reflected "the ideas that shaped it, and finally the results" that would emerge from it.[21] It went on to enumerate the political, ideological, economic, and military benefits that the agreement would produce.

> It is a solution from which many diverse benefits have resulted. . . . On the theoretical and ideological level, the solution affirms the conceptual originality of the party. Its progressivism and its humanism are clearly revealed in the face of all forms of demagoguery and in particular that of Zionist ideology. In the political realm, a new level of patriotic life is being attained, one that will build a solid patriotic front, bringing together all progressive forces and making Iraq a model of national democracy for those Arab countries where it is lacking. On the economic level, the immense hemorrhage that was wasting Iraq's abundant resources has

been stopped and it has become possible to undertake a victorious struggle against underdevelopment and the deprivations imposed by the previous reactionary regime. In the military domain the solution gives the
Iraqi forces the opportunity to assume their rightful place on the battle-
field in Palestine and in the defense of Arabism in the Gulf. It shores up
the Arab forces and brings them together with the patriotic Kurdish
movement in the struggle against the common enemy.

The seriousness with which the party regarded the March 11 manifesto and the sincerity with which it sought to find a peaceful and permanent solution to the Kurdish question are best evidenced in its internal
literature. Such literature reveals a clearer picture on important issues
than most public announcements.

A major article published in 1971 in the third issue of *Al-Thawra al-
Arabiyya*—the party's main theoretical organ, which is distributed only
to its members—stated the party's position regarding the Kurdish question. The article had the following goals:

• To explain the Kurdish problem to Party members and to indicate
the correct stand they should adopt toward it;

• To defend the March 11 manifesto by affirming the party's support
for it against the chauvinist and ultra-nationalist elements within the
party who felt that the government had made too many concessions to the
Kurds;

• To inform the membership of expected developments resulting from
the solution;

• To draw a blueprint for action to help implement the manifesto.[22]

The link between Kurdish and Arab nationalist movements was
stressed, and Kurdish nationalism was viewed as a basic element in the national liberation movement of Iraq.

> The Kurdish issue is a genuinely nationalistic one which reactionaries
> and imperialists have sought to distort and weaken by dividing the Kurds
> and subjecting their masses in the countries in which they live to the
> fiercest forms of racial and reactionary repression at the hands of back-
> ward and agent governments. The fight for the Kurdish cause has taken
> many forms. At times it is through war; at other times it is through the
> denial of the Kurdish national existence and yet at other times through
> social assimilation.

The article then declared that the July 17 Revolution could not deny
"the legitimate national rights of the Kurdish masses," who, in its view,
represented "an important segment of its base and its goals." Since the
Iraqi masses, comprising both Kurds and Arabs, were the core of the Rev-

olution, to deny Kurdish nationalist and liberationist demands would be to deny the Revolution, its goals, and its principles. On the contrary, the adoption and implementation of these demands by the Revolution merely reflected the sincerity of the goals and identity of the Revolution. "This is not only the duty of the Revolution, but the condition of its success and survival as well." The article stressed Arab-Kurdish brotherhood. "We can say that the methods of repression and the war aimed at [the Kurds] were generally condemned by the masses of the people. Arab-Kurdish brotherhood is history, while the struggle between the two peoples was a distortion of history." As a result, said the article, true support from the people for anti-Kurdish governments simply could not exist.

The article described the basic characteristics of the Kurdish national struggle as an "important nationalist and revolutionary movement, consecrating Iraq's independence and strengthening the positions of struggle against imperialism and reaction." The Kurdish struggle was described as one that began to "affirm Kurdish national rights" through the participation of various social classes and political forces. The article adds that the Kurdish nationalist movement goes beyond the boundaries of nationalism since it has, contained within it, an element that "linked the Kurdish cause to the basic interests of Kurdish toilers."

One of the main differences between the Arab and Kurdish nationalist movements brought out in the article was the different background which went into the formation of each movement. It indicated specifically that although the Arab nation was divided into several states, it remained "a nation represented in a group of countries which are recognized as states, while the Kurds, because of certain objective conditions were distributed in a number of countries and have not had a state of their own."

The article went on to point out, however, that the reason the Arab nationalist movement had been able to continue and advance its struggle to a higher plane was because it was able to recognize the varying levels of development within the Arab social structure. Through the process of historical progress, it had been able to identify its basic social forces, thus allowing them to assume control of their own struggle. These same social forces would "prevent exploitation by the classes and leaderships which blocked the path of the march and sought to push it backward in a policy contradictory to historic development."

The article added that because of the variety of classes within the Kurdish movement, it contained contradictory forces, some "revolutionary and liberationist," and others "backward and reactionary." Unlike the Arab nationalist movement, the Kurdish movement had not been able to rid itself of those forces which "trade on and exploit emotional and nationalist feelings." The failure on the part of the Kurdish movement to purge itself of these reactionary and feudal elements was attributed to "conditions of persecution under which the Kurds have lived." These conditions, had covered the contradictions and postponed the social struggle within the Kurdish movement. "The removal of the influence of feudalism, the bourgeoisie, the power brokers, and the pockets of imperialism and monopoly" increase the responsibility of the "toiling Kurdish masses, a responsibility that goes beyond the narrow nationalist framework. . . . To the extent that the role of Kurdish strugglers is increased by embracing the Kurdish nationalist movement and leading it on a progressive revolutionary road, it becomes possible to remove the outer covers and the hangers-on and to push aside everything that opposes the progressiveness of the Kurdish nationalist movement."

The "correct way" to solve the Kurdish nationalist question was then suggested. The article stressed that the realization of legitimate Kurdish aspirations could not be achieved in isolation from the common struggle of the people of the area. "Arrogance and national chauvinism will not lead to any results favorable to the nationalist cause but, on the contrary, will corrupt it. . . . The nationalist struggle must be a driving force against imperialism and reaction . . . otherwise, it condemns itself to failure."

The forces that had sought to derail and block peace were identified as the "big landowners, feudalists who have been hurt as a result of the implementation of the land reform program, beneficiaries among the military men who became rich as a result of the civil war, as well as other war profiteers such as the leaders of cavaliers who used to collect money illegally or to trade in arms." It also listed those forces which sought to weaken the revolution's influence among the masses and which would thus profit from continued warfare.

The activities of these forces were then linked to "imperialist powers, Zionism, Iranian reaction, and local reaction within one conspiratorial movement," which would oppose any steps to "strengthen peace and guarantee Kurdish rights. The struggle against these forces and the forces using them is an important link in the chain protecting national unity and peace."

Peace, defined according to Baathist principles, was "not simply stopping the war but goes beyond that. Peace must carry within it the factors for continuity and survival." The following factors were listed as essential for peace:

• The elimination of causes of war that were rooted within the history of the people and its enemies on the one hand, and in unresolved national relations on the other;

• The realization of national unity and the strengthening of the unity of struggle among the Kurds and Arabs;

• The liberation of the masses from the domination of reactionary, feudal, and suspect elements;

• The establishment of strong state authority to ensure the security and return of normal life to the region;

• The liberation of the Kurdish masses from the social and economic backwardness they had experienced accompanied by an educational process that would make apparent the contrast between their previous living conditions and the improved standard of living they could experience under peace;

• The reconstruction of the North and development of economic, health, political, and cultural activities which would bring homogeneity to the Iraqi region;

• The fulfillment of the basic interests of the Kurdish masses, guaranteeing national unity, achievement of peace, and establishment of Kurdish rule, all of which would serve to strengthen national unity and consecrate Iraqi sovereignty;

• The elimination of all traces and vestiges of war.

Peace could not be secured before two important issues were resolved: "the realization of common struggle among the masses" and "the struggle against isolationist trends regardless of where they are."

Guidelines were laid out for the achievement of the common struggle, which could not occur "apart from the masses, their progressive political organs, and their revolutionary leaders." Since the class struggle was at the center of the conflict, the Kurdish and Arab peasants, workers, and progressive forces must unite in one revolutionary struggle to achieve economic as well as political independence and to defeat the reactionary forces, whether among Kurds or Arabs. The article asserted that the "Kurdish revolutionary movement must therefore be linked to the Iraqi revolution and to Arab revolutionary forces within the Arab homeland and expanded to include all anti-imperialist, anti-reactionary, and progressive forces."

The emphasis then shifted to the need to purge the national struggle of "all rightist trends, chauvinist practices, isolationist activities, and authoritarian tendencies." In a warning to elements within the party opposed to the formula reached with the Kurdish leadership, the article stressed that the "Arab revolutionary movement must cleanse its ranks of all behavior foreign to its nature and unmask all elements that seek to exploit mistakes and stir conflicts under the guise of protecting the Arab people."

The article went on to emphasize the second requirement for securing peace: the struggle against isolationist tendencies. It called for condemnation and exposure of attempts to contain the Kurdish masses and to prevent them from interacting with Arabs. The thrust of this argument was aimed at "discriminatory practices" among some government officials and at proposals advanced by some Kurdish leaders to "divide the national wealth . . . in proportion to the percentage of any nationality." In a defense of the Baathist slogan, "Arab oil belongs to the Arabs," the article described it as a revolutionary slogan — serving both Arabs and Kurds — which did not reflect a selfish or isolationist view but which, rather, was directed against the exploiters of Arab oil. "It is part of the overall struggle to liberate and develop a strong national economy in each Arab country and thereby strengthen the Arab revolution. A strong, unified Iraqi economy benefits Arabs and Kurds alike."

The article also responded to the demands of some Kurdish leaders to set up a separate army in Kurdistan by saying that the "Iraqi Army, composed of both Kurds and Arabs, must work to defend both Arab and Kurdish regions. No attempt must be made to distribute assignments or forces by nationality or national region."

The implementation of the March 11 manifesto would await the judgment of history, which would determine whether it was to be a victory for Arab–Kurdish brotherhood. The article stressed that the manifesto's implementation depended on full preparation for all eventualities and the following results would have to be taken into account:

• Since the civil war only delayed and covered up the class struggle by placing all classes of Kurds together to fight for the national cause, the implementation of the manifesto, by solving the national question, would advance the class struggle and "lead to the creation of contradictions between the old and new forces."

• The "social struggle" would separate the "feudalists from the peasants and the exploiters from the exploited."

• As the revolution moved through its various stages (national, national democratic, popular democratic, etc.), those social and political forces which were unresponsive to the dynamics of the continuous revolutionary process would retreat and flee.

The article declared that the Kurdish people must defend themselves against the infiltration of "certain opportunistic elements" who would seek to profit from the manifesto and would attempt to hold office; and reactionary forces, particularly the Iranians, who in the past were linked to the Kurdish movement out of necessity.

The article stressed the need for firm guarantees in the implementation of the manifesto. These included:

• A "serious alliance between the KDP and the Baath based on "mutual trust, understanding, and cooperation";

• "The implementation of the manifesto in text and spirit";

• An objective, thorough, and painstaking assessment of the agreement, which would eliminate any hasty misjudgments or reactions;

• A revolutionary interpretation of the problem.

The article concludes that the Baath party "believes deeply in the right of the Kurdish people to enjoy all of its national rights and to actively participate alongside the Arab people in the development and progress of Iraq . . . from the same standpoint our party affirms that concern for securing peace is totally linked to the creation of a healthy environment for the implementation of national rights, and that this alone reflects the concern to preserve the revolution and progress."


## IMPLEMENTATION OF THE AGREEMENT


The Baath leadership and the *Revolutionary Command Council*, as the above statement and declaration reveal, were anxious to find a peaceful solution to the Kurdish problem and to reaffirm their rapport with the Barzani leadership through the implementation of the manifesto.

Within one month of the agreement, a nine-man high commission, composed of four Arabs and four Kurds under the chairmanship of Saddam Husain was established and charged with the task of carrying out the agreement.[23]

One of the first acts of the government after the signing of the agreement, was to reshuffle the cabinet, appointing five prominent Kurdish leaders administrators in accordance with Article Two of the manifesto concerning Kurdish participation in the government. The five ministers were:

• Nuri Shawis, a member of the KDP's Politburo who was appointed minister of housing and public works

• Muhammad Mahmud Abd al-Rahman, an engineer and a member of the KDP's Politburo, who was appointed minister of northern affairs

• Ihsan Shirzadi, a former professor of engineering, who was appointed minister of municipal and village affairs

• Colonel Nafiz Jalal, minister of agriculture

• Salih al-Yusufi, a member of the KDP's Politburo, who was appointed a minister without portfolio[24]

The government, in accord with Article Four, also appointed a number of Kurds governors, vice governors and district directors. Ali Amin, a member of the KDP's Politburo, was appointed governor of Sulaimaniyyah province, and two members of the KDP's Central Committee, Abd al-Wahhab al-Atrushi, and Hashim Aqrawi, were appointed governors of Arbil and Duhok provinces. Thirteen other prominent Kurds were appointed *qaimmaqams*. Four Kurds were appointed vice-governors and thirty-nine others were appointed district directors.[25]

In addition, the government appointed three Kurdish police chiefs for the three Kurdish provinces of Sualaimaniyya, Arbil, and Duhok, and named a number of Kurds to head municipalities.[26]

On April 23, 1970, the government appointed a number of Kurds to the Foreign Service, including two with the rank of ambassador. On April 25, the RCC named a Kurd director general of the newly established Cultural and Information Directorate. These appointments were made in addition to those Kurds already serving in the government.[27]

At the end of April, the ministry of education announced the implementation of Article One of the manifesto concerning the use of Kurdish as the language of instruction in Kurdish schools, and the teaching of the Kurdish language, grammar, and literature as primary subjects in intermediate schools in the North.[28] Orders were given to all official and semi-official institutions in the North to accept transactions in the language of the citizen's choice. The use of Kurdish as the official language of communication in intergovernment agencies in the northern provinces, however, was postponed. Kurdish language newspapers and magazines and cultural institutions began to appear in accordance with Article Three of the manifesto. A union of Kurdish writers was formed and a Kurdish cultural society was founded. Publication of *al-Taakhi,* the KDP's organ, was resumed on May 1, 1970, along with the weekly newspaper, *Hawkari,* and a magazine, *Bayan.* The RCC ordered the ministry to take action to start a Kurdish publishing house. In addition, the government permitted a resumption of studies for all students who wished to continue their education, and granted a pardon to those students who had been fined upon leaving school to join the Kurdish movement.[29]

The government allowed the Kurdish provinces in accordance with Article Four, to form Kurdish student, youth, women's, and teachers' unions. Civilian workers, officials, and military personnel were allowed to return to their jobs, a large number of whom were transferred at their request to the Kurdish provinces. Time served by the military in the Pesh Merga was to be counted toward future promotion and retirement.[30]

Normalization of the North, in accordance with Article Seven of the

manifesto was enhanced by the opening of health, administrative, and social services. The government allocated 11 million dinars ($33.1 million) to
rebuild 100 villages devastated by the fighting since 1961. As the people resumed their normal commercial activities, various development projects
were undertaken. Three carpet factories were set up in Koisanjaq, Mosul,
and Arbil. A cigarette factory was established in Sulaymaniyya. Water,
telephone and electricity projects were completed in several Kurdish
towns and villages and a number of roads, bridges, laboratories, and
health centers were opened. Plans were made for the expansion of existing factories and the initiation of new cement and marble factories.
Money was allocated for the construction of new hotels, campsites, and
movie houses in order to encourage the resort and tourist industry, which
had suffered during the fighting.[31] The army, the Pesh Merga, Arab and
Kurdish peasants, students and members of the Baath and KDP parties
all participated in this effort. The government declared its recognition of
the cultural rights of the Turkoman and Assyrian minorities by allowing
the publication of newspapers, magazines, and books and the broadcast
of radio and television programs in Turkish and Syriac.[32]

The government in accordance with Article Eight, sought to quicken
the pace of agrarian reform. In a number of cases, it cancelled the back
taxes that Kurdish peasants owed on their property. Areas were set aside
for the construction of villages for the peasant refugees, and lands formerly under government control were distributed in Diala, Sulaymaniyya, Balik, and other provinces. Plans were made to dig artesian wells
in the province of Arbil.[33]

In action resulting from what may have been one of the secret points
agreed upon by the two sides, the government ordered the shutdown of
*Al-Nur* newspaper, which represented the Talibani-Ahmad faction of the
KDP. This action came at the insistence of the Barzani leadership after the
Baathist failure to get Barzani to negotiate with these opponents.[34] Ahmad had left Iraq for medical treatment in London, and Talibani was reportedly under house arrest.[35] Following the closing of *Al-Nur,* Barzani is
reported to have made overtures to Talibani and his followers and persuaded them to join him. This decision was a result of the unenviable position of the Talibani faction, which had been ostracized by both the Barzani group and the government. One leftist faction, however, remained
on the sidelines and refused to join Barzani. It was later to form the Kurdistan Revolutionary party.[36]

On May 21, the high commission for the affairs of the North fulfilled
what was believed to have been another one of the secret clauses of the
agreement by disarming the Cavalry of Salah al-Din. The Cavaliers were

traditionally Kurdish opponents of Barzani who formed irregular units and fought alongside the government. The disarming of the Cavaliers was believed to have been one of Barzani's first demands. The government called on the governors of al-Najaf, Kirkuk, Sulaymaniyya, Arbil, and Diala to collect the weapons given to the Cavaliers by no later than June 1, 1970.[37]

On July 16, 1970, the government took another step toward the implementation of the agreement when President al-Bakr announced the promulgation of the provisional constitution in accordance with Article Nine of the manifesto. This declaration was preceded by a three-hour meeting between Saddam Husain and Mulla Mustafa which paved the way for amending the provisional constitution. In a report from the Iraqi News Agency, Husain said, "We reviewed with our Kurdish brothers what had been implemented in accordance with the manifesto. We have discussed the best means to build Arab-Kurdish relations on a solid basis in order to guarantee self-rule for the Kurds."[38]

The government, while declaring its commitment to the realization of one Arab state, affirmed its promise to the Kurds. Paragraph A of Article Five declared that Iraq was a part of the Arab nation and paragraph B emphasized that the "Iraqi people are composed of two main nationalities, Arab and Kurdish." Article Seven declared that "(a) Arabic is the official language and (b) Kurdish will be an official language side by side with Arabic in the Kurdish region." Article Nineteen stated that "all citizens are equal before the law regardless of race, color, language, social origin or religion," and that "equal opportunity is guaranteed to all within the framework of the law."[39]

It was during this atmosphere of relaxation of tensions and improved ties between Barzani and the Baath that the KDP decided to hold its congress in Kallala during the first half of July 1970. Representatives of Kurdish organizations from Syria and Iran, as well as members of different Iraqi, Arab, and Communist parties and organizations arrived at this town near the Iranian and Turkish borders to celebrate the agreement with the government.[40] The Kallala Congress was expected to name Barzani as the first Kurdish vice president of Iraq, but it failed to do so. Some reports spoke of disagreements among the Kurds over a vice-presidential candidate after Barzani declined. Denying this report, informed Kurdish sources explained that because the government had decided to have more than one vice president, the Kurds would register their displeasure by failing to select their candidate for this office.[41] Mahmud Uthman minimized the importance of the vice presidential issue by pointing to the fact that the Kurds had five ministers to represent them already.[42]

In a secret session of the KDP that lasted some five hours, Barzani was unanimously elected president. After his election, he called for increased cooperation with the government in the name of all Iraq. He asked for social justice, basic social and economic change, and condemned what he described as the "destructive elements which are trying to sow dissension among the citizens of one country with the aim of disrupting national achievements."[43] The congress ended by affirming Arab-Kurdish friendship and Kurdish support for the government.

During the last months of 1970, both sides moved quickly to resolve potentially divisive problems concerning the methods by which the Kurds were to share in the legislative process. An agreement was reported in *Al-Thawra* to have been reached in December 1970 allowing Kurdish participation in the legislative process through the formation of a National Council of 100 members. The council was to include representatives of the Kurdish and Arab popular organizations and "progressive and patriotic personalities."[44]

The KDP's *Al-Taakhi* declared that the council would be a temporary body, which would prepare the way for free elections and draw up a permanent constitution.[45] The government also promised to incorporate 6,000 Pesh Mergas into the armed forces as border guards. Barzani declared that the remaining forces which continued to carry arms, would be paid from a monthly government grant of 90,000 Iraqi dinars. In addition the government provided Barzani with a monthly stipend for personal use to range from 35,000 to 50,000 dinars.[46]

The first year of the agreement was the honeymoon period between the government and the Barzani leadership, although there were some difficulties, which will be discussed in the following chapter. While there were reports of some Kurdish dissatisfaction with the sluggishness of the government's rehabilitation of the Kurdish areas[47] this was not reflected in Kurdish official statements. Quite to the contrary, Mahmud Uthman stated that despite the government's depleted treasury, construction had begun on hospitals and schools, and over 2,700 houses had been built or rebuilt in the affected areas. Al-Atrushi, Irbil's governor and a leading figure in the KDP, announced that half of the 100 villages that had been completely destroyed in the province had been rebuilt.[48]

Kurdish as well as Arab leaders continued throughout 1970 and early 1971 to emphasize publicly their determination to keep the peace agreement. In an interview with the *Los Angeles Times* in December 1970, Barzani declared his optimism: "For the moment we are optimistic. After ten years of fighting the Iraqi government offered us autonomy last March, and so far they seem to be implementing the agreement. We too are trying to cooperate with the government. Both sides need peace and security after all the fighting. I don't feel there is full security yet but maybe some day perhaps."[49]

Baathist leaders continued to express optimism and support for the agreement during the same period. Saddam Husain described the settlement as "a completely substantial, political, and constitutional settlement ensuring brotherhood for all time between Kurds and Arabs."[50] However, such a statement was to prove overly optimistic.

# 6

# DETERIORATION OF RELATIONS
# BETWEEN THE BAATH AND THE KDP

Relations between the Baath and the KDP improved considerably following the signing of the March 11 Manifesto and the implementation of a number of its clauses. Although disagreements and tensions began to surface in the summer of 1971, both sides continued to affirm their commitment to the agreement. The situation entered a new stage, however, in the summer and fall of 1972, when the Barzani leadership, backed by aid and promises of support from Iran, Israel, and the United States, consolidated its control over much of the Kurdish area and escalated its demands. This deterioration of relations continued unchecked until 1974, when the government granted self-rule to the Kurds in areas under its control and resumed a full-scale war with Barzani's forces.

The difficulties and disagreements between the Barzani leadership and the Baath centered on such issues as the delineation of the Kurdish areas, the manner of KDP participation in the government, and continued Kurdish relations with Iran.

The question of the nomination of a Kurdish vice president for Iraq (Article Twelve of the agreement) was never resolved. The Kurds submitted the name of the KDP's secretary, Habib Muhammad Karim, as a candidate for the office.[1] The Baath, however, rejected the candidacy of Karim on the grounds that he was of Iranian origin and that his family continued to live in Iran. The Kurds were asked to nominate someone else, but they could not agree on another candidate.[2] There was also a feeling that the office was relatively meaningless since the real power rested in the Baathist Revolutionary Command Council.

The matter of a census to determine the exact number of Iraqi Kurds (Article Fourteen) was another issue of contention. The census was scheduled to take place in December 1970, postponed by mutual agreement until the following spring, and then postponed again. This measure was one of the most important in the agreement, since the government was pledged to grant autonomy to the Kurds in the areas where they formed a majority. The Kurds were acknowledged to be the majority in Arbil, Duhok, and Sulaymaniyya provinces.

Kurdish claims to oil-rich Kirkuk, however, were disputed by the government since the region's inhabitants included Arabs, Kurds, and Turkomans. Because of the animosity between the Kurds and the Turkomans, the latter did not wish to be included within the Kurdish areas. The Kurds accused the government of resettling Arab tribes in the Kurdish region to influence the outcome of the census. Barzani accused the government of seeking to Arabize not only Kirkuk but the districts of Khanqin and Sinjar as well.[3] He claimed that Arabs from the Tay, Shammar, and Ubayd tribes as well as bedouins from the Ratba and Ramadi areas were brought in and given identity cards. He further charged that the government had forged the population records of Kirkuk and refused to allow the Kurds to register.

These charges of Arabization were denied, however, by Saddam Husain, who offered Barzani the use of the 1965, and later the 1957, census figures to determine the future of Kirkuk.

The dispute over the census also involved Iranian Fayly Kurds who were living in Iraq but who had not been granted Iraqi citizenship. The Kurds wished to include this population in the census. Also to be considered was the number of Kurds who had fled to Iran during the fighting. The government feared that the Kurds were seeking to augment their numbers by bringing in Turkish or Iranian Kurds, particularly in those areas where such infiltration might tip the population figures in their favor, such as Kirkuk.

Despite these disagreements, Kurdish and Arab leaders were still speaking favorably of the agreement in 1971. On the first anniversary of the March 11 Manifesto, Iraqi and Kurdish leaders praised the alliance between the two sides. The Baath party's assistant secretary general, Shibli al-Aysami, praised the alliance between the KDP and the Baath party and expressed the hope that the two parties would continue to work together.[4]

The secretary general of the KDP, Habib Muhammad Karim, told *Al-Jumhuriyya* newspaper that the Baath-KDP alliance had put an end to foreign interference. "The declaration has strengthened our independence and no foreigner has any chance to interfere in Iraq's internal affairs," he said. He also praised the Baathist government for ending the civil strife.[5]

On May 11, 1971, Radio Baghdad broadcast a decree by President al-Bakr establishing a higher committee with full powers to implement the provisions of the March 11 agreement. The decree appointed Saddam Husain, who was then deputy chairman of the RCC and assistant secretary general of the Baath party, the chairman of the new committee. The decree gave the committee the same powers as the RCC in directing implementation of the agreement. The decisions of the committee were to be binding on all ministries once they were issued.

Other members of the committee were Lieutenant General Sadun Ghaidan, an RCC member and minister of the interior; Foreign Minister Murtada al-Hadithi; and three members of the National Command of the Baath party — Naim Haddad, Samir Najm, and Muhammad Fadil. While there was no official explanation for the replacement of the joint committee set up to carry out the March 11 agreement with the new committee, the government's decision to speed up implementation may have been prompted by complaints from the Kurds that certain crucial portions of the treaty were not being fulfilled. In his interview with the author, Barzani expressed his belief that the formation of the higher committee was only a "maneuver" by the government.

The formation of the higher committee did not significantly ease the tension between the government and the Kurds, for little more than a week later the dispute over the Iranian Kurds came to a head. In anticipation of the proposed census to determine areas of Kurdish majorities, the KDP newspaper, *Al-Taakhi* published a report claiming that the Iraqi government had promised to give Iraqi citizenship to 100,000 Iranian Kurds who were currently living in Iraq. *Al-Jumhuriyya,* on behalf of the government, denied this report, adding that the number of Iranian Kurds in Iraq did not exceed 15,000 in any case.[6] It was reported that as a result of this dispute, copies of *Al-Taakhi* were confiscated for three days on the orders of the minister of the interior. The newspaper, however, continued publication.[7]

Barzani was reported to have sent a letter to President al-Bakr accusing the government of resorting to delay tactics with the intention of bringing more Arabs into the Kirkuk area to dilute what Barzani reportedly regarded as a Kurdish majority there. He also charged that certain Christian leaders in the north were collaborating with the regime by encouraging Christians to move to Kirkuk and identify themselves as Arabs.[8]

In his reply, President al-Bakr warned that Iraqi troops would be able to reestablish law and order throughout the country. This was taken by the Kurds as a threat. Barzani, "irritated by al-Bakr's reply, summoned an extraordinary session of the congress of the KDP. A number of Kurdish leaders at the congress called for restraint in order to avoid a showdown with the government. The general view inside the congress was that the

Kurds at that time were not prepared for another armed action against the Iraqis."[9]

Still another cause of friction was the Middle East situation. The government criticized *Al-Taakhi*'s stand in favor of a peaceful solution to the Arab-Israeli conflict and in support of President Nasir's acceptance of the Rogers plan.[10]

On April 28, 1971, Turkey's minister of justice, Ismail Arar, announced that he had uncovered a Kurdish independence movement allegedly set up and supplied by Barzani,[11] but in an interview in the Egyptian weekly, *Roz al-Yusif,* Barzani continued to affirm the unity between the Iraqis and the Kurds. When asked if he planned to bring about national unity among the Kurds in Iraq, Turkey, and Iran, Barzani replied, "We are Iraqi Kurds operating in Iraq only. We have no relations with others. We wish good to all, but we do not interfere in the internal affairs of others."[12]

In the same interview in *Roz al-Yusif,* another Kurdish leader, Mahmud Uthman, said, "We are part of the Kurdish people, but at the same time part of the Iraqi Republic. We are proud of the unity between our Kurdish nationalism and Arab nationalism in Iraq."

When Barzani was asked if he was satisfied with the implementation of the March 11 agreement he replied, "You cannot eat a whole chicken in one bite." Uthman added that the process was slow, but the provisions of the agreement were being fulfilled.[13]

Nevertheless, relations worsened during July 1971, and clashes erupted between the government forces and Barzani. The Kurdish forces were opposed to the presence of the Iraqi army in the Barzan region. The government forces reportedly had attacked the region, using airplanes, tanks, and artillery.[14] Al-Bakr and Barzani exchanged memoranda seeking to solve the problem. Kurdish sources blamed the incidents on the government. They claimed that the Iraqi army had not only remained in the Kurdish areas but had increased its numbers there following the withdrawal of Iraqi forces from Jordan and Syria. The government, on the other hand, justified these actions as "preventive measures against the continuing Iranian threats on the Iraqi border, and in preparation to repel any attack."[15]

Clashes and artillery exchanges between Iranian and Iraqi forces did occur when Iran escalated the conflict by using its air force, thus bypassing the Pesh Merga forces, which had been inducted into the Iraqi forces as border guards. When the government ordered the border guards to wage counterattacks against Iranian border posts, they refused to obey and informed Barzani of the situation. Barzani, in a telegram to the RCC, declared that "the duty of the border guard is not to wage attacks but to prevent any infiltration of the borders."[16]

The refusal by the border guards to obey government orders and the opposition to the Iraqi army's presence in the Kurdish areas increased government suspicions concerning Barzani's intentions and the sincerity of his promises to restore state authority and normalcy to the north. The government, which was facing an inter-party struggle, was powerless to do more than protest.

The situation deteriorated further when on September 29, 1971, an attempt was made to kill Barzani and to thereby destroy the agreement between the Kurds and the Iraqi government. Nevertheless, both sides continued to express their interest in the survival of the agreement. Both Saddam Husain and Mulla Mustafa stressed the need to implement the provisions of the agreement and to end the conflict "for all time."[17]

"The attempt on my life was aimed at blasting the March 11 declaration, which settled the Kurdish problem last year, and the national unity of the Iraqi people," Barzani said. He added, "We leave the investigation of the case to the authorities, and we shall put at their disposal all the information we have."[18]

Although the attempt on Barzani's life did not wreck the agreement, it did sow seeds of suspicion on both sides. Recriminations, charges, and countercharges appeared in *Al-Taakhi* and *Al-Thawra*.[19] A second assassination attempt in 1972 was only one more of a series of incidents which increased the Kurdish leadership's apprehension about the government. These incidents included an attack on KDP offices in Mosul and the ambush of a car belonging to Idris al-Barzani on December 7, 1970, in Baghdad.[20] In a case of mistaken identity, a friend of Idris was wounded while driving his car when Idris was out of the city on an unexpected trip. At the time, Barzani and KDP leader Mahmud Uthman declared that they suspected the conspirators were followers of Jalal Talibani.[21] Information since then has offered the possibility of another suspect — the then-powerful Nazim Kazar, Iraq's security chief. Kazar as well as a small group of Baathist and pan-Arab officers opposed the party's decision to solve the Kurdish problem in accordance with the March 11 Manifesto. Kazar felt that the government had made many unnecessary concessions to the Kurds. He also opposed the government's decision to improve its relations with the country's Communist party. Consequently he waged a ruthless campaign against communists, Kurds, and other dissidents, leading to the disappearance of many people considered to be enemies of the regime.[22]

The situation continued to deteriorate as the government arrested a number of Kurdish supporters of Barzani in the early part of November 1971, accusing them of participating in "criminal acts such as sabotage, assassinations, and kidnapping." The government decided to try them before a revolutionary court to ensure "just punishment."[23] These announcements, published in *Al-Thawra,* came in response to an accusation by *Al-Taakhi* charging that a number of KDP members and supporters had been arrested and that the authorities had failed to follow the "required procedures" concerning their detention.[24]

*Al-Thawra* then published the text of two telegrams sent on November 14 by the government's High Committee for Northern Affairs to Barzani explaining the arrests of the KDP members and supporters.[25] The first telegram indicated that the arrests followed the discovery by the government of plans to commit acts of sabotage such as "the blowing up in Arbil of ammunition stores, oil pumps, the military intelligence center, and the military airport in Kirkuk," as well as plans to assassinate the director of security in Arbil and a number of leading citizens and Baath party members in the area. The telegram claimed that the conspirators had confessed and that they were directed by the intelligence agency of the KDP. The second telegram, sent on the same day, spoke of the arrest of a number of Kurds in Bashiqa, Nineveh province (formerly Mosul province) after they had fired on security forces killing one police sergeant and wounding another. It claimed that these men had fired at the police from the headquarters of the KDP.

At the same time the question of KDP participation in power emerged to further cloud relations between Barzani and the government. On November 15, 1971, President al-Bakr announced the formation of the National Action Charter in an attempt to broaden his base of support by moving toward the formation of a united front of political forces to include the Iraq; Communist party (ICP) and the KDP. The charter declared, "The political system built by the July 17 Revolution under the leadership of the Baath party, which seeks the realization of the broadest coalition among all the national, patriotic, and progressive forces . . . is a democratic and popular system."[26]

On November 16, *Al-Taakhi* published an article declaring that the Baath party and the government had failed to consult with the KDP prior to the proclamation of the charter.[27] The government, however, had consulted various parties and groups, including the KDP.[28] The Kurdish representatives questioned the need for an alliance with the Communist party.[29]

The situation was further complicated when a letter sent by Barzani to President Ahmad Hasan al-Bakr warned that unless the Kurds were allowed broader military and political authority, they would have to take another look at the "peaceful dialogue which began after March 11, 1970."[30] The Barzani memorandum demanded the following: that the Kurds not only have five ministers in the cabinet but also have representatives in the RCC and the army, adding that the promised vice-presidential office was meaningless unless the Kurds shared in the decision-making process.

The Kurdish memorandum admitted that the regime had fulfilled much of the March 11 Manifesto but added new demands. Since large portions of the Iraqi army were stationed in the North, a withdrawal of these forces was demanded. A quick investigation into the attempt on the life of Barzani in September was also sought as well as the ouster of leading government officials who, it claimed, were responsible.

The government replied that it was investigating the assassination attempt and reaffirmed its right to train and station troops in all parts of the country. In answer to Barzani's demand for participation in the military authority, President al-Bakr said in a press conference on November 7, 1971: "The responsibility of the army and its political guidance belongs to the leadership of the Revolution alone and there will not be in the army any political front or party organization except for the Baath Arab Socialist party. There may be other individuals who may belong to some political movements but they will be inducted into the army on an individual basis and not on the basis of party or political affiliation."[31]

Barzani responded by toning down his demands and promised that his party would first study the charter from all angles and then express its position toward it. He also declared his support for an interpretation of the Kurdish problem in the Charter that delegated equal responsibility for its solution to all national groups.[32]

Barzani further called for a united effort in building healthy relations to end the "rumors" and "divisions." He added: "We have asked all sides to put an end to divisions and conflicts which progressive and nationalist forces have gone through and to reach an agreement on a coalition. We are absolutely ready to play our full role on this basis. The patriotic forces must appreciate the historic stage through which our country is passing."

These statements by Barzani did contribute to an easing of tensions. While certain points remained unresolved, both sides continued their peaceful dialogue toward implementing the March 11 Manifesto. The government continued to work toward carrying out the unimplemented sections, and the Kurds promised both to surrender some of their weapons and to restore government authority in their area.

In an interview published on April 14, 1972, Saddam Husain discussed the Kurdish question and the implemented as well as the unimplemented sections of the manifesto. Concerning Article Eleven, in which the Kurds promised to surrender their radio transmitters and their heavy arms, Husain said that the "Kurdish side has not implemented it, and we have not insisted that they do so because we don't consider it urgent. The Kurdish people are our people and if they have weapons they will be used to defend the cause of the Revolution."[33]

Concerning Article Twelve, referring to the appointment of a Kurdish vice president, Husain said: "This matter is up to them until they nominate someone. We are ready." He added that Article Thirteen, dealing with amending the law affecting the governorates, had not been implemented but that a committee was working to remove any contradiction with the March 11 Manifesto."

As for Article Fifteen, dealing with Kurdish participation in the legislative process, he said that the Kurds had nominated their candidates for the National Council and "we are waiting for the end of the dialogue to announce the names of the members of the National Council, which will include the names of the Kurdish candidates."

Husain emphasized that autonomy did not mean secession, an issue which was becoming of growing concern to the government. He declared that Iraq "lies within the map of the Arab world and that does not conflict with the rights of minorities living in the Arab homeland. But this does not mean delineating lands for these minorities because this means that they want to secede from the Arab homeland. This we will not allow. Iraq is part of the Arab nation and the Kurds are a nationality coexisting in a brotherly way with the Arab nationality. The constitution will guarantee the rights of minorities and will include the March 11 Manifesto, agreed upon by Arabs as well as Kurds."

He denied Kurdish charges that attempts were being made to Arabize their areas. "If this means settling Arabs in Kurdish areas, I can assure you that there is no truth to it."

Husain declared that: "A census is essential to the implementation of self-rule and to the delineation of the administrative border for the Kurdish self-rule area."

He denied charges that the government had delayed developing the Kurdish areas. He said the Iraqi government had promised that 19 percent of the funds of the current Five Year Plan in addition to 11 million Iraqi dinars (about $30 million) would be spent in the areas where the Kurds formed a majority, adding that the number of houses already built in the North exceeded the number built in the rest of Iraq. Ninety percent of the Kurdish refugees had returned to their villages, he said, and the rest refused to return either because of their conflict with the Kurdish leadership or for personal reasons. He concluded by saying that the government would grant the Kurds immediate autonomy in the case of Iraq's unification with another country.


## DETERIORATION OF RELATIONS


Despite the slight improvement in relations in late 1971 and early 1972, the situation began to deteriorate badly in the summer and fall of 1972 following the nationalization of the Iraq Petroleum Company (IPC) in June 1972. Armed clashes erupted in Sulaymaniyya, resulting in the deaths of three Kurds. The government accused Abd al-Rahman Ramash of the uprisings, but Barzani denied that Ramash was connected with his group.[34]

On July 3, the RCC ordered the formation of a special committee and court in Mosul to investigate and try the perpetrators of a number of incidents which had occurred in Sinjar. The court ordered several KDP members to appear before it on charges of inciting and participating in the incidents. Among those cited were such high KDP officials as Ali Sinjari, vice governor of Duhok and head of a branch of the KDP, and Isa Sawar, commander of a Pesh Merga division in Zakho. Both refused to appear before the court and were reported to have responded that they had no trust in the fairness of those who would be trying them.[35]

On the morning of the same day, the government also announced that a district director in Sinjar and his chief of police had been attacked and were wounded. When the district governor went with a small force to investigate, he and a sergeant were shot and killed, and three soldiers were wounded. The government responded by sending in a large force and arresting thirty people it described as "agents of imperialism and the oil companies."[36]

These incidents were attributed to a number of causes. Many of the Yazidi Kurdish tribal leaders (not among Barzani's followers) were incensed at the loss of some of the revenue-producing concessions they had received from the IPC after Iraq nationalized the company on June 1, 1972. At the time of the nationalization, the government was also attempting to extend to Sinjar its efforts to disarm the North, creating still another source of tension. Another problem was the Kurdish protest over the inclusion of Kurdish-claimed Sinjar and Shaykhan districts in the predominantly Arab Nineveh province and not in the Kurdish Duhok province. The Kurds claimed that the government was settling Arab tribes in these two districts, a charge that was denied by the government.[37]

Clashes were also reported to have erupted between Yazidi and Arab tribes, causing the government to use the air force against both sides and the Iraqi army to send reinforcements to the area. It was reported at this time that Barzani sent a group of his followers to help the Yazidis even though they were not considered to be on his side. Estimates of the number of people killed in these conflicts ranged between thirty and fifty on each side.[38]

To prevent the conflict from accelerating, the Iraqi government sent several Kurdish ministers to contact Barzani and to inform him that the government still adhered to the March 11 agreement and did not wish the situation to worsen. Barzani responded by telegram to President al-Bakr, saying that the situation "is unclear to us and to the members of our party within and without the region." Barzani said that the Kurds were willing to cooperate with the government to discover those responsible for the clashes, despite the fact that the government had accused the Barzani group even before the investigation was complete and had sent additional forces from Mosul to Sinjar on July 4. Barzani requested the government to put an end to these military operations before they led to a wider explosion and promised to cooperate in finding and punishing the guilty.[39]

The situation took a turn for the worse when Jalal Harizi, the Kurdish minister of agriculture, was killed in a car accident on July 11. The RCC later combined the ministries of agriculture and agrarian reform and gave the position to a Baathist, Izzat Ibrahim al-Duri.[40]

A battle between the two party organs ensued, deepening the rift between the Baath and the KDP as the discord moved into the arena of public polemics. In an article in *Al-Thawra,* the government replied that the combining of the two ministries was necessitated by agricultural conditions in Iraq and had nothing to do with the question of Kurdish rights. It added that since the Ministry of Agrarian Reform was a temporary post whose aim was to divide lands among the peasants, and since its purpose was about to be fulfilled, a combination of the two ministries was justified. The newspaper added that the KDP had not nominated anyone to replace Harizi, although it had the right to nominate anyone it wished to fill a cabinet post.[41]

*Al-Thawra* went on to criticize *Al-Taakhi*'s stand in the matter, saying that the Baath party had always avoided a narrow point of view by refusing to consider a citizen's ethnic background (implying that this was *Al-Taakhi*'s attitude). It added that even though a ministerial post was occupied by a Kurd, this did not mean that the ministry should be solely concerned with Kurdish matters. Nor did it mean that the minister should ignore the affairs of the Kurdish area, for his position was one of public trust.

## THE BAATHIST MEMORANDUM TO THE KDP

The Baath party expressed its growing concern over the anti-government positions adopted by the Barzani leadership. On September 23, 1972, the regional leadership of the Baath party sent a memorandum to the KDP's Central Committee reviewing relations between the two sides, citing Baathist grievances, and expressing the desire for "forestalling any future deterioration in our relations and facilitating the reconstruction of these relations." The memorandum stated that the causes of the deterioration had been repeatedly discussed with the majority of the members of the KDP's Politburo and Central Committee and particularly with Barzani.[42]

The memorandum emphasized that the March Manifesto comprised two closely linked issues that had been agreed upon by both sides as the basis for settlement. These were "guaranteeing the legitimate national rights of the Kurds" and consolidating the unity of Iraq.

The memorandum enumerated the implementations of Kurdish demands that had taken place after the March 11 Manifesto. It then reiterated the clauses of the agreement not yet in force. Concerning the question of Kurdish participation in legislative decisions, the memorandum said that although what it sought to achieve was a "natural right" it had established the National Council following the agreement on the National Action Charter in order to form the basis for a coalition among the KDP, Baath, and the ICP. It also expressed a willingness to study "all proposals submitted by you in this respect."

Concerning the question of appointing a Kurdish vice president, the memorandum said that it was the KDP's right to nominate a representative, but that the government should not be forced into a difficult situation (the nomination of Habib Muhammed Karim). It added that the Baath had nominated two Kurds, one who was a member of the KDP's Central Committee, but had not received any Kurdish response to the nomination.

Referring to the matter of appointing directors of security, the memorandum said that while "reaffirming our concern for the participation of our Kurdish brothers in all state institutions, including security organizations, we cannot ignore the fact that the present conditions dominating the Kurdish area and the nature of the relations and the connections of the Kurdish movement [with Iran] do not encourage the prompt application of this clause." It promised to reconsider the clause as soon as "appropriate conditions" prevailed.

Concerning the amendment of the Governorate Law, the memorandum declared government readiness to implement this clause and to consider any Kurdish proposals concerning it. Regarding the question of the census, the memorandum stated: "We are still prepared to enforce the clause of the [March 11] Manifesto pertaining to carrying out a population census in the mixed areas to determine those populated with a Kurdish majority. We have discussed with you the question of postponing the census only after Mr. al-Barzani had told Comrade Murtada al-Hadithi that you were not prepared to recognize the results of the census if they indicated the presence of an Arab majority in the enumerated areas." The government declared that it was ready to go back to the 1957 census. Earlier it had offered the option of using the 1965 census [which Barzani had rejected as forged] as the basis "for determining whether or not a citizen is a resident of these areas" and insisted on the termination of "operations of settling Arab and Kurdish citizens in the mixed areas."

The memorandum reaffirmed the Baathist commitment to implement self-rule within the four-year period determined in the Manifesto or even earlier. It, however, added that the KDP as "the main quarter shouldering self-rule, you must naturally be required to honor your commitments to . . . attain that goal in the shortest possible time."

The memorandum then delved into the main issues behind the government's concern over the development of its relations with the Barzani leadership, i.e., its ties to Iran and the failure of the KDP to allow the government to function in the areas under its control.

Concerning the second clause of the March 11 Manifesto pertaining to the upholding of the unity of the people and the land of Iraq it stated, "We do not part from the truth when we say: you have not taken a single step along this path." It charged the Kurdish leadership with gross violations of the principles of national unity and Iraqi national sovereignty by entering into and continuing relations with Iran. It added: "If the leadership of your party could manage a self-justification for past relations with the Iranian and the reactionary government, it is in no way acceptable to continue that relationship after the March Manifesto." Severing these ties was the least that could be expected following the declaration of peace and the stages of implementation of the March 11 pact since "Iranian reaction was the first to conspire simultaneously against the Revolution and the Kurdish masses in order to prevent" peace and the March Manifesto.

It specifically mentioned the following evidence of Kurdish-Iranian ties:

• The flow of Iranian arms into the north, including heavy and light weapons;

• A new broadcasting station supplied by Iran;

• Kurdish attendance in Iranian military colleges and the training of Pesh Merga forces in the use of arms, particularly heavy arms;

• The communication of military information concerning the Iraq army to Iran;

• Collaboration with Iranian forces in frontier clashes, particularly in the Khanaqin area;

• The harboring of members of Iranian intelligence;

• The circulation of counterfeit Iraqi currency printed by Iran;

• Medical treatment of Kurds in Iranian hospitals;

• Exit of Iraqi citizens via Iran despite a RCC ban on travelling abroad as well as the admission of foreigners into the northern area through Iran;

• Iranian intelligence aggravations in Kurdish-held areas, including kidnappings and killings;

• Extradition of Iranians fleeing the Shah's government;

• Exchange of visits between KDP and Iranian officials.

Charges that the KDP had persisted in undermining the authority of the Iraqi government included the following:

• Refusal to hand over frontier posts on the Iranian border to the armed forces;

• Prevention of the armed forces from training and stationing in certain areas;

• Denial of access to government officials in performing their official duties, including those offering medical services to the Kurds;

• Establishing prisons and arresting, imprisoning, and executing citizens;

• Imposing taxes.

Attacks against the security of the state were cited as follows:

• Attempting to blow up the oil pipe lines during the ultimatum served to the oil companies in May 1972;

• Attempting to explode certain air bases;

• Blowing up railway lines;

• Inciting riots and disorder (the Khaniqin, Bashiqa, Sinjar incidents, etc.);

• Attempts against the lives of administrative officials, and kidnapping, torturing, and killing citizens suspected of sympathizing with the government;

• Large-scale acts of rape committed by the Pesh Merga, and burning of villages whose inhabitants were known to be loyal to the government.

The KDP was accused in the memorandum of hindering the implementation of the Agrarian Reform Act by deliberate obstruction, including the kidnapping and harassment of officials entrusted with carrying out the operations of the reform. The Pesh Merga was implicated in the collection of agricultural taxes falsely presented as a "zakat."

The inherent contradiction of the KDP playing the role of the opposition at a time when it was participating in the government was illustrated by examples of negative statements issued in KDP publications and the failure of the KDP to support major Iraqi government positions, particularly on the question of the Iran-Iraq border clashes.

The Baathist memorandum accused the KDP of actually hindering the enforcement of the March Manifesto by handing over only one installment of weapons instead of the full amount agreed upon. It also blamed the KDP for preventing the repatriation of some displaced Kurdish families because of a "policy of persecution exercised by your party against elements unwilling to comply with your orders."

A new list of conditions to be met by the KDP concluded the memorandum and was presented as a necessary prerequisite for "commencing new relations." These conditions included:

• Severance of relations with Iran, the sealing of the borders, and a transfer of frontier posts to the government to prevent smuggling and the infiltration of foreigners into Iraq;

• Termination of expatriation of "Iranian patriots" to Iran;

• Condemnation of all acts of political assassination, disorder, and sedition;

• Banishment of Kurdish tribal leaders who endanger the northern area or Baghdad;

• Noninterference with the functions of the armed forces, security, and intelligence organs operating in the northern area;

• Closing of all KDP prisons, a release of prisoners, and establishment of a policy opposed to the killing, kidnapping, or torture of citizens supporting the Revolution;

• Dedication of KDP policy toward "cementing peace and national fraternity and safeguarding national unity and the unity of the struggle";

• Enforcement of the laws and regulations of the country by all KDP administrative staff members;

• Ending the state armament in all areas inhabited by Kurds, including the handing over of heavy weapons to the central authorities;

• Acknowledgement that the responsibility for state authority rests with state organizations;

• Cooperation with authorities in criminal investigations of murder and kidnapping;

• Resistance to counter-revolutionary trends;

• Repatriation of all Kurds;

• Enforcement of the Agrarian Reform Law;

• Noninterference with the granting of cultural and administrative rights to national minorities (Assyrians, Turkomans, etc.).

Special conditions were enumerated in the memorandum pertaining to the Frontier Guard. In the future, it was to function directly under the Ministry of Defense, to be trained by Kurdish officers and NCC's of the Iraqi army, and to be strictly confined to duty along the Iraqi frontier.

## THE KDP MEMORANDUM

New attempts were made to alleviate tensions when Abd al-Khaliq al-Samarai, a member of both the regional and national commands of the Baath party and a leading Baathist theoretician and Kurdish Minister Muhammad Mahmud Abd al-Rahman made contacts with the KDP. Results, however, were indecisive, and the KDP Politburo responded by sending a memorandum to the regional command of the Baath on November 28, 1972. The memorandum declared:

> There is no doubt that the relations between us have reached a major rift. We have previously brought this to your attention more than once during the past year, either through the peace committee, through the party meetings held between our representatives and yours, or through memoranda sent by the president of our party to the RCC. But the carelessness and the lack of concern which met our efforts and the trespasses against us since the middle of last year have pushed the situation toward constant deterioration until the general situation threatens an explosion which may damage the security of our Iraqi people, both Arabs and Kurds, damage its safety and achievements, and subject the future relationship between our two parties to great damage and harm.[43]

The KDP summarized its stand, saying, "It is no longer a secret that the alliance between our two parties has become questionable and that all the important positions in government and the armed forces have been monopolized by your (the Baath) party." As for the Kurdish movement's commitment to a return to normalcy, the memorandum declared that, while unwritten, evidence could be seen in the return of normal conditions to the area and the establishment of the central government's authority in the region. This had been accomplished by the formation of the border guards and the dissolution of the "institutions of the Kurdish Revolution," including its RCC, executive, military, administrative, judicial, education, health, and other bureaus. It added that although the spirit of cooperation had lasted for more than a year, future progress in relations would have to be tied to sincere and truthful cooperation between the two sides.

The KDP also objected to Baathist actions. These actions included:

•Failure to take legal action against the criminals involved in the shooting incidents at the KDP headquarters in Mosul and on the car of Idris al-Barzani in Baghdad;

•Arabization policy in Kurdistan, particularly in the provinces of Kirkuk, Diala, and Nineveh, where Kurdish inhabitants were repatriated away from the area;

• Failure to allow the Kurds to share in legislative authority and in the planning of general state policy on internal as well as foreign levels;

•Carrying out a comprehensive policy to destroy the leadership of the KDP and shatter its unity, including two attempts on the life of Barzani, the kidnapping, arrest, and torture of party members, the delivery of explosive packages and bombs to party headquarters, and the transfer of active elements of the KDP from the central and southern parts of Iraq in order to weaken the party. Also included in these tactics was the formation of pseudo-Kurdish organizations set up to publish and disseminate false party literature;

•Obstruction and postponement of the census;

•Creation of armed pockets in the Kurdish area supported by government money and weapons and used against the Kurdish people, particularly in Sbilik, Aqrah, and Sinjar;

•Expulsion of tens of thousands of Fayli Kurds and the confiscation of their property;

•Surveillance of KDP members in the armed forces;

•Formation of the National Guard to include mercenary elements and not members of the KDP;

•Bombing of peaceful villages by artillery and planes and the levelling of entire Kurdish villages by bulldozers;

• Arrests and threats exercised against the employees of *Al-Taakhi*;

• Reversal of some of the gains achieved after the March 11 Manifesto, including the denial of KDP authority in the army, attacks on Kurdish national rights, and efforts to dissolve the ministry of northern affairs by tying its directorates to other ministries;

• Harassment of mass Kurdish organizations, particularly in the trade unions and peasants' organizations.

In response to the charge that the KDP had adopted a negative attitude toward the National Action Charter, the memorandum denounced the government decision to announce the charter unilaterally instead of "jointly as was agreed upon between us."

The KDP memorandum then discussed the implemented and unimplemented clauses of the March Manifesto. It agreed that the following clauses had been implemented successfully:

• Article One, concerning the use of Kurdish as an official language;

• Article Five, concerning the establishment of Kurdish organizations;

• Article Six, concerning the return of Kurdish officials, soldiers, and employees to their posts, but added that hundreds of Kurdish soldiers had since fled the military because of the army ban on any KDP political activity in its ranks;

• Article Nine, concerning agrarian reform;

• Article Ten, concerning amendments to the Constitution.

The Fourth Article, which provided for the appointment of Kurdish officials to administrative posts in areas where the Kurds formed a majority, was said to be implemented in the provinces of Duhok, Sulaymaniyya, and Arbil but not in the provinces of Kirkuk, Nineveh, and Diala.

The memorandum raised questions about Article Eight, concerning the return of Arab and Kurdish villagers to their homes, saying that only the residents of two out of twenty-two Kurdish villages were allowed to return. It further accused the government of seeking to Arabize Kirkuk by bringing officials, policemen, workers, and other Arabs from outside the province and giving them local identity cards.

Arabization was also the charge made concerning Article Fourteen, which dealt with the census. Beside charges of postponing the census for a year, the KDP accused the government of waging "a campaign of Baathization and Arabization which was the primary cause for shattering confidence and precipitating clashes. It is considered to be an undeclared war against the Kurdish people." A delineation of the Kurdish regions, the memorandum added, would solve many of the problems on both sides.

In reference to Kurdish participation in the legislative process and sharing of government power (Article Fifteen), the memorandum reiterated the fact that the RCC, which did not include Kurds, still exercised primary legislative power. Although four Kurdish ministers and three under-secretaries had been appointed, "It is well known that state policies are generally set by the RCC, which only represents the Baath leadership, and no measures have been taken to guarantee participation by the Kurds or the KDP in governing. The Kurds are participating in administration but not in decision-making."

Concerning the return of radio transmitters and heavy weapons to the government (Article Eleven), the KDP said that it had surrendered one radio transmitter and some heavy weapons but would wait before surrendering the rest.

The memorandum agreed that the government had asked the KDP to nominate a vice president but that it had refused in view of the lack of authority allocated to the post. It promised that the KDP would nominate another candidate if the situation improved.

Still not implemented by the government was the amending of the Governorates Law (Article Thirteen), according to the memorandum.

It denied Baath charges that counter-revolutionary elements were being welcomed by the KDP as "untrue and greatly exaggerated." Accusations of large-scale KDP connections with local and foreign enemies of the government were denied, but the memorandum added that a justification for such relations did exist, due to "the negative atmosphere between our two parties," and it cited the period between March 11, 1970, and September 22, 1971, as an example. It promised that the KDP would stop smuggling.

To charges that the border guards were failing to comply with government orders, the KDP memorandum pointed out major differences in interpretation by saying that unlike the Baath, the KDP felt that the guards should be linked to the ministry of the interior through its own directorate and not the ministry of defense. It also insisted upon maintaining command in the hands of the border guards instead of relinquishing it to an army commander, particularly in matters of investigation and leave.

The memorandum also found fault with the granting of national rights to the Assyrian and Turkoman minorities and accused the government of deciding on this policy for "tactical" reasons.

The KDP submitted its own list of conditions to improve relations between the two sides. These included:

- Releasing arrested, convicted, and kidnapped persons;
- Ending hostile activities, including propaganda;

• Ending attacks and pressure applied to the KDP, their supporters, and other national minorities in the Kurdish areas;

• Ending Arabization and Baathization;

• Creating a strategic alliance between the KDP and Baath leadership;

• Consulting with the KDP on the appointment of security officials in the area;

• Increasing the percentage of funds allocated for the Kurdish area in the Five-Year Development Plan;

• Defining the format for self-rule and the date for its implementation;

• Granting citizenship to Kurds without Iraqi citizenship including the Faylis, the Koyans, and Omiryans, and allowing those expelled from the country to return;

• Speeding up the investigation of the attempt on Barzani's life.


## OPEN DISCORD


The ties between Baghdad and the Kurds deteriorated further as differences began to be aired publicly in a series of articles published by *Al-Thawra* from October 19, 1972, to November 13, 1972. The series presented the government's views on obstacles impeding the settlement of the Kurdish question as well as proposals for reconciliation. Entitled, "To Safeguard Peace and Consolidate National Unity," the series was designed to acquaint the Iraqi public with developments in the North and relations with the Kurdish leadership. In addition, the government sought to get broader support for the National and Nationalist Progressive Front (NNPF) it was seeking to form under the National Action Charter. The series was written in response to the KDP memorandum and reiterated many of the government's previous positions as reflected in the Baath memorandum and earlier statements.[44]

The paper also reported that Iraqi Foreign Minister Murtada Abd al-Baqi (al-Hadithi) in his capacity as chairman of the peace committee entrusted with implementing the March Manifesto, had offered Barzani the option of a new census. Barzani replied that he was not prepared to recognize the results of the census if it yielded certain results. He was reported to have said "Kirkuk is part of Kurdistan. If the population census shows that the majority of the inhabitants are not Kurds, I will not recognize this. I will not bear . . . responsibility for relinquishing Kirkuk. Maybe this can take place after me."[45]

The situation in Kirkuk itself had worsened after a bomb was thrown in one of the cafes on November 16, 1972, causing the death of one Iraqi sergeant and the wounding of 27 other people, including an army officer.[46]

On November 2, *Al-Thawra* levied new and sharp attacks against the Kurdish leadership, charging it with maintaining and strengthening its ties with Iran. The newspaper stated that the severance of these ties was "foremost of the conditions" presented by the government during the talks preceding the March Manifesto and agreed to by the KDP leadership. The article went on to say that instead of those relations being terminated or limited, they were in fact being strengthened and expanded. It reiterated much of the same evidence of Kurdish-Iranian ties as had appeared in the Baathist memorandum, adding the following: the flooding of the northern area with Iranian and Israeli commodities, resulting in a very strong Iranian economic influence that extended to the local Kurdish markets in the region; the smuggling of certain Iraqi Jews to Iran in preparation for their onward escape to Israel.[47]

Another article appeared on November 5, dealing with the military dimension of Iraq's troubled relations with the Kurds. The government accused the Barzani leadership of encouraging Kurdish soldiers to desert the armed forces in order to go to Kurdish areas, "one time under the pretext of 'strained relations,' and another time in connection with the allegation of 'the arrest of Kurdish soldiers.'"[48] The paper continued that the military authorities could not allow such acts to go unpunished. "But brothers in the KDP considered these acts as a political issue and insisted either upon absolving the soldiers concerned of the punishment they deserved or retaining them in the KDP areas."

In the same article, the government charged the Kurdish leadership with the following hostile acts:

• Plans to blow up military bases;

• Preventing the armed forces from being stationed in the Kurdish areas under their control;

• Enabling more than 120,000 individuals, including some Arabs, to escape from military service by furnishing them with documents stating they belonged to the Pesh Merga (the government gave the Pesh Merga, whose numbers were estimated at 21,000 after the March 11 Memorandum, exemption from the draft);

• Continued use of the Pesh Merga, which had been made border guards and equipped by the government, as an official armed force ignoring the authority of the government;

• 379 murders, 5,110 kidnappings, 419 assaults, 29 robberies, and 157 rapes of Kurdish citizens opposed to the KDP by the Pesh Merga;

• Establishment of nineteen prisons and detention centers in the areas under Barzani's control;

• The burning and shelling of Kurdish villages whose inhabitants did not back the KDP;

• Expulsion of Kurds who did not support the Barzani leadership from their homes, including 34,000 in the province of Nineveh;

• Preventing other national minorities from exercising their national rights;

• Acts of sabotage against rail facilities, electric power installations, roads, bridges, dams and other public property.

The newspaper concluded its series by affirming government intentions to implement self-rule and suggested other political parties and groups participate in the KDP-Baath dialogue. It also called on the Kurdish leadership to end its foreign contacts and allow the government to restore normalcy to the North.[49]

One possible result of the renewed tensions was the reappearance of the Kurdish Revolutionary party (KRP). This can be attributed to increased disillusionment with Barzani among some of the more urban and leftist elements. It is important to note that the KRP, under the leadership of Abd al-Sattar Sharif, had taken a strong leftist stand before it joined the Barzanis after the March Manifesto and was more radical in its economic and social approach. It is probable that its original split with the KDP was due to dissatisfaction with the pace of Barzani's activities, for the KRP charged that he had blocked agrarian reform in the North by being both "feudal and tribal."[50]

## SOVIET MEDIATION EFFORTS

Relations between the KDP and the Baath failed to improve, despite reports of attempts by the Soviets to mediate the dispute. The Soviets, at Iraqi urging, promised to use their influence with Barzani to encourage him to continue his dialogue with the Baath and to work toward reaching a new format for cooperation with the Iraqi government. In an editorial in *Pravda,* the Soviet government expressed its support for the idea of forming a national progressive front in Iraq which would include the three main political forces in Iraq: the Baath, the KDP, and the ICP.[51]

The Soviets issued an invitation to Mukarram Talibani, the communist minister of irrigation and a leading Kurd, for talks in Moscow. An invitation was also sent to Barzani to visit the USSR, but Barzani denied ever receiving an invitation.[52] Nevertheless, Mukarram Talibani contends that he brought an invitation from the Soviets to Barzani but that Barzani had refused to accept it.[53] Talibani claimed that Barzani, who was afraid of being arrested or assassinated if he left his headquarters, asked that the Soviet ambassador go to Kallala and pick him up in his own car. Talibani contended that Barzani had nothing to fear from the government which simply wanted him to listen to what the Soviets had to say. Finally, two Kurdish members of the KDP's Politburo were dispatched to the USSR. These visits and subsequent contacts led nowhere. The Soviet mediation efforts continued although the discussions between Baghdad and the Kurds remained static as both sides continued to consolidate their positions throughout the winter months of 1973.

The situation broke down further when serious clashes initiated by Barzani's forces erupted in April and late June 1973 near the Kirkuk oil fields. Barzani's forces attacked and dislodged Kurdish forces led by Ahmad Talibani, a pro-government Kurdish leader in Kifri and Tozkhumatu, south of Kirkuk.[54]

Barzani was reported to have threatened a full-scale Kurdish attack on Iraqi forces unless they withdrew from the areas he considered to be inhabited by a Kurdish majority. There were reports from Tehran, where Barzani was getting increasing aid, that Barzani had ordered the mobilization of 28,000 regular fighters of the Pesh Merga. The *Tehran Journal* reported the killing of eleven Kurds and the wounding of twenty others in the first days of the fighting, which was reported to have lasted for several days.[55]

Barzani's decision to order his forces into action appears to have been motivated by his desire to prevent the government from securing and further developing the northern oil fields. He feared that this would strengthen the government economically, allowing it to solidify its position at home and thus challenge his control in the Kurdish area.

The outbreak of fighting in June may have been partly influenced by the visit of a Soviet delegation to the Iraqi oil fields in Kirkuk as the result of a Soviet promise the previous September to send some of their best oil experts to help Iraq work its oil fields. One week earlier Mulla Mustafa had expressed a preference for a U.S. presence in the area when he told an American correspondent that if the U.S. "support were strong enough, we could control Kirkuk and give it to an American company to operate.

It is in our area and the nationalization [of the IPC] last year was an act against the Kurds."[56]


## THE FORMATION OF THE NATIONAL
## AND NATIONALIST PROGRESSIVE FRONT (NNPF)


Iraqi-Kurdish relations were greatly affected by the government's increased cooperation with the Iraqi Communist party (ICP) and with the Soviet Union following the abortive coup at the end of June 1973 of Colonel Nazim Kazar, the Iraqi chief of security. Kazar had strongly opposed Baath party members such as Saddam Husain who wished to strengthen ties with the Communist countries and the ICP and grant self-rule to the Kurds.

Kazar's background explains his anti-communist and anti-Kurdish orientation. He came from a village in Iraq where the communists were in the majority and the Baathists in the minority. The Baathists were subjected to harassment and imprisonment under Qasim. Several of Kazar's friends and associates were believed to have been killed by the communists and the Kurds who supported the Qasim regime. Kazar himself had been a leading underground Baathist fighter during the struggle against Qasim and his communist supporters.[57] He never forgot these experiences and waged, upon the Baath's return to power, his own personal vendetta against the Kurds and the communists. Kazar was given a free hand as security chief during the first three years of Baath rule. The Baath leadership, faced with the insecurity of plots and threats against the regime, was more interested at the time in remaining in power than in checking Kazar's activities.

As the party began to consolidate its authority, however, Kazar's excesses became a source of embarrassment and concern. This was particularly apparent at a time when the government was seeking to improve its relations with the ICP, to come to an agreement on the Kurdish problem with the KDP, and to form a united front with the two parties. The leadership began to plan for the removal of Kazar, who had established his own power center as chief of internal security. Kazar apparently became aware of these efforts and decided to strike first.

On June 30, the day that President al-Bakr was due to return from a visit to Poland, Kazar invited General Sadun Ghaidan, the interior minister, and General Hammad Shihab, the defense minister, to a luncheon at his home. His plan was to invade the airport with his security forces and to shoot or take hostage al-Bakr and Saddam Husain, who was to meet the president at the airport with other senior party officials.

When generals Ghaidan and Shihab failed to show up at the airport, Husain became suspicious and called al-Bakr, urging him to delay his arrival. Kazar, alerted to Husain's suspicions, fled toward Iran with the ministers as hostages. En route, Kazar sent a long message to al-Bakr by a radio transmitter in his car in which he explained his demands. He wanted Iraq to resume the war against Barzani, to take tougher measures against Israel, to provide firmer support for the Palestinian resistance, and to give power back to the party's National Command. He threatened to shoot his hostages unless the demands were met.[58] His group, however, was apprehended near the Iranian border by Iraqi military units. In the fighting that ensued, General Shihab was killed and General Ghaidan was wounded.

It became clear afterward that Kazar had no support from the army. Only two high party officials were involved: Muhammad Fadil, head of the party's military branch, and Abd al-Khaliq al-Samurai, a leading Baathist theoretician. It seems that Fadil had informed al-Samurai of the planned coup but had failed to inform other party leaders. Kazar, Fadil, and thirty-four others were tried, sentenced to death, and executed. Al-Samarai's execution was commuted to life imprisonment as a result of intercession by Aflaq and other party figures because of his past contributions to the party.

The Baath leadership was shaken by the coup attempt, seeing it as a reflection of the desire by some elements in the army for a bigger say in government affairs and for a firmer stand against the Kurds and the communists.[59] Since the communists and the KDP had suffered greatly at the hands of Kazar, both groups quickly expressed their solidarity with the government. Al-Bakr told Barzani that 2,000 missing Iraqis were thought to have been Kazar's victims.[60]

The coup attempt was believed to have swung the government position over to the camp of Husain, who wished to move quickly but cautiously to improve relations with the ICP and the KDP. Efforts were made to institutionalize participation in power for the communists and the KDP through the speedy formation of the National Front.

When the Baath party and the ICP announced an agreement to cooperate politically through the National and Nationalist Progressive Front, the KDP was left out in the cold. The two sides issued a statement signed by Baath Secretary General al-Bakr and ICP Secretary General Aziz Muhammad, which described the formation of the Front as a "great achievement" stemming from agreement between the two parties on the National Action Charter. It expressed the two parties' belief in the "necessity of having the KDP as a major and active partner in the Front" and promised to continue the dialogue with the KDP to that end.[61]

The ICP-Baath coalition promised to achieve self-rule for the Kurds, but Barzani remained suspicious and refused to join the Front. A statement published on August 19 in *Al-Taakhi* said the KDP's Central Committee promised to continue the dialogue with the ICP and the Baath but expressed resentment against the pressure applied on the Kurds to join the Front.[62] The KDP was apparently alarmed by the alliance and sought to prevent its formation, fearing it would limit the KDP's influence in the areas under its control.

Following its refusal to participate in the National Front, the KDP's relations with the government and the ICP now began to deteriorate rapidly.

# 7

# FOREIGN INTERFERENCE

The Kurdish situation entered into a new phase during 1972 as a result of internal as well as external factors. As we have seen, the internal factors focused on differing perceptions of the March Memorandum between the Baath party and the Barzani leadership and the overall policies adopted by the government. The external factors involved the decisions of the United States and Israel to aid Barzani in his struggle against the government, the commitment of Iran to expand its aid to him.

The underlying causes of Barzani's search for aid from the United States, Iran, and Israel — countries viewed as hostile powers by the Baath government — can be found in the evolution of events inside Iraq, which were seen as major achievements of the government and which contributed greatly to the consolidation of its power.

The March 11 Manifesto had offered autonomy to the Kurds and a permanent and peaceful solution to the costly Kurdish problem. This was the first time a Middle Eastern government had offered a solution to the problems of a minority by guaranteeing it autonomy. By this approach, the government had gained widespread backing among many Arabs and Kurds.

Internally, the Iraqi government was able to solidify its ranks following several unsuccessful coup attempts and after the ouster or demotion of such leading Baathist military figures as General Salih Mahdi Ammash, General Hardan al-Takriti, and others. These moves allowed the civilian wing of the Baath party to solidify its control of the state organs and the party apparatus.

The Baath party had proclaimed the National Action Charter and had presented it for discussion among other political parties (ICP and KDP) and other well-known political forces and figures. The charter and the debate that followed were intended to produce wider political participation in the country by allowing other political forces to share in the decision-making process.

The government had also appointed two communists and other non-Baathist nationalists to the cabinet.

The Iraqi-Soviet treaty of April 9, 1972, had helped consolidate ties with the socialist camp. There had also been improvement of ties with leftist, Arab, and international forces, due to the government's continued opposition to a peaceful settlement with Israel.

The nationalization of the Iraqi Petroleum Company on June 1, 1972, and the decision of April 7, 1972, to exploit Iraqi oil with Iraqi companies had also been important. These moves were in response to demands by radical Baath elements as well as other leftist forces. Through these decisions and their successful implementation, the government was able to get backing from most Iraqi forces (except the KDP), and to lay a firm foundation for its economic independence. The significant income from oil allowed the government to begin its development programs—prerequisites for stability.

As the government solidified its control within the Arab areas of Iraq and consolidated power in Baghdad, the possibility of creating the economic, social, and political framework for a stable regime increased. The rise in oil income became an additional factor in helping achieve stability, and with it came the chance to modernize the army. These developments were generally seen as major gains for the Iraqi government and were viewed with increasing alarm by Barzani, Iran, the United States, and Israel.


## BARZANI'S MOTIVES AND ACTIONS


During the first two years of efforts to implement the March Manifesto, it became obvious that Barzani was not anxious to see the successful implementation of the agreement and the return of normalcy and peace to the North. This stance was manifested in a number of steps taken by the Barzani leadership, which included:

• Refusal to close the borders with Iran, continued importation of arms to the Kurdish areas, and resistance to allowing the return of normalcy in the North;[1]

• Consolidation of control over the Kurdish area, accompanied by a tough campaign against Barzani's opponents;

- The establishment of a sophisticated intelligence apparatus, Parastin, through the aid of the Israeli Mosad and the Iranian Savak, in order to gather information on the Iraqi government and its armed forces and to intimidate opponents;[2]
- The constant escalation of demands against the government;
- The establishment of contacts with Israel, a country hostile to Iraq and to the Arabs;
- The public promises to turn Kirkuk oil fields over to American companies in return for United States aid;
- Appeals for aid from the United States even during the honeymoon period with the Iraqi government. The Otis Pike Congressional Committee report revealed that Barzani made an appeal for United States aid in August 1971 and again in March 1972.[3] It also revealed that the 1971 proposal of aid was not the first but the second made by the Kurds.[4]
- The Barzani leadership was quick to support its followers regardless of the justice of their case and the seriousness of the situation. This position was revealed in the incidents of Khaniqin and Sinjar. Such a stand may be attributed to the nature of Kurdish society and its leadership, which was greatly influenced by religious, clan, tribal, class, and family relations and the reliance of the leadership on these ties to consolidate authority.
- The prevention of government agencies and personnel from returning to the Kurdish area under Barzani's control. Permission to enter this area was required for government officials.[5]

In addition to these factors the Iraqi government was greatly concerned over the views of a number of KDP leaders concerning the return of normalcy and the reestablishment of central authority in the Kurdish areas. These KDP leaders felt:

- That the return of normalcy was a manifestation of the supremacy of national authority. Consequently, it was necessary for the KDP to take up a bargaining position by deliberately refusing to change its stand prior to the implementation of all the clauses of the March agreement;
- That the return of law and order to the north would weaken the KDP, its leadership, and the Kurdish movement, whose growth and survival depended on a continued state of tension and crisis in the area;
- That the return to normalcy would cause a relaxation within the ranks of the Kurdish movement and consequently a loss of the state of mobilization needed to confront any emergencies.[6]

The Baathist government was also greatly concerned about KDP statements raising questions about the Kurdish leadership's ultimate objectives. One of these statements was issued in the KDP's theoretical organ *Al-Kadir:*

> The central objective of our KDP and the liberation movement of our
> Kurdish people at the present phase is the realization and practice of self-
> rule. The March agreement specified certain measures and steps . . .
> leading to self-rule. But neither the substance nor the general guidelines
> of self-rule were spelled out in the agreement. . . . Self-rule is not a sub-
> stitute for the Kurdish people's right to self-determination. But the ob-
> jective realities of the development of the Kurdish liberation movement
> together with the circumstances and conditions surrounding it necessi-
> tate raising the self-rule slogan so as to enforce the common struggle
> against the two nationalities.[7]

This and similar statements were seen as a direct challenge to the
March agreement and meant that the Kurdish movement had not accepted voluntary union instead of separation as its ultimate objective.

In addition to these factors there was the feudal, religious and tribal
nature of the Kurdish leadership as personified in the conservative and
authoritarian personality of Mulla Mustafa al-Barzani. He understood
that the return of stability and real peace to the North would have meant
the end of his control and that of his tribal allies. With normalcy would
come the implementation of agrarian reform, which he had blocked at the
insistence of some of his tribal and feudal allies; economic development
projects under a socialist government; and the slow but inevitable crum-
bling of the base of his authority over the tribal-feudal structure. Normalcy would also lead to the emergence of leftist Kurdish forces because
Barzani had wrested control of the KDP from the hands of leftist leaders
only through the military superiority of his tribal allies.

Consequently, it was only natural that Barzani viewed the March
agreement as tactical rather than strategic. It was a temporary cease-fire
to secure his control in the Kurdish area, to arm and reinforce his soldiers, and to augment his financial and political resources.

The main question, however, is of Barzani's ultimate aim and whether
he was seeking the creation of an independent Kurdish state, as his Iraqi
and some Kurdish opponents charge; or the establishment of a federation
as his autonomy proposal indicated; or whether, as he claims, he was
seeking autonomy for the Kurds and democracy for Iraq. In response to a
question on whether he was seeking separation or autonomy, Barzani
claimed, "We were seeking self-rule, not separation. The initial aim of the
Kurdish nationalist movement was not separation. Separation was never
one of our slogans, which indicates that it was not our goal."[8]

But whether or not separation was Barzani's initial goal, it became
obvious, through his insistence that the Pesh Merga obey Kurdish orders
and not those of the central government, and through his promises of

turning over the Kirkuk oil fields to American or Western companies in return for military aid, that he was seeking more than autonomy.

Iraqi leaders were becoming fearful that Barzani was seeking secession from Iraq. Tariq Aziz said later: "The Kurdish leadership wanted the (March) manifesto to be a stage for something else they didn't even dare tell the Iranians—secession. Barzani cannot retain his leadership unless there is separation or disorder and anarchy in Iraq. To have self-rule succeed limits his authority and activity."[9]

Regardless of the real motives behind his moves, Barzani found that his opportunity for outside aid grew out of Iranian-Iraqi enmity.

## IRANIAN-IRAQI RELATIONS

Relations between Iraq and Iran had been characterized by suspicion and hostility since the return of the Baath to power in 1968. The quarrel between the two neighboring countries was deep and complex. It was one between a conservative non-Arab Iranian monarchy whose ruler was seeking both to preserve his throne and to play a dominant role in the region, particularly in the Arab/Persian Gulf, and an Arab nationalist and socialist regime aiming at maintaining itself in power, spreading its ideology to other Arab regions, and thwarting Iran's aims in the Gulf. The reasons behind the conflict were not limited to ideological factors but had historic and geographic causes as well. The roots of the historic conflict go back to the political struggle between the Ottoman and Persian empires manifested in clashes over borders until 1913, when Britain and Russia helped mediate a border agreement between the two states.[10]

But as soon as World War I ended and Iraq emerged as an independent country, Iran began to question the border agreement, claiming that it was made when Iran was weak and under pressure and had no choice but to accept. In 1934, after Iraq gained its political independence and after a number of Iranian border incursions, Iraq threatened to complain to the League of Nations. But Turkey mediated and the conflict was temporarily resolved.[11]

In addition to the border dispute it must be remembered that historic antagonism existed between Arabs and Persians before, during, and after the spread of Islam. Culturally, Iran was not submerged by Sunni Islam, and the Persians did not assimilate or unite with the Arabs. Historically, Iran preserved its distinct personality linking Shiism with ancient indigenous cultural and linguistic traditions. In twentieth-century nationalistic terms, the differences were accentuated.

In addition to the historical factors, the political developments in both countries affected relations between the two countries, especially after the 1958 revolution in Iraq. Before 1958, Iraqi-Iranian ties had improved, following the Saadabad Pact among Turkey, Iran, Iraq, and Afghanistan, which secured their borders and which was partly directed against the Kurds.[12] Ties between the two countries were further strengthened when they joined the pro-Western Baghdad Pact in 1956.

Following the revolution of 1958, however, there was fear in Iran that a similar coup might take place there or that Iraq might join the UAR. Such developments would have threatened the Iranian regime and put an end to its dream of border changes because the balance of power would shift to Iraq. It was natural, therefore, that tensions increased. But as soon as Iraq's ties with Nasir's UAR were broke, relations between Iran and Iraq began to improve, because an anti-Nasir Iraq no longer posed a serious threat to the Iranian regime. The situation, however, worsened again as talks began over the formation of a union among Syria, Egypt, and Iraq, and the three countries signed an agreement in April 1963. At that time, Iran raised the border question again and renewed support of the Kurdish movement.[13] Relations improved slightly under the Arif regime. The foreign ministers exchanged visits in April 1967 and June 1968. But despite friendly statements and visits there was little movement on the border question.

The situation reached a new low following the Baath's return to power. Iran viewed the new socialist and Arab nationalist regime — which advocated the "Arabization of the Gulf" and the rejection of any Western-sponsored security system — with hostility and suspicion. Baathist aspirations ran directly counter to Iran's goals in the Gulf. Following Britain's decision to withdraw from the area, Iran hoped to adjust its borders and to play the role of guardian of Gulf security.[14] Iran's demand for revision of the treaty covering the Shatt al-Arab — the extension of its boundaries to the median line and its unilateral abrogation of the 1937 treaty following Iraq's attempt to enforce its territorial rights — contributed greatly to the deterioration of relations between the two countries.[15] Iran also increased its aid to the Kurdish insurgents and reached an agreement with Barzani promising him military and economic help on the condition that he not allow Iraqi Kurdistan to be used as a base for the Iranian Kurdish movement.[16]

Iraq retaliated by expelling thousands of Iranians living in Iraq and giving asylum to such Iranian political opponents of the Shah as Ayatullah Khumaini, perhaps the most respected religious figure among the Shiis, with connections to underground groups in Iran. Other leftist factions opposed to the Shah also found support in Iraq. In addition, support was given to an Arab group calling for the liberation of Arabistan (Ahwaz) and to a secessionist group in Baluchistan.

Another factor that may have contributed to Iranian enmity was the fear that, if a settlement was reached, Iraq might use the Kurdish area to infiltrate men and material into Iran to support dissidents or to carry out subversive activities. Barzani told this writer that one of the reasons for the mutual mistrust between him and the government was that "immediately following the agreement I was asked to allow the Baathists to infiltrate into Iran and begin acts of subversion. I refused."[17]

This charge was denied by Tariq Aziz, but regardless of its truth or falsity, Barzani must have carried this information to the Iranians; inevitably this would further heighten Iranian suspicions of their neighbor.

The Iraqi government also welcomed former Iranian General Taimur Bakhtiar, who had been the former head of the internal security apparatus in Iran. Bakhtiar's connections may have worried the Shah. Bakhtiar was killed in a hunting accident in Iraq in August 1970, and some believe that he may have been executed on the orders of Savak.[18]

Attempts at mediation by Jordan's King Hussein and his prime minister in 1969 proved unsuccessful.[19] In the hope of counter-balancing Iran's influence in the Gulf and of strengthening its position in the Shatt al-Arab dispute, Iraq also sought to improve its relations with Saudi Arabia. It also advocated nonintervention in the domestic affairs in any Gulf state. But both of these efforts only served to escalate Iranian fears.

In addition, Iranian-Iraqi hostilities were influenced by Iraq's attempt to strengthen its ties to Arab radical forces in the Gulf; the Iranian military takeover of the Greater and Lesser Tumbs and the Abu Musa islands from the newly-formed United Arab Emirates; the Iranian intervention in Oman against the Dhofari rebels; the Iranian-supported coup attempts against Iraq; and Iranian cooperation with conservative Arab governments such as Kuwait, Saudi Arabia, and Jordan, which were fearful of a Baath regime.

Expecting hostilities from each other, Iran and Iraq sought out opportunities to act against each other. For Iran the Kurdish situation offered an opportunity to tie the hands of the Iraqi regime or even to overthrow it. The Shah's support to the Kurds tended to confirm Iraqi views of the existence of a hostile alliance against the Baath government among Iran, Israel, and the United States, whose aid was enlisted by the Shah in his Kurdish operation.

## THE ROLE OF THE UNITED STATES

It is difficult to say precisely when United States support for the Kurds began. Despite the part the United States and Britain played in the collapse of the Barzani-backed Kurdish Mahabad Republic in Iran, Mulla Mustafa began to ask the United States for aid early in the 1960s without any public response.[20]

In an article criticizing the U.S. role in the Kurdish defeat of 1975, the former U.S. consul in Kirkuk, Lee Dinsmore, who was in charge of contacts with the Kurds, hinted that CIA aid may have started long before 1972: "Still, the CIA probably counts the operation a success; it kept the Iraqis occupied for fifteen years. And nobody gives a damn about the Kurds."[21]

But the return of a Baath government advocating socialist and Arab nationalist principles and hostile to U.S. allies and clients such as Israel, Iran, and the oil-rich conservative Arab states must have been a matter of concern for the United States. The Kurdish insurgency would have served as an effective means of destabilizing the Iraqi regime. The first credible report of U.S. aid to the Kurds claimed it occurred in August 1969.[22] Barzani was reported to have welcomed two American officers working with CENTO — General Anthony Devery Hunter and an officer named Perkins, whose rank was unidentified. They were reported to have come by a special American plane, which landed near Barzani's headquarters. After long discussions the officers left. Within two days Perkins returned, accompanied by four other Americans, to sign a secret agreement by which Mulla Mustafa al-Barzani received $14 million.[23]

The secret agreement was reported to have included the following points:

• The subject of United States aid must be kept secret from all, including high-ranking members within the Kurdish movement;

• The main aim of the insurgency was to overthrow the Baath regime;

• The decision to continue or discontinue the movement following the overthrow of the government was to be made by the United States;

• The United States would back the Kurdish struggle for autonomy, but the Kurds must not go beyond the limits of autonomy outlined in the agreement;

• The Kurdish movement must not undertake any act contravening United States directives. If this occurred, the United States would be free to discontinue its aid through Iran;

• The Kurdish movement must not cause any harm to Iran in the future, particularly by supporting Iranian Kurds. In return, the Iranian government would not take any actions hostile to the Kurdish movement;

• Doors would be closed to communists seeking to join the movement; the Kurdish movement must not protect them;

• There must be no present or future links between the Kurdish movement and the Soviet Union. The movement should oppose communism and support a free and democratic system;

• All Soviet aid offers must be rejected and the United States immediately notified of such offers;

• United States aid would increase with the increasing effectiveness of the movement;

• The United States government would decide the amount of assistance it would grant. Such aid would be both financial and military;

• Financial aid must not be spent on consumer goods or it would be cut off. Bills for spending the aid must be sent annually to verify the way the assistance was spent;

• Political and military boards for the movement must be formed. The military board would include Iranians for coordination purposes;

• No flags, including that of the Kurdish movement, would be raised in the Kurdish areas;

• The aid would be paid back as long-term loans with 2 percent interest, but if there were no violations of the agreement, the aid would be considered a grant;

• The United States government considered Barzani the man responsible for the movement and would accept only his objections.[24]

The documented phase of the United States role begins in May 1972, when the Shah asked President Richard Nixon and Secretary of State Henry Kissinger to join Iran in aiding the Kurds. The details of this venture were revealed by the unauthorized publication of the Pike House Committee hearings in the *Village Voice*. Nixon and Kissinger agreed to study the proposal. They thought the matter over and agreed to cooperate, despite previous CIA and State Department opposition. The Pike Report reveals "highly unusual security precautions and the circumvention of the forty Committee by the President and Dr. Kissinger that details of the project would otherwise leak — a result which by all accounts would have mightily displeased our ally. It is also clear that the secrecy was motivated by a desire that the Department of State, which had constantly opposed such ventures in the region, be kept in the dark."[25]

The report also reveals that the United States, and Dr. Kissinger in particular, had turned down at least two Kurdish requests for aid in 1971 and 1972 because such aid would have had the effect of "prolonging the insurgency, thereby encouraging separatist aspirations and possibly providing the Soviet Union the opportunity to create difficulties for (two other U.S. allies),"[26] i.e., Turkey and Iran, which had large Kurdish minorities.

Furthermore, the report indicated that the Shah, Nixon, and Kissinger hoped that "our client (Barzani) would not prevail. They preferred instead to sap the resources of our ally's neighboring country (Iraq). This policy was not imparted to our clients, who were encouraged to continue fighting. Even in the context of overt action, ours was a cynical enterprise."[27]

The Shah was informed of the American agreement to his proposal not through the U.S. ambassador but through John Connally, who was sent to Iran to inform the Shah. The United States agreed to pay $16 million in arms and cash. The idea was to purchase from Israel the Soviet and Chinese weapons which had been captured from the Arab states during the June 1967 war.[28] These arms as well as arms purchased later from Cambodia[29] would give the Kurdish forces the ability to renew their campaign against Iraq—and they would lead the Iraqis to believe that the Soviets were the actual suppliers. There is no evidence to show that the Iraqis believed this. On the contrary, it served to strengthen their preconceived views of Iranian-United States designs against them.

Barzani welcomed the U.S. aid which had been denied him previously because he needed help and did not trust the Shah. On this issue Barzani declared: We wanted American guarantees. We never trusted the Shah. Without American promises we wouldn't have acted the way we did. We knew Iran could not do it all on its own. We accepted American aid in what we believed was the interest of the Kurdish people.[30]

This view was supported by the Pike Report, which indicates that the U.S. "acted in effect as guarantor that the insurgent group would not be summarily dropped by the foreign head of state (the Shah)."[31] The report states, however, that actual U.S. aid was "dwarfed" by Iranian aid.

There were a number of reasons why the U.S. decided to join the Shah in backing the Kurds and encouraging the embroiling of the Iraqi government at home.

The timing of U.S. aid was significant since it suggests that oil was one of the motives. After rejecting Kurdish requests for aid in August 1971 and March 1972, the U.S. agreed to cooperate two weeks after the IPC nationalization. In addition, Barzani promised that if he won he was "ready to become the fifty-first state."[32] He also promised, if successful, to turn over the oil fields to the U.S.,[33] and that the U.S. could look to a friend in OPEC once oil-rich Kurdistan achieved independence.[34]

But the Iranians and the Americans were more interested in seeing the fighting prolonged than in seeing Kurdish victory achieved because of the implications such victory would have for Turkey and Iran. Instead, Nixon and Kissinger may have had something else in mind. They saw Iraq as a Soviet client and wanted to achieve a significant cold war victory by toppling the Baath regime. American journalist Aron Latham advocates the view that the United States hoped the Kurdish rebellion "would be the functional equivalent of the truckers' strike in Chile. They intended that Saddam Husain go the way of Salvador Allende. Once Saddam Husain and his revolutionary council were toppled, Nixon and Kissinger hoped a more friendly regime would take over Iraq. And this new regime might let us back into the oil fields."[35]

The Iraqi regime was aware that it might face the same fate as the Chilean regime. In a speech on September 24, 1973, discussing the proposal for Kurdish autonomy, Saddam Husain said:

> There is yet one other point which is merely a comment on the experiment of Allende. We can confidently say that the 'anti-Allende' will be buried here in Iraq. Allende's experiment will not be repeated in this country—neither by work nor act . . . on this basis we realized that imperialism—having been surprised by the 1972 measures—reviewed its stand to launch a counter attack. Consequently we prepared for it additional forces which (it had) not taken into account in its plans and we can assure our nationalist brethren here in Iraq that the 'anti-Allende' will be buried in Iraq and will not emerge from amongst us as was the case in Chile.[36]

Another U.S. motive was to prevent Iraq from taking any action that could be considered hostile to the interests of the United States and its allies in the region. CIA memos and cables mentioned in the Pike Report characterize the Kurds as "a uniquely useful tool for weakening (our ally's enemy's) potential for international adventurism."[37] The Pike Report also offers another reason for U.S. action. It says that "the project was initiated as a favor to our ally who had cooperated with U.S. agencies, and who had come to feel menaced by his neighbor."[38]

Other reasons offered by a high U.S. official for U.S. involvement in the project included:

• To make it difficult for the Soviets to use Iraq to infiltrate the Gulf region.

• To prevent Iraq from aiding radical and Arab nationalist forces in the United Arab Emirates, Oman, Kuwait, Saudi Arabia, and the Yemens.

• To prevent Iraq from challenging Iran in their border dispute and from aiding anti-Shah dissidents and minorities seeking secession.

• To prevent the Iraqi regime from playing a major role in the Middle East conflict in opposing a peaceful settlement, and to limit its participation in any future Arab-Israeli war.[39]


## THE ISRAELI ROLE


Israeli support of the Kurds prior to 1972 is as difficult to document as U.S. aid. But reports of Israeli aid go as far back as 1965. Aziz Aqrawi, one of the top military leaders in the Kurdish movement since 1961, and who remained with Barzani until the end of 1973, said that Barzani's contacts with Israel and the West started as far back as 1965 but that they were known only to a few people in the movement.[40] An Israeli member of Parliament, Luba Eliav, has recently documented the early phase of Israel's contacts with Barzani. In an interview with the Israeli newspaper *Yediot Aharonot,* Eliav said that Barzani, who was seeking to establish an independent Kurdish state, sought international aid for his cause, and that Israel responded to his appeals in late 1966.[41] Eliav said that Prime Minister Levi Eshkol asked him because of his government position and close personal relations to undertake a journey to Kurdistan with a "medical team" which included three doctors and three male nurses. The team crossed the Iranian border to Iraq at Haj Umran. Eliav met with Barzani and offered him a golden medallion commemorating the seventh opening of the Knesset. Eliav's discussion with Barzani in Russian, a language known to both, focused on the condition of the "Kurdish state and people, and on the best means to give technical and economic Israeli aid to Barzani."

Israeli Prime Minister Begin has recently admitted that Israel provided Kurdish guerrillas with "money, arms, and instructors" and that some military advisers were assigned to Barzani's headquarters.[42] Barzani reciprocated by mounting a large-scale offensive during the 1967 war, preventing Iraqi troops from bolstering Syria and Jordan. Begin also confirmed information given by Aziz Aqrawi that Barzani visited Israel several times, toured collective farms and met newspaper editors and political figures, including Begin, who were sworn to silence. Other Kurdish leaders, including supporters of Talibani and others who backed the government, say that Barzani's intelligence apparatus was set up by the Mosad.[43]

Reports published in *Al-Ahad* magazine in 1969 revealed that Iran

and Israel were cooperating in support of Barzani. Israeli Colonel Morde-
chai Hud was reported to have been appointed an adviser to the Iranian
General Staff responsible for coordinating activities with Barzani.[44] Hud
later became the chief of staff of the Israeli army. Another Israeli officer,
Major Eliahu Kohen, was reported to have been attached to Barzani's
headquarters as liaison officer.[45]

Charges of Israeli aid to the Kurds surfaced again in September 1972.
This time, however, they came from the well-known American syndicated
columnist, Jack Anderson. In his column of September 17, 1972, Anderson wrote: "Every month, a secret Israeli envoy slips into the mountains
(of Northern Iraq) from the Iranian side to deliver $50,000 to Kurdish
leader Mulla Mustafa al-Barzani. The subsidy ensures Kurdish hostility
against Iraq, whose government is militantly anti-Israel."[46]

Anderson based his information on a Central Intelligence Agency report which said: "An Israeli intelligence officer . . . went to Barzani's
headquarters at Hajji Umran to deliver to Barzani the Israeli government's
monthly subsidy. . . . (The agent) regularly delivers to Barzani Israel's
$50,000 monthly subsidy. . . . Upon his return to Tehran, (the agent) re-
ported that Barzani was continuing to gather men and equipment together in anticipation of a probable encounter with the Iraqi army."

Anderson's report went on to add that General Zevi Zamir, Israel's
intelligence chief, had, at least on one occasion, called on Barzani in his
mountain stronghold. One of the reasons for Zamir's visit, according to
the CIA, was "to discuss the possibility of having Barzani assist Iraqi Jews
to emigrate from Iraq. General Zamir also was seeking assurance from
Barzani of continued Kurdish hostility to Iraq."

Concerning the Anderson article, Barzani said that he "could never
have compromised Arab-Kurdish brotherhood for $50,000 from Israel.
Our future lies with the Arabs, what affects them affects us, even if indi-
rectly. Our future lies with the Arab, Turkish, and Iranian people. What
happens to them happens to us."[47]

Zayd Haydar, member of the Baath National Command and head of
its foreign relations section, told this writer that Iraqi intelligence had received reports about the arrival of Israeli officers to the Kurdish areas,
and that Barzani had received Soviet weapons from Israel as well as Israeli weapons.[48] He further stated that he was informed by KDP Politburo member Hashim Aqrawi, who also broke with Barzani in 1973, that
Barzani had personally made two visits to Israel, including one in 1973.[49]

Israel appears to have been motivated by its desire to keep Iraq em-
broiled in an internal conflict in order to minimize Iraq's military potential and to help get Iraqi Jews to Israel.[50] Lee Dinsmore, former U.S.

Consul in Kirkuk, writes that "Israel has trained Kurdish insurgents on Iranian territory."[51]

Israel's role in the project is neglected in the Pike Report, however, except for the following brief paragraph:

> It is particularly ironic that, despite President Nixon's and Dr. Kissinger's encouragement of hostilities to keep the target country (Iraq) off-balance, the U.S. personally restrained the insurgents from an all-out offensive on one occasion when such an attack might have been successful because other events were occupying the neighboring country (Iran).[52]

The report refers to the Arab-Israeli war of 1973 which saw Iraqi forces, following an improvement in relations with Iran, sent to the Syrian front. Israel apparently suggested that Barzani launch his own war against Iraq at the time. Barzani apparently sought U.S. advice. The Pike Report reveals that Secretary of State Kissinger asked that the following note be sent to the Kurdish leadership: "We do not, repeat do not, consider it advisable for you to undertake the offensive military action that (another government) has suggested to you. For your information, we have consulted with (our ally) through the ambassador and they have both made the same recommendation."[53]

Pro-Israeli writers in the U.S. have charged that Kissinger's decision was a disservice to both Israel and Barzani because Israel lost a chance for Barzani's help during the war and because Barzani lost his chance for dramatic military success.[54] Barzani, however, denied that he wanted to wage war at that time: "This is totally false. If this was our goal we would have waged the war in 1967 and 1973. In 1973, we totally froze our military operations. We don't accept orders from Kissinger."[55]

Kissinger's decision to urge Barzani not to use his forces against Iraq in the 1973 war is reported to have been motivated by Kissinger's "fear of a stunning Israeli victory" following the Israeli breakthrough in Suez which would have made them intractable in the negotiations.[56] It is more likely, however, that Kissinger's decision followed his realization that Israel had won and there was no need for Barzani to launch his war.

While this action by Kissinger is portrayed as putting Israel's interest at a secondary level compared to that of the U.S. and Iran in the relations with the Kurds, it has become evident since that time that Israel's interests have been a major factor behind U.S. support for the Kurds.

A cable sent by the CIA chief of station in Iran to Washington declared "only a few Kurdish leaders knew that until recently they had our secret support for their military resistance because it diverted Iraq from Israel."[57]

Another factor in Kissinger's calculation was Iran's opposition to such a move at a time when the Shah was trying to improve his relations with the Arab world and to get support for his decision to raise oil prices. To have the Iranian-backed Kurds wage a war against Iraq at a time when the Arabs were fighting a war against Israel would have caused embarrassment if not actual trouble for the Shah among his devout Muslim subjects. It was with these factors in mind that the Shah decided to accept, during the first days of the October war, Iraqi proposals offering to restore diplomatic relations and to reach a peaceful solution of the border disputes.[58] Iran accepted and halted its propaganda warfare against Iraq and opposed Israeli urgings to Barzani to launch his war against Iraq.

In addition to the support from Iran, Israel, and the U.S., it has been reported that some Arab countries may have given aid to Barzani. In this author's interview with Tariq Aziz, he said that he has received reports that one Arab country knowingly allowed representatives of Barzani to receive material through their country, that another country contributed some financial aid to Barzani, while a third Arab country has aided and continues to aid Kurdish opponents of the Baath government.[59] Barzani, however, denied receiving aid from the Arab countries, although some Arab governments "wanted us to continue."[60] He also claimed that he sent notes and memoranda to the Arab states asking them "to use their influence on the regime which was against both Kurds and Arabs." But there was no response to these urgings, or to a call to the Arab Summit Conference at Rabat in 1974 to send a delegation to Iraq.[61] In a second interview, Barzani gave a new reason for his aid request to the West: "We have complaints against the Arab states. They didn't say to the Iraqis 'give them equality.' This is why we were forced to turn to the West."[62]

## IMPACT OF EXTERNAL AID TO BARZANI

The Barzani alliance with Iran, Israel, and the United States dramatically influenced Kurdish-Iraqi ties and had the following consequences:

 • Barzani was strengthened militarily and financially and encouraged to escalate his demands against the government, ultimately refusing autonomy and waging war in 1974.

 • Iraqi fears were greatly heightened, leading them to increase their dependence on Soviet military aid and to prepare for a new confrontation with Barzani.

• Contradictions emerged within the Kurdish movement, for although under Barzani's traditional leadership, it still contained many urban and leftist elements opposed to the tribal, religious, and conservative elements. It ultimately led to the defection of leading KDP elements at the end of 1973 and prior to the resumption of fighting. These included Barzani's own son Ubaidullah; Hashim Aqrawi, a member of the KDP's Central Committee and governor of Duhok province; Ismail Mulla Aziz, a leading KDP Central Committee member; and former Iraqi Army Colonel Aziz Aqrawi (no relation to Hashim) a member of the KDP's Politburo and a leading military commander of the Kurdish forces that had defected to the Kurdish movement in 1961. These actions led to a split within the KDP and to the formation of a separate KDP and of the Kurdistan Revolutionary Party.[63]

• The isolation of the KDP from leftist Iraqi and international forces which had previously viewed the Kurdish movement as a national liberation movement.

• Growing Soviet backing for the National Front formed in Iraq which was described by Soviet premier Alexei Kosygin as a "basic guarantee for the perpetuation of the regime and its consolidation."[64] Pravda saw the implementation of self-rule in 1974 as "an event that has great historical significance for the country" and criticized "the activity of rightist agents which have penetrated the KDP as a result of its class heterogeneity and which is trying to arouse separatist sentiments.[65] Soviet support of the Baath government was translated into important military aid to the government.

# 8

# AUTONOMY AND THE RESUMPTION
# OF FIGHTING

Despite Barzani's growing foreign entanglements and his establishment of a de facto state in the Kurdish areas under his control, the government repeatedly called on the Kurdish leadership to participate in the National Front and in the formulation of the Kurdish autonomy plan.[1]

Throughout 1973, the government sought to avoid the resumption of fighting. The KDP-Preparatory Committee, a Kurdish group led by Mahmud Uthman who broke with Barzani in 1975 but continued to oppose the government, revealed in a study seeking to assess the causes behind the demise of the Kurdish movement that in mid-1973 Saddam Husain called on Barzani to send his son Massud to Baghdad for further negotiation to clear up their differences.[2] When these calls were ignored, Husain sent a message to Barzani, through a member of the KDP Politburo, asking him not to adopt stands which would eventually force the Iraqi government to make border concessions to Iran in the Shatt al-Arab and other areas in order to bring an end to the Kurdish problem.[3] In addition to ignoring the warnings, Barzani kept this message a secret by failing to inform other KDP leaders of its contents. The Preparatory Committee's report describes this incident as a "turning point" in the relations between the government and the Kurdish movement since it led to a complete breakdown of confidence between the two sides.[4] The report further accused the Barzani leadership of arrogance and of not making any serious attempts at negotiations when the government was desperately seeking to avoid the conflict.

It is significant that the Baath government had previously been approached by the Iranian government after the initiation of the United States–Iranian project to aid Barzani and that Iran had promised that it would abandon the Kurds if Iraq agreed to abandon its claims to Shatt al-Arab. The Pike Report cites the following CIA memo sent on October 17, 1972: "(Our ally) has apparently told (another government's) foreign minister that he would be willing to allow peace to prevail (in the area) if (his enemy) would publicly agree to abrogate (a previous treaty concerning their country's border)."[5] The government's reluctance to resume the fighting was attributed to the following causes: The fear of the ruling civilian wing of the party that war would lead to the ascendancy of the army or of the party's military wing; The fear of a defeat and ultimately the overthrow of the regime—particularly since the Soviet Union was discouraging the government from seeking a military solution to the problem; and Concern that the Arab nationalist Baath, with its pretensions of leading the Arab nation, might have to make embarrassing territorial concessions to Iran.[6]

Instead of heeding calls to join the Front and help formulate the self-rule plan on the basis of a Baathist draft, the KDP leadership proposed its own self-rule proposal to the government in the early fall of 1973. The KDP's proposal included recommendations which were seen by the government as leading to the creation in Iraq of a federation, or a confederation, instead of an autonomous region.[7] The KDP proposals (and the government objections) were as follows:

• The "Kurdistan Region enjoys self-rule." (The government draft proposal had used the word "area" instead of "region.")[8]

• That the Region of Kurdistan must be composed of the governorates and administrative units where the Kurds formed the majority on the basis of the 1957 census. (This meant that the KDP wanted villages or forums in mixed areas—such as Kirkuk, Diala and Nineveh, where the Kurds did not form a majority—to join the autonomous area.)[9]

• That the Iraqi Republic is formed through "a voluntary union" between Kurds and Arabs. It also called for a change of the flags and insignia to reflect the national makeup. (The government's proposal, however, stated that the Kurdish area was an "indivisible part of Iraq.")[10]

• The KDP demanded a capital for the Kurdish region, preferably Kirkuk. (The government plan proposed an "administrative center" for the area in Arbil.)[11]

• The KDP proposal envisioned two constituent organizations for the Kurdish region: a legislative assembly and an executive council. (It was, as a whole, similar to the government law as amended, but there were two differences: "The promulgation of the text of laws creating taxes and duties to be imposed upon the province, in conformity with the constitution and central laws, would be included among the legislative assembly's prerogatives; The ratification of the province's annual and special budget would likewise be among the legislative assembly's powers."[12] These two points gave financial control to the legislative assembly.

The KDP text concerning the executive council did not differ greatly from the government proposal. It, however, suggested the following amendments: "Among the council's subsidiary organs, the cabinet would be replaced by a directorship, the investigations bureau by an inspections bureau, and the bureau of planning and census by the provincial planning council. Two new subsidiary organs are proposed: a bureau of industry and a bureau of planning. The role of the first would be to stimulate and oversee the development of the province's industry. An exception was made with respect to the extraction of petroleum, which would remain within the central government's control."

With regard to the executive council's prerogatives, it suggested the government proposal would be modified as follows: "The Executive Council would have the power to name those functionaries of the autonomous government's directorship, the nomination of which is not made by Presidential decree, or subject to approval by the President of the Republic according to the laws of the public sector. Such functionaries would be subject to the laws in effect for functionaries of the Iraqi Republic on condition that functionaries of localities with a Kurdish minority be Kurds. This condition shall apply to functionaries up to the rank of directors of the province's central organisms; Article three of this law shall be observed on condition that a regional civil service replace the Iraqi civil service."

The KDP text includes two additional paragraphs that supplement the foregoing: "The nomination of those functionaries, the nomination of which must be by Presidential decree, would be included among the council's prerogatives"; and "The naming of Iraqi and foreign experts according to the laws in effect at the time, and within the framework of the State's general policy."[13] The latter point was considered a very dangerous proposal by the government, which feared that in light of the close ties between Barzani and Iran, Israel, and the United States, Barzani might invite experts from these countries to work in Iraq.

• Concerning the budget and the treasury of the region, the National Development Plan be calculated in proportion to the number of inhabitants of the region. To the resources envisaged by the governmental law, the counter proposal text adds: ". . . a part of the aid and loans accorded Iraq for its development."[14] always in proportion to the percentage of Kurds in relation to the country's entire population. Additionally, a special sum must be set aside from the State's general budget for the purpose of "eliminating underdevelopment in Kurdistan."

These demands, together with the supplementary propositions formerly drawn up, support the belief that the Barzanian directorship was not striving for autonomy at all, but rather for a federal republic completely subject to its power.

• Other differences appear between the opposing parties' proposals regarding security and police measures to be implemented within the region. The government proposal ties the police and security apparatus to the minister of the interior's central administration. Authors of the counter-proposal would tie said apparatus to the autonomous government. In the latter case, the units involved would depend on the central government for technical and moral support only, as well as for nomination to, and promotion of, its ranks.[15]

• The KDP proposal conferred control over the legality of the decisions arrived at by the organs of the autonomous government to a high court made up of a president and six members chosen from prominent men of law. The choice of these members would result from an agreement between the President of Iraq's legislative assembly and the President of the Kurdish legislative assembly.

The KDP proposal also charged the High Court with a supplementary role—that of being the tribunal of supreme recourse in the event of unilateral modification of the autonomy law. This proposal was phrased in the following terms: "The autonomy may be modified by proposal of the legislative assembly of the province, and with the consent of the central legislative body. In the event of amendments to said law being enacted by the central legislature without the legislative assembly's consent, the High Court's decision shall be determinative of the propriety of such amendment."[16]

The government proposal confers the oversight role upon the Iraqi Court of Cassation assembled in special session and made up of a president and four members of the court chosen for a term of three years, renewable only once. The minister of justice or the minister of state have the power to contest decisions taken by organs of the autonomous government which they feel to be in violation of the Constitution or laws and regulations in effect at the time, before this tribunal. Such process must be instituted by the aforementioned ministers within thirty days following the date upon which notification of the allegedly unconstitutional or nonconforming decision was provided them.

The KDP proposals demonstrated that the central authorities must be placed on an equal footing as the autonomous authorities in regard to the choice of the High Court mentioned above.

• The KDP proposal suggested that the chairman of the autonomous region's Executive Council be accorded the rank of vice-premier or vice-president and its members the rank of ministers. The government proposal, however, stated that the chairman and the member be accorded the rank of ministers.[17]

• The Barzani leadership proposal suggested that the judiciary must be independent and the only authority above it is the constitution. The government proposal added to the above that the judiciary in Kurdistan is an "indivisible part of the judicial organization of the Republic of Iraq."[18]

• The KDP proposal called for the establishment of a mixed administration to administer disputed areas in Kirkuk, Nineveh, and Diala governorates.[19] The government opposed this provision, but later made some concessions on these issues as we shall see later on.

Saddam Husain rejected the KDP's plan because "that proposal, as we see it, is far removed from the concept of autonomy."[20] Another high Baath official was more explicit in explaining the reasons for the rejection when he declared: "The Kurds don't want self-rule, but a state above the state. We remained silent over the existence of a state within the state in the hope that it would disappear with the disappearance of the circumstances which led to its creation. But to have a local state above the central state is neither reasonable nor acceptable. . . . The Kurdish proposal . . . states in several articles that if the laws of the central government conflicted with those promulgated by the Kurdish government, the state laws would be considered inapplicable and the local law would go into effect."[21]

For its part, the government decided to go ahead with formulating its own plan within the framework of the National Front. The government's draft proposal of the autonomy law was formulated by the Baath and later submitted for discussion during a series of symposiums in September 1973 to various government officials and representatives of state-sponsored public organizations.[22]

The draft was then submitted to representatives of ethnic minorities, and a special symposium was dedicated to 600 independent and anti-Barzani Kurdish leaders for discussion.[23] In addition, the dialogue was going on with Barzani and the KDP.[24]

During the conference with the KDP representatives, Saddam Husain indicated that suggestions made by other non-Baathist representatives were taken into account and that changes were made in the Baath's proposal.[25]

The official response to the KDP proposal, however, came at the end of the Eighth Regional Congress of the Baath party held in Baghdad January 8–12, 1974. The congress, which reelected al-Bakr and Husain as chairman and vice chairman of the Baath's regional command and the RCC, issued a three-point program for action: economic development, using increased oil revenues; Kurdish autonomy; and closing national ranks on a more democratic basis within the framework of the national progressive front.[26]

Each of these points had important implications for the Kurdish question since the major issue of contention was the control of Kirkuk and its oil fields. Oil production had been increased both in the national-ized IPC field in Kirkuk and Mosul and in the nationalized southern fields. During the 1973 October war, Iraq nationalized 52 percent of the southern fields owned by the American, British, Dutch, and Gulbenkian companies but did not nationalize the shares of the French company as a reward to France's Middle East policy.

Revenues from oil were expected to reach close to $8 billion, or ten times the revenue prior to nationalization in 1972. Consequently, the gov-ernment, with its plans for major development, opposed the decentraliza-tion of petroleum resources. It was backed in its stand by the Iraqi Com-munist party. Both parties were willing to allow the government of the Kurdish autonomous region to have its own budget and plan its own eco-nomic development but were opposed to turning over a share of the oil solely on a proportional basis. The government wanted the KDP to join the National Progressive Front and to participate in government decision-making as well as the planning of regional development. But it wanted the central authorities to control natural resources and revenues since it con-sidered them national resources and not regional ones as did the Barzani leadership. Ultimately, the Baath saw the Kurdish proposal for the pro-portional sharing of oil revenues as tantamount to the establishment of a confederation in Iraq and rejected it.[27]

The second major point of national action called for by the congress focused on the question of Kurdish autonomy:

> Notwithstanding certain . . . isolationist reactionary tendencies . . . which, in part, are . . . (linked) with the imperialist and reactionary circles — the Kurdish movement in Iraq is fundamentally and essentially a national movement. Within the limits of demanding the legitimate na-tional rights of the Kurdish people (with self-rule in the forefront) within the framework of the Iraqi Republic, it has a concrete and ideological *raison d'etre*. And in this context it is a main part of the national move-ment of Iraq.[28]

Baath party representatives met on January 16, 1974, with representa-tives of the ICP, the KDP, and several nationalist and left-leaning Iraqi personalities, both Kurds and Arabs, to finalize agreement on the Baath self-rule plan. The Kurdish representatives included Habib Muhammad Karim, the KDP's secretary general, and Mahmud Abd al-Rahman. The National Front's representatives included Saddam Husain and Ghanim Abd al-Jalil on behalf of the Baath party and Mukarram Talibani on behalf of the ICP.[29] In addition, the meeting also included independent nationalists, such as Hisham al-Shawi and Abd al-Latif al-Shawwaf and independent Kurdish political figures such as Ihsan Shiraz and Fuad Arif.

Both sides restated their previous views. A major disagreement arose when KDP leader Karim hinted that if an agreement, in accordance with KDP demands, was not reached, the KDP was ready to take its case to the UN. The Baathists responded that they were "discussing a proposal for autonomy, not a proposal for the creation of a new state in Iraq.

A discussion on the demarcation of the administrative borders took place. The National Front plan offered the demarcation of the border on the basis of the "national presence and population density of the region" and the 1957 census. The KDP delegates, however, insisted that Kirkuk must fall within the region. The National Front delegates then proposed that Kirkuk be managed by a mixed administration affiliated with the central government. When this proposal was also rejected by the KDP representatives, the Baathists suggested that Chimchimal and Clar districts of Kirkuk province — which had clear Kurdish majorities — be affiliated to the self-rule area, with the remaining parts affiliated to the central administration. The KDP rejected this and suggested a mixed administration affiliated with the self-rule region. This proposal was rejected by the government. Since no agreement was reached, Baath representatives offered to submit the KDP plan and the National Front plan to the people to express their views through a referendum, but this plan was rejected by the KDP at a later session. Nevertheless, both sides agreed to hold another meeting on March 2, 1974. KDP representatives failed to show up on the appointed date, and the National Front delegates decided that the autonomy plan should be promulgated on March 11, 1974, even if the dialogue failed to produce any agreement with the KDP. But new mediation efforts were made and Idris al-Barzani came to Baghdad to meet with Saddam Husain on March 8, 1974.

Al-Barzani expressed the KDP's desire to reach agreement with the Front and said the Kurds had no intention to fight and were willing to reach a peaceful solution. He also emphasized that the restoration of confidence was fundamental for reaching an agreement. Husain replied that the restoration of confidence would be met by the KDP's abiding by its commitment to put autonomy into effect on the agreed date of March 11.

He summarized the government's position as follows: "From today, the ninth of March, 1974, and until noon March 11, 1974, discussion of any serious formula will be accepted. It is our concern that you should be among the national forces that have approved the draft law on autonomy, so that the law may be issued in the name of all national parties. After noon on March 11, 1974, we will be unable to discuss any proposal you may submit. . . . Nevertheless, the door will remain open to you for a period of fifteen days, following the promulgation of the law of autonomy for the Kurdistan area, to allow you to join the National Front and abide by the law of autonomy. Until that time we will consider you as allies, provided that there are no extraordinary acts that violate security and the law. If such acts occur, we will withdraw our undertaking. At the same time, we will not seek an alternative to you in this connection, before the expiration of the stipulated fifteen-day period. After that, we will not be your allies."

One day later, two Kurdish leaders, Ihsan Shiraz and Dara Tawfiq, met with National Front leader Ghanim Abd al-Jalil offering to sign the self-rule proposal "if our point of view with respect to Kirkuk is accepted." On March 10, Saddam Husain sent them the following telegram for Barzani: "Until now your proposals have not included any changes essentially different from your view point as explained at several previous meetings, and the Front's opinion regarding this viewpoint has already been clarified. We hope that new positive proposals will reach us before noon tomorrow."

The KDP's response came in a telegram sent to Ghanim Abd al-Jalil by Idris al-Barzani: "We believe that what we have proposed is correct. Hence, we have no new proposals. We will be committed to the preservation of the law."

## THE SPLIT IN KURDISH RANKS

In the meantime, the government's stand was boosted by the breakaway of several prominent Kurdish leaders. These included KDP Central Committee members Mulla Aziz and Hashim Aqrawi, and Politburo member and military commander Aziz Aqrawi, who had sent a letter to Barzani on January 29, 1974, accusing him of harming Iraq and the Kurdish people and serving imperialism. The letter stated: That Barzani had rejected democratic and legitimate party practices within the KDP itself; That the policies followed by Barzani did not reflect the spirit of the KDP and its "liberationist revolution" and allowed the infiltration of elements hostile to the interests of the Kurdish people; That Barzani had ordered the execution and kidnapping of a number of Kurdish leaders; That Barzani was linking the destiny of the Kurds to himself by showing hostility to the KDP and to any form of collective leadership; and That Barzani was attempting to isolate the Kurdish cause from the Iraqi national movement and linking it to foreign elements well known for their violent hostility to the national rights of the Kurdish people and to the Iraqi people.[30]

Another Kurdish faction under the leadership of Tahir Sattar Abd al-Sharif re-established the Kurdish Revolutionary party.[31] These Kurdish leaders favored cooperation with the National Front and accepted the autonomy law. Aziz Aqrawi explained his reasons for breaking with Barzani: "I joined the movement in 1961 because it was in the interest of the Kurds, not of the Mulla or any other person. We did our duty militarily and politically for the Kurdish people, but for the reasons I mentioned earlier, I came to realize that it would be treasonable to follow the Mulla's reactionary leadership. He has a tribal mentality and the Kurds supported him in the past because [previous] governments oppressed them. We realized it would be treason to wreck the March 11 declaration and to become tools in the hands of Israel, Iran, and imperialism."[32] When asked to comment on Mulla Mustafa's charges that the self-rule plan offered by the government was insufficient, he replied: "Of course there are things which are lacking, but these could be solved by trust on both sides and by working together to do what is needed. Barzani's claims are far from reality. He does not seem to realize that he is being supported by forces that work against Iraq and do not want to see the Kurds enjoying their national right. . . . Every backward people wants a revolution to bring about a change in their status and not a revolution for the sake of destruction."[33]

Mulla Mustafa's eldest son Ubaidullah also broke with his father for reasons similar to Aqrawi's. He charged that the Mulla "does not want self-rule to be implemented even if he was given Kirkuk and all of its oil. His acceptance of the law (autonomy) will take everything from him, and he wants to remain the absolute ruler."[34]

He further expressed his anger over his father's alliance with Iran because it "does not sincerely seek to support the Kurds. On the contrary, it oppresses them. There are no Kurdish schools in Iran that teach the Kurdish language. There are no hospitals and no agrarian reform laws in the Kurdish areas. The Mulla is riding the wave of conflict so he can remain on top."[35] Aziz Aqrawi set out further to reorganize his supporters in the KDP into a new Kurdistan Democratic Party.

The stands adopted by these leaders, in addition to the ones adopted by a number of the powerful tribal elements traditionally opposed to Barzani, served to bolster the government's position.

In the meantime, Barzani set his own deadline — March 25 — for the Iraqi government to decide to share the oil revenues of Kirkuk on a proportional basis between the Arabs and the Kurds. He threatened that if this did not happen, he would order sabotaging the country's oil installations.[36] Both sides continued to prepare for a military confrontation. There were reports of clashes between ICP members and the KDP over the communists' attempts to promote the National Front and its self-rule proposal among the Kurds. The ICP charged that Barzani's forces were waging a campaign to destroy it, and that its members and supporters were being kidnapped and tortured.[37]

## THE AUTONOMY DECLARATION

On March 11, 1974, President Al-Bakr announced the law enacted by the Revolutionary Command Council for the implementation of self-rule in the Kurdish region along with the pertinent constitutional amendments. He declared that the law was being implemented in confirmation of historical Arab-Kurdish ties and in compliance with the March 11 Manifesto and the National Action Charter.[38]

The autonomy law issued by al-Bakr included a number of noteworthy features:

• The law stated that the Kurdistan area shall enjoy autonomy (Article One). This autonomy is limited by the legal, political, and economic unity of the Republic of Iraq.

• The law provided in Article Two that Kurdish be the official language beside Arabic in the region, and that it be the language of education, should but the teaching of Arabic would be compulsory at all stages. Furthermore, Arabic was to be the official language of correspondence between the government of the Kurdish region and the central authorities.

• Article Three guaranteed the rights of non-Kurdish minorities within the region in accordance with the constitution.

• Article Four guaranteed that the judiciary conform with the legal system of Iraq.

• Articles Five through Nine dealt with the financial independence of the region within the "financial integrity of the state." It provided for a separate budget and said that the sources of this budget would consist of its local revenues in addition to allocations from the state budget and the annual investment program.

• Part Two of the law (Articles Ten through Fifteen) provided for the establishment of a Legislative Assembly and an Executive Council to be the governing organs of the autonomous region. The Legislative Assembly was to consist of eighty members directly elected by the people, except for the first assembly, which was to be appointed by the president because of the conditions prevailing in the Kurdish area at the time. This assembly had the authority to adopt legislation concerning the development of the area, the promotion of local culture and economic development, and the adoption of legislative resolutions concerning the semi-official departments and the local administration.

It also had the authority to submit budget proposals on the special budget in conformance with the development plans and laws of the state.

The Executive Council was to consist of a chairman and vice chairman and between ten and twelve members. The chairman and members had the rank of a minister. The governorates of the area were attached to the Council. The following bureaus were also linked to the Council: education, public works and housing, agriculture and agrarian reform, internal affairs (police, civil defense, civil affairs), transportation and communications, culture and youth, municipalities and resorts, social affairs, economic and financial affairs, and religious trusts (awqaf). The Council's functions included: securing the implementation of laws and regulations, abiding by judicial rules and the establishment of justice, maintenance of security and public order, the spending of the region's budget in accordance with the laws of the state, and drawing up detailed plans for economic and social development.

• Part Three of the Law (Articles Sixteen through Twenty-one) covered the relationship between the central government and the autonomous authorities. The autonomous bodies were seen as an integral part of the state in the sense that the central authority extended to all parts of the state, including the autonomous region. These bodies function within the limits of the laws established by the central government. Autonomy was seen as a joint participation in the exercise of authority. Therefore, the relationship between the government and the autonomous bodies was defined as one of supervision and of coordination. Article Nineteen provided that the Supreme Court of Iraq supervise the legality of the resolutions of the autonomous authorities. The ministers of justice or state could object to the resolutions of the autonomous bodies before the court. The president of the republic had the authority to abolish the Legislative Assembly if the latter did not abide by the constitution.

The coordination between the central authority and the autonomous bodies was to be brought about through the appointment of a minister of state or any of the ministers entrusted with this task to coordinate activities between the two authorities. Coordination also included consultation between the government and the central authorities.

• Article Seventeen stipulated that police, security, and nationality agencies be attached through their directorates to the ministry of interior and be subject to the laws and regulations of the central government. The president of Iraq had the authority to dissolve the Assembly and to appoint the Legislative Council chairman. The Council chairman had the right to attend the Iraqi cabinet sessions.[39]

The autonomy law promulgated by the Iraqi government, after consultation through the National Front, acknowledged the existence of the Kurds as a distinct national group in a region of their own where they form the majority of the population. It also granted them certain rights and opportunities in running their own local affairs. It, however, imposed limits on the autonomous government and retained final authority in the hands of the central government.


## REACTIONS TO THE AUTONOMY LAW


On March 12 and 13, there were reports of Kurdish attacks against government garrisons in the North.[40] The clandestine "Voice of Kurdistan" radio rejected the autonomy law, accused the government of intriguing to divide the Kurds, and called on the Kurds to "wrest your land by force of arms."[41]

Senior Turkish officials reported that the Kurds killed an Iraqi army officer and wounded three others and that the Kurdish forces were seizing border posts along the 207-mile stretch of the Turkish-Iraqi border and were beginning to push south.[42]

The Iraqi government was reported to have pushed its crack Eighth Division of commandos and paratroopers to Kirkuk, Mosul, and Sulaymaniyya.[43]

On March 18, however, the negotiations to reach a peaceful settlement were continuing despite the tension, and Al-Nahar stated that reports on the fighting had been exaggerated.[44]

On March 23, a KDP delegation was in Baghdad to participate in the negotiations with the government as the Soviet Union attempted to play a mediating role and prevent the resumption of a full-scale war by sending

Defense Minister Andrei Grechko to Baghdad on March 23. Grechko sought to meet with Barzani, but Barzani refused to see him.[45] The Soviets had long supported the KDP but their close ties with the Baath following the establishment of the National Front led them to support the autonomy proposal, which was hailed by *Pravda*.[46]

On March 27, President al-Bakr told a news conference that the Kurdish leaders continued, following the 15-day government deadline, to reject the autonomy law. He said that the main dispute centered on KDP demands for Kirkuk, which were rejected by his government.[47] Behind Barzani's rejection of the government's self-rule proposal were the promises of aid he received from the United States and Iran. When the deadline for Kurdish self-rule approached in March 1974, Barzani contacted U.S. officials in Iran and gave them a list of the arms possessed by the Iraq forces. He is reported to have told these officials: "This is what they have to use against us. If you will give us arms to match those arms, we will fight. Otherwise, we will make peace. We don't want to be massacred."[48] Barzani said that he was promised weapons and that is why he decided to fight.[49]

Barzani confirmed this information in a subsequent interview with this writer. He said that "Without American promises, we would not have acted the way we did. Were it not for the American promises, we would never have become trapped and involved to such an extent."[50]

In a letter to President Carter, sent on February 9, 1977, he admitted that he could have reached an agreement with the government were it not for assurances from top U.S. officials. He wrote: "Mr. President, I could have prevented the calamity which befell my people had I not fully believed the promise of America. This could have been done by merely supporting Baath policy and joining forces with them, thereby taking a position contrary to American interests and principles and causing trouble for Iraq's neighbors. The assurances of the highest American officials made me disregard this alternative."[51]

Lee Dinsmore writes that the U.S. government assured the Kurds they would continue to receive aid through Iran, and that these assurances came from CIA operatives in Baghdad and, according to Kurdish sources, from the White House itself.[52]

An indication of U.S. support to Barzani was the opening in the spring of 1974 of U.S. Army Team House in Rezayieh near the Iranian-Iraqi border, not far from Barzani's headquarters. The members of this Team House were reported to have regularly visited the border to advise the Kurdish forces on how to conduct their war effort.[53] Other reports speak of the establishment of a CIA station in Haj Umran inside the Iraqi border and near Barzani's headquarters.[54] Ubaidullah al-Barzani has stated that he had seen foreign advisers, including Israelis and Americans, in his father's headquarters.[55] Aziz Aqrawi told a U.S. reporter that for many months there had been an Israeli mission of four men equipped with radios linked to Tel Aviv.[56]

In addition to the promises of military and financial support from the West, Barzani was counting on other favorable factors:

• The Pesh Merga was strong and well trained. The number of the regular forces reached 40,000 and of the militia about 60,000.[57]

• The Kurdish movement was bolstered by a high number of Kurdish intellectuals and professionals, some of whom left their jobs in Baghdad and other Iraqi cities to join Barzani in the mountains. These included 60 doctors, 4,500 teachers, 30 professors, 5,000 policemen, 160 engineers, and about 100 army officers.[58]

In the meantime, the Iraqi government had followed a defensive military strategy by relinquishing untenable positions and fighting to prevent the Kurds from consolidating their positions. The Kurds cut off, or forced into submission, close to 12,000 Iraqi soldiers stationed in strategic camps inside the Kurdish areas.[59]

The reasons for this policy were that the Soviet ministers visiting Baghdad in April urged the government to follow a conciliatory path with the Kurds and to make one more attempt at negotiations, and that the government wished to prepare its own strategy for a push on the Kurdish areas.

Politically, however, the government went on the offensive by reshuffling the cabinet and ousting the five pro-Barzani Kurdish ministers from the cabinet, and five anti-Barzani Kurdish ministers who had backed the autonomy law were appointed. These were Hashim Aqrawi, Aziz Aqrawi, Ubaidullah al-Barzani, Abd-Allah Ahmad, and Tahir Abd al-Sattar Sharif.[60] This move was followed on April 22 by the appointment of Taha Maruf, Iraq's ambassador to Rome and a prominent Kurdish figure as Iraq's vice president.[61]

## THE ESCALATION OF FIGHTING

The military situation in northern Iraq moved close to an all-out confrontation in April. The Kurds were reported to have moved their forces from the mountainous areas into the central plains as fighting was reported near Kirkuk and Khaniqin, about seventy miles south of Baghdad.[62] Government control of two important dams, Dukan and Darbindikhan, which regulate water flow to eastern Iraq, were threatened. Fighting was also reported on the road between Kirkuk and Sulaymaniyya as the Barzani forces controlled all the areas near the Iraqi-Turkish borders and about half of the area on Iran's borders.

Iraqi jets went into action on April 23 and 24 in support of armored units trying to reinforce a garrison of 600 men in the town of Zakho near the Turkish borders.[63] In the meantime, Barzani continued his calls for aid from the West. In an interview published in the *New York Times* on April 1, 1974, he repeated his offer to allow Western oil companies to exploit Iraq's northern oil field and added: "Kurdistan has become an important factor in the military and political equation of the Middle East. It is the duty of the Western powers to advise us what role it should play."

In another interview published in the *Christian Science Monitor* on April 1, 1974, he declared that in return for U.S. help he would guarantee that the Kurds in Iran and Turkey would not agitate for an independent Kurdistan.

The Iraqi government made a major push in late April to rescue Iraqi soldiers cut off near the Turkish borders. On April 30, it was reported that the Iraqi forces had retaken the city of Zakho and the Khabur Bridge on the Turkish-Iraqi border.[64]

Kurdish sources claimed that the Iraqi government was mobilizing all its reserve forces and that it was sending its 100,000-man army against the Kurdish forces.[65] Barzani's demands for foreign aid reflected his dissatisfaction with the amount of aid he was receiving. Consequently, he sent a two-man delegation to Washington to plead for heavy weapons he felt necessary to continue the offensive against the six Iraqi divisions facing him.[66]

United States Secretary of State Henry Kissinger, however, refused to meet with the delegates. Smith Hempstone, a journalist who visited the Kurds during the summer of 1974, attributes Kissinger's refusal to meet the delegation to his concern for the success of the Sinai agreement which he was trying to put together. Syria opposed the agreement and the most effective way to put pressure on Syria was by not weakening its rival, Iraq. The second reason, however, was attributed to his concern over the growing Soviet influence in Iraq. Consequently, the Kurdish delegation met with other high U.S. officials but received a non-committal response to pleas for arms and ammunition.[67] Kurdish sources, however, believe that the delegation was promised limited military and financial aid and told that the United States would study their other requests.[68]

Barzani expressed the need for sophisticated weapons in order to achieve his military and political objectives. He felt that the political and diplomatic circumstances were as favorable as they were ever going to be. Iran, Israel, and the United States were concerned about the potential threats from a secure and stable Baath regime with close ties to the Soviets. Consequently, Barzani played on the fears of the Shah who was seeking to tame or overthrow the Baath regime.

Barzani believed that if he had the sophisticated weapons, he could interfere with the flow of oil from Iraq.[69] If he was able to achieve this by sabotaging oil installations and holding on to his own territory, he could impress any Iraqi government and outside forces that he was a real force to be reckoned with. Such a situation would cause problems in Baghdad and might lead the army to overthrow the "fascist Baath dictatorship" as Barzani and the Voice of Kurdistan described the government in Baghdad.[70] A new government would come into power and might accede to the type of autonomy Barzani was seeking.

There were, however, indications that Barzani may have had another more difficult objective in mind. He hoped that if he received the sophisticated weapons he wanted, he might be able to hold the oil installations, at least for a while, get outside help and ultimately win recognition for an independent Kurdish state. In an interview with David Hirst of *The Guardian,* he expressed the belief that he might get outside help if the Kurds controlled Kirkuk: "Kirkuk has been taken by the Arabs. Because this oil-rich area is in their hands, they are attracting people to help them. Perhaps if it were in our hands we, too, would have outside help."[71]

These and similar statements reveal Barzani's reasons for insisting that Kirkuk be included in the Kurdish region. Furthermore, Kurdish leaders interviewed during this period by foreign reporters were speaking more of independence and no longer of autonomy.[72]

In order to achieve this objective, according to pro-Iraqi sources, Barzani, with the help of foreign advisers, developed a new strategy. He moved his forces to control most of the Kurdish areas in Iraq from Salah al-Din to the east and south, the area from Derbendikhan to Jalwa that then stretched northwest to Zakho and Duhok on the Turkish borders.

This crescent-shaped area was an easy one to defend because of its rugged and strategically placed mountains. Behind this area, the Iraqis had stationed about eleven battalions or somewhere between 8,000 and 12,000 men in strategic positions on the mountain tops.[73] Iranian, American, and Israeli advisers suggested to Barzani to surround these bases until they surrender, while, at the same time, blocking all Iraqi efforts to relieve them.[74] These advisers estimated that it would take about three months for the bases to surrender although Barzani estimated it would take close to six months. It was decided that the Kurdish forces would tighten their siege around the camps, fight mainly in a conventional manner instead of relying on guerrilla tactics, and prevent the Iraqi army from advancing along all strategic axes, fronts, and passes. After the surrender of the Iraqi mountain forces, the Kurdish movement and its allies planned to wage a major propaganda campaign and submit the Kurdish case to the United Nations. Practical steps would then be taken toward a declaration of independence.[75]

The government's military strategy was at first aimed at relieving the garrisons trapped in the Kurdish areas, particularly on the axes of Zakho-Duhok-Aqra, and Arbil-Ruwanduz. Plans for this offensive were completed by April 6, 1974, and the government forces were able in a few days to take back Zakho and relieve some of the Iraqi forces trapped in Shaqlawa and Salah al-Din near Arbil. However, heavy fighting continued around Aqra and Duhok and near Gali Ali Beg near Ruwanduz.[76]

The Iraqi army scored some quick successes in this area primarily because the Kurdish leadership and its advisers had not expected any major push before late April with the melting of the snow. Consequently, the government captured the four important strategic mountains of Zozak, Handarin, Tatan, and Hasnan, allowing the government to divide its forces between the Surani-speaking Kurds living in the northeast and the Bahdinani Kurds (to whom the Barzanis belong) living in the northwestern areas.[77]

The Kurdish forces, however, were able to quickly recover and a war of attrition began until the last week of June 1974, when Iraqi army forces in division strength were reported to have smashed through Kurdish defenses after more than two weeks of ferocious fighting and took up valley positions in the Kurdish heartland.[78]

The government forces were thus able despite heavy casualties to reach most of the forward outposts occupied by their garrisons and scatter Kurdish resistance before the fall of winter when heavy snows would give the Kurdish forces an advantage in mobility. The important cities of Ruwanduz and Qal at Diza fell to government forces as a result of successful armor attacks, creating new communication and supply problems for the Kurdish forces who retreated higher into the mountains.

The reasons for Iraqi successes included the determined Iraqi armor attacks against which the Kurdish anti-tank weapons lacked killing power beyond short ranges; the fact that Iraqi troops were fighting with more determination and sophistication than in previous years; and new ways of overcoming natural obstacles by modern tactics devised by the Iraqi army in mountain areas which used to favor the Kurds' defensive maneuvers and wars of attrition. In the Ruwanduz battle, Iraqi engineers built new roads under difficult conditions, allowing tanks to bypass Kurdish fire bases on mountain tops near Gali Ali Beg, one of the most rugged passes in Iraq, and to take the city which is the gateway to Shuman Valley, the Pesh Merga's principal supply route from Iran. Pontoon bridges and other engineering devices allowed Iraqi forces to quickly overcome Kurdish mine squads and snipers trying to block Iraqi advances through nearly impassable hills.

The Iraqi push allowed the government to regain control of all major Kurdish cities and towns, including Aqrah, Zakho, Amadiyyah, Ruwanduz, and Raniyah by the end of the summer and to gain control, by Barzani's admission, of more Kurdish areas than at any time since the beginning of fighting with Iraqi governments in 1961.[79]

The fighting, which pitted close to 60,000 Iraqi troops against about 12,000 Pesh Mergas was described by Kurdish representatives as "the fiercest and most concentrated attacks" by government forces since 1961.[80] Iraqi strategy was aimed at cutting the only major supply line left to the Kurds—the road to the Iranian town of Piranshah before the coming of winter snow. If this line was cut, the Kurdish forces would be left with little food, fuel, and heavy-weapons ammunition.

Iraqi military successes alarmed the Iranian government, which had urged Barzani to fight conventional warfare against the Iraqi government without giving him all the necessary weapons to fight this kind of war.[81] Consequently, the Shah began to escalate his aid. Iranian army troops dressed as Kurds and Iranian Kurds joined Barzani's forces. Long-range heavy artillery support was also given from within the Iranian borders, particularly 175-mm cannons, which the Iraqis could not match, as well as anti-aircraft guns.[82]

On August 28, Iraq complained to the United Nations Security Council over the amassing of forces by Iran on its frontier in violation of the UN Security Council's three-month-old resolution calling for the withdrawal of troop concentrations from both sides.[83] The Iraqis charged that Iranian military strength reached three armored divisions, two infantry divisions, and an independent infantry brigade. Iran also reported that Iranian border troops destroyed three Iraqi tanks and killed three Iraqi soldiers in border clashes on August 28 when they fired in retaliation against Iraqi armored and artillery attacks on Iranian border towns.

In response to Iran's escalation of its aid, the Iraqi air force began to increase its reconnaissance flights over the Iranian bases near the transit points to the Kurdish-held areas. The Iraqis were further reported to have bombed some Iranian border villages and scattered anti-Shah leaflets. On September 6, the Iraqis bombed the Iranian village of Kohneh Lahijan near the border, killing fifteen people.[84]

The Iraqi strategy seemed to be aimed at bringing an end to the insurrection before the winter even if it meant bombing Kurdish supply routes and bases inside Iran and risking a more direct response from the Shah.[85] However, the Shah did not want at the time to risk an all-out confrontation with Iraq. His forces were still taking delivery of the sophisticated weapons purchased from the West, and their training was incomplete. Risking a defeat at the hands of the seasoned Iraqi forces would have meant courting disaster.

The Shah was also courting other Arab states, such as Syria, Egypt, and Saudi Arabia, and did not want to alienate them by waging a direct war with his Arab neighbor. As a result of the Shah's successful diplomacy, these countries expressed little or no protest of his massive support to Barzani's forces fighting their fellow member of the Arab League.[86] In befriending these countries, the Shah probably hoped to weaken and isolate Iraq and to protect his borders from Soviet and Iraqi encirclement. He, like Barzani, was gambling that if the Kurds were able to hold their position against the Iraqis before the winter, the Baath regime would be undermined. There were rumors of a growing dissatisfaction within the Iraqi army. The transfer of Iraq's air force chief to another post was viewed as a sign of growing unrest in the military as the Kurds reported that a number of other officers had been demoted or executed.

In any case, whether the rumors were true or not, military operations came to a standstill from November 1974 until December 1975. The Iraqi forces, however, held their ground and did not retreat to the plains as was the case during previous campaigns.


## THE POLITICAL OFFENSIVE


Along with its military successes, the Iraqi government was anxious to advance its political and diplomatic moves to end a war costing it thousands of casualties and over $2.5 million daily.[87] On the Iranian Front, Iraqi Foreign Minister Shazil Taqah indicated on October 3 that Iraq wanted to cool border tensions with Iran and said that an "open conflict" was not in the interest of either side. He, however, denied the attacks on Iranian border villages and issued an implicit warning to Iran to stop its aid to

Barzani: "It's nice to feel warm by the fire but it is too dangerous to play with it."[88]

Reports of new efforts at negotiations with the help of Egypt surfaced a few days later.[89] Iraq's relations with Egypt, which had reached a low level following President Sadat's signing of the Sinai agreements and his acceptance of the principle of a peaceful solution to the Arab-Israeli conflict began to improve as a result of the mediation efforts by Shaikh Zayed of the United Arab Emirates and the Algerian ambassador in Baghdad.

In an attempt to end its isolation in the Arab world and to gain backing for its confrontation with Iran, the Iraqi government reached a $1 billion economic agreement with Egypt and another one to allow newspapers from each country to enter the other. The Egyptians, badly in need of financial aid, accepted the deal but urged Iraq to tone down its attacks on Egypt's Middle East policy, if it could not renounce them altogether. Egypt also expressed its support for Iraq's Kurdish policy and promised to seek to improve Baghdad's ties with Saudi Arabia as well as Iran.

Despite the mutual suspicion between Saudi Arabia and Iraq, the Saudi leaders were becoming increasingly concerned over Iran's role in Oman and the Gulf.[90] The Saudi leadership wanted to make it clear to Iran that the Gulf was not a Persian lake but that it was an Arab Gulf, at least on its western coast. Consequently, the Saudis supported Egypt's attempts to improve relations with Baghdad and play a mediating role in the conflict with Tehran. Turkish mediation efforts, which led to negotiations between the foreign ministers from Ankara and Baghdad in late August and early September, ended in failure.

An Iraqi delegation traveled to Tehran in early October to resume the negotiations over the border disputes. A few months earlier the Shah had rejected an agreement reached in Geneva between his foreign minister and a member of the Iraqi RCC. The Shah had rejected the agreement because he was still hoping to overthrow the Baathist regime or to weaken it severely. He was aware of Iraq's isolation in the Arab world and therefore was seeking to tell Baghdad that he had the upper hand in the Gulf and could solve the problem any time he wished. Baghdad, however, scored major military successes against the Kurdish insurgents and escalated its attacks against Iranian border towns. The Shah nevertheless waited to see how the Iraqis would fare militarily during the winter and again rejected the Iraqi offer to reach an agreement.[91]

In another attempt aimed at calming the fears of Iran and conservative Arab governments fearful of the close Iraqi-Soviet ties and of the consequences of the emergence of a radical Iraq free from the Kurdish problem in the region, the Baath government allowed reports of its differences with the Soviet Union to surface. Reports in the Arabic press indicated that Baghdad and Moscow did not enjoy the best relations despite their advocacy of similar socialist and foreign policies.

Moscow urged Baghdad to scale down its offensive against the Kurds since it had made major military advances and enjoyed wide support from other Kurdish sectors. Moscow was also fearful that a prolonged war would strengthen the military's hand and lead them to confront the party's civilian rule. The Soviets supported the government's Kurdish proposal but urged Baghdad to give a chance to Barzani to return to the central government's fold.[92]

Iraq also may have been irritated by the arrival in Moscow in the early fall of 1974 of a Kurdish representative sent to negotiate with Soviet officials and try to get the Soviets to mediate between the government and Barzani.[93] Soviet policy appeared to favor a compromise solution both because the war had sidetracked the energy of the Iraqi leadership in its efforts to counteract the influence of the United States and her allies in the region; and because victory for either side would have weakened Soviet influence in the Iraqi government.

Other points of disagreement between Baghdad and Moscow included the following:

• Soviet demands that the Iraqi communists be given a bigger share in decision-making in recognition of their support for Baath policies.[94]

• Iraqi complaints that the Soviet Union had remained silent in the face of Iran's intervention in their internal affairs. Baghdad believed that Moscow could have put leverage on Iran with which it had significant economic ties to end the support to Barzani.[95]

• Soviet concern over the growing economic ties between Iraq and Western companies at the expense of the Soviets and their East European allies.

But while it was true that the Soviet and Iraqi leaders had some important differences, relations between the two countries remained strong as Iraqi officials stated that differences with Moscow focused on a proposed solution to the Middle East conflict but not on the Kurdish question which was an internal problem.[96] The Soviets continued to send arms and supplies to Iraq, including the MIG 23, which was introduced to Iraq for the first time in October 1974.[97] The arrival of the MIG 23s was believed to be in response to Iran's military buildup and the growing tension between Iraq and Iran. The planes were sent following the visit to Baghdad of a Soviet military delegation to assess Iraq's military needs. The Soviet visit was preceded by visits of the Iraqi foreign minister and the Iraqi chief of staff to Moscow. It appears that Iraq permitted, even encouraged, the reports of Iraqi-Soviet differences in order to end its isolation in the Arab world and to allay the suspicions and fears of its conservative neighbors.

At the same time, Iraq escalated its attacks against Iran and its policies. Anti-Iranian conferences were held in the fall and winter months of 1974–1975 by Iraqi and civic organizations representing students, lawyers, historians, women, doctors, and nationalist groups.

Government efforts concentrated also on winning the confidence and support of the Kurds. The government went ahead with implementing self-rule for the Kurdish region in the areas under its control. On July 30, the RCC appointed sixty prominent Kurds to the Legislative Assembly in accordance with the autonomy law.[98] Moreover, the RCC announced an amnesty on August 25, 1974, to all Kurdish fighters who would surrender to the government.[99] On September 25, the government nominated twelve new members to the Kurdish Legislative Assembly, including Hashim Aqrawi, who was named by President al-Bakr to head up and form the Executive Council.[100]

Furthermore, the High Committee for Northern Affairs, headed by Saddam Husain, kept in close touch with the military and political developments in the north. The committee adopted a policy designed to avoid alienating the Kurds and, if possible, win them to its side, as follows:[101]

• The government should encourage the Iraqi soldiers to pursue fair treatment of non-combatants and to try to win the confidence of the Kurds.

• It was decided that the army should not play the role of policing the Kurdish areas which they cleared of insurgents, nor were army officers to become the military governors in the Kurdish areas with the authority to arrest and execute. Instead, regular police were assigned to recaptured areas. Any difficulties were to be solved by the political and not the military authorities.

• The government encouraged Kurdish supporters of Barzani to join the government side by offering them financial aid and automatically returning them to their villages and places of work.

• Kurds fighting on the government's side were permitted to advance to all ranks. One Kurdish officer became a division commander.[102]

• The government continued its development projects in the Kurdish areas and initiated new ones. Agrarian reform laws were implemented, and construction was encouraged. The war victims were compensated. In addition, steps were taken to allow the population to resume normal life by distributing food, medicine, and other materials.

• While following a lenient policy against the Kurdish civilians and deserters, the government followed a harsh policy against the insurgents themselves.

The government also went ahead with the establishment on August 31, 1974, of an eighty-member Legislative Assembly to be followed later by a twelve-member Executive Council for the autonomous government.[103] In addition, the government achieved a major gain when Shaikh Uthman Ahmad, nephew of Mulla Mustafa and the spiritual leader of the Barzanis, defected with 500 of his men in the summer of 1974.[104]

The Iraqi policies were implemented at the urging of the political leadership, which also emphasized discipline and harsh punishment for those violating the government directives. Saddam Husain ordered that "erroneous behavior," even if committed with well-intentioned purposes or by Baathists, must be reported to the highest political authorities in order for the party to maintain "the right direction, discipline, and control."[105]

The tough policy adopted by the party's political leadership is believed to have gone a long way toward gaining the neutrality if not the support, of many Kurds. On the military level, 20 percent of the Iraqi army was reported to be composed of Kurds, in addition to several thousand anti-Barzani tribal irregulars and Kurdish members of the ICP who fought alongside the government.[106]

For its part, the Kurdish leadership launched its own diplomatic offensive to win international support. On January 3, it was reported that Kurdish representatives asked to attend the International Red Cross conference in Geneva and submitted an application for observer status to the International Labor Organization.[107] The status of these requests was to be discussed in February or March and thus came at a time when the Kurdish movement was nearing its collapse and, therefore, were consequently rejected.

## RESUMPTION OF MILITARY ACTIVITIES

The fighting escalated again in December and January of 1975 when the government decided to push the remaining 5,000 to 6,000 Kurdish troops from the strip they still controlled near the border with Iran.[108] Barzani's forces were desperately seeking to prevent the Iraqi army from making any further advances into Shuman Valley. The Kurds, however, were undisguisedly backed by two regular Iranian artillery battalions possessing heavy howitzers operating inside Iraq's borders.[109] These forces were also armed with sophisticated ground-to-air missiles and anti-aircraft guns.[110] Iranian forces on the border were also reported to have provided the Kurdish forces with heavy 75-mm and 130-mm guns. On the other side, the Iraqis could not reach the Iranian borders with their 155-mm Russian field guns.

Using what then were believed to be U.S. Hawk missiles, Iranian forces had on December 14 and 15 shot down two Iraqi warplanes inside Iraqi territory.[111] Iranian planes and torpedo boats were also said to have violated Iraqi waters and air space.[112] The Iraqis were further incensed when Iranian forces used 175-mm guns to shell Qalat Dizah, inflicting heavy losses in life and property. The office of the Iraqi chief of staff issued a statement repeating previous warnings and pointing to the dangers of such escalations.[113]

The Iranian intervention prevented the Iraqi army from destroying Barzani's forces and allowed the Kurdish forces to shell the city of Arbil with their new artillery. Iraqi General Munim Lifta, commander of the Iraqi forces in the Ruwanduz sector, said: "Now it all depends on the Iranians. If they withdraw their support, we can finish the rebels off within a week. If the Iranians increase their support, I suppose there could be war between our two countries, but that would also depend on other political factors."[114]

The escalation and the consequent Iraqi requests for heavy artillery from the Soviet Union came after the failure of another attempt at Iranian and Iraqi negotiations in Istanbul.[115] The Shah was reported by Arab sources to have told Egyptian President Anwar Sadat in Cairo in mid-January that, while the border problem with Iraq could be negotiated, he saw no hope for reaching any agreement with the Baath government, which he described as a threat to the whole area.[116]

During the same period, Iraq escalated its pan-Arab public campaign against Iran. In late January through early February twenty-five Arab political organizations, including representatives of the Palestinian resistance, held a conference in Baghdad to support Iraq in its confrontation with Iran.[117] Other solidarity conferences were held in Baghdad by the Asian Peace Congress and other international organizations.[118] Iraq also gained important Arab support during the Arab Information Ministers Council held in Cairo on February 15, 1975. The council called on the Arab mass media and the Arab League to "confront Iranian aggressions" against Iraq's eastern borders and called on Iran to take religion and good neighbor policies to account.[119]

## THE IRAN-IRAQ AGREEMENT
## AND THE COLLAPSE OF THE INSURGENCY


In the meantime, King Hussein of Jordan and President Sadat of Egypt continued their mediation efforts and were later aided by the Algerians.[120] These efforts culminated in the March 6, 1975, agreement between the Shah and Saddam Husain at the OPEC meeting in Algiers to settle and solve permanently all their disputes. On March 15, 1975, the Iraqi News Agency repeated that the two leaders agreed to the following:

• Definite demarcation of their land frontiers on the basis of the Constantinople Protocol of 1913 and minutes of the Frontier Demarcation Commission of 1914.

• Demarcation of river frontier according to the Thalweg Line.

• The re-establishment of mutual security and confidence along their joint borders and an undertaking to conduct strict and effective control along the joint borders to put a final end to all subversive infiltration from either side.

• The two parties also agreed on considering the aforementioned arrangements as indivisible elements for a comprehensive settlement and consequently the violation of any of the provisions will naturally contradict the spirit of the Algiers Agreement; the two parties will remain in constant contact with President Houari Boumedienne who will, when necessary, offer Algeria's brotherly assistance for the implementation of these decisions.

Less than two weeks later, the foreign ministers of Iran, Iraq, and Algeria began extensive discussions in Tehran to complete work on the details of the agreement. Other high level meetings and visits followed between officials of the two countries and the final agreement was signed in Baghdad on June 13, 1975.

The agreement, which came as a surprise to the outside world as well as to the Kurdish insurgents, offered gains for both Iran and Iraq. For Iran it meant that Iraq would accept Iran's demands that the border between the two countries on Shatt al-Arab should run along the Thalweg Line, the deepest point of the waterway instead of along the Iranian bank as the 1937 Shatt al-Arab Treaty stipulated; stop aiding Baluchi and the Arab secessionist movement in Iran; and·cut off aid to leftist and Muslim anti-regime Iranians operating inside and outside Iran. There were also reports, denied by the Iraqis, that Iraq also promised to cut off aid to the Dhufari insurgents operating against the Sultanate of Oman.[121]

For Iraq the agreement meant the withdrawal of Iranian forces backing the Kurdish insurgency and the cut-off of all aid to the rebels. Concerning the land frontiers, the agreement upheld the status quo in accordance with the Constantinople Protocol of 1913 and the minutes of the Frontier Demarcation Commission of 1914. The agreement also achieved two common objectives for both countries: the establishment of a stable frontier; and avoidance of any disruptions of oil production and the establishment of a strong front within OPEC calling for high oil prices.

The Algiers Agreement revealed a change in the position of the Shah. He had rejected Iraqi offers to settle the border disputes along similar lines as late as December 1974.[122] This change stemmed from Iran's realization that even with extensive Iranian support the Kurds faced inevitable defeat.[123] Iran had calculated that its direct intervention would not be necessary and that by aiding the Kurds, they would severely weaken the Iraqi regime or cause it to be toppled. However, the Iraqi army was able to reach the outskirts of Kallala and other new positions during the first year of fighting. During the winter, the Kurdish forces did not gain ground as in previous campaigns. The Iraqis did not retreat but held their ground and continued to make small advances in December, January, and February in spite of the introduction of Iranian forces on a larger scale with sophisticated weapons.

As a result, Iran was confronted with the choice of increasing military aid, possibly permitting the Kurdish insurgents to hold for one more year, or doing nothing and allowing the Iraqis to win.[124] Such a development would have led to new political and military realities not favorable to Iran, or would have forced Iran to escalate its intervention and thus become more involved in a declared or undeclared war with Iraq. Iranian escalation would have been considered a *causus belli* by Iraq and would have triggered a direct and open war between the two neighbors with serious consequences for both countries and the world.

A war between Iraq and Iran would have meant, in addition to normal human and property losses, the shelling by Iraq of the Abadan oil field and the bombing of Iraqi oil fields by Iran.[125] In a speech at the Pan-Arab anti-Iran conference held in Baghdad on February 2, 1975, Saddam Husain warned publicly about this situation when he declared that: "Oil is a very flammable matter."[126]

Furthermore, the war might have led to the closing of the Gulf since both Iraq and Iran had the capability of doing so; the involvement of other Arabs in the conflict; and the possible involvement of Israel. A direct war between the two countries, the destruction of oil fields, and the closure of the Gulf would have confronted the industrialized countries with a severe crisis. Any Western attempt to occupy the oil fields carried with it the possibility of a Soviet-U.S. confrontation.[127] The Iraqis believe that this scenario led to Iranian-U.S. consultations and to subsequent agreement between the two countries. Therefore, the Shah made the deal which netted him several important gains and avoided a major war with Iraq. The Iraqis also avoided a wider war with Iran and gained the opportunity to end the most serious Kurdish uprising in Iraq's history. According to official government estimates, the war losses included 1,640 soldiers and officers killed and 7,903 wounded, while the Kurds lost 7,600 killed or wounded.[128]

Within hours of the signing of the Algiers Agreement, Iran began to withdraw its forces from Iraq and to cut off aid to Barzani.[129] Immediately afterward, the Iraqis mounted a major offensive against the Kurdish forces.

The Iraqis were able to break through the Ruwanduz Valley and to occupy the important mountain ridges of Sartiz and Hasen Beg, threatening the Kurdish military headquarters at Haj Umran.

Stunned by the Algiers Agreement, Barzani vowed that 60,000 Pesh Mergas would carry on the fight but admitted that the agreement affected his ability to carry on the war.[130] In the meantime, the Iraqi government, in accord with the agreement reached with the Shah, offered a cease-fire from March 13 to April 1, to allow the Kurdish forces to go to Iran or to surrender.[131]

A few days after the Algiers agreement, Mulla Mustafa, after a brief visit to Iran to meet with the Shah, announced that he would not resume the fight. He was informed by the Shah that Iran's borders were going to be tightly sealed because the accord was "vital to Iranian interests in the Middle East." Barzani was given three options by the Shah: to surrender; to fight on without Iranian support; or to tell his people to move to Iran.[132]

Upon his return, Barzani sent a telegram to the government asking for a renewal of the dialogue.[133] The government's response came in a cable sent by President al-Bakr which declared: "The only possible thing for you to do is to profit from the general amnesty declared by the Revolutionary Command Council which expires April first."[134]

Following the rejection, Barzani called for a meeting of the KDP's leadership to decide what action to take. The meeting was held for three days from March 20–23, and it was decided to give up the fight.[135] The decision, however, was not unanimous. Some of the KDP's military and political officers favored a return to partisan warfare, and a new Kurdish RCC was formed. In its first decision, the new leadership renounced Barzani and some of the leaders and their men went high into the mountains vowing to continue the fight.[136]

The movement, however, collapsed when Barzani gave orders to stop the fighting and withdrew with his family, close associates, and several thousand Pesh Mergas and their families to join close to 100,000 Kurdish refugees already living in Iran.[137] Barzani also asked the United States for asylum and later went to the United States where he began to receive medical treatment for cancer. He was asked to refrain from any political activities.[138] Thousands of other Kurdish fighters surrendered with their arms as the government paid 150 dinars for each cannon, 75 dinars for each machine gun, and 50 dinars for each rifle.[139]

The estimates both in human lives and in material cost were high on both sides. To the government's reported $2.5 million a day the Kurds spent over $9 million a month. Accurate casualty figures are difficult to determine exactly, nevertheless, they were certainly very high. Zayd Haydar estimated that the Iraqi army lost close to 10,000 dead and wounded.[140] Iraqi Irrigation Minister Mukarram Talibani quoted Saddam Husain as saying that the Iraqis lost close to 10,000 men,[141] while Babakr al-Pishdari, former chairman of the Executive Council of the Autonomous Areas, and minister of labor and social affairs said that there were 14,000 casualties on the government side and about 20,000 on the insurgents' side.[142]

On January 15, 1979, *Al-Thawra* stated that the Iraqi army had suffered about 16,000 casualties. Kurdish sources claimed that the government had lost 30,000 dead and wounded, while they lost only 2,000 of their men.[143] The representative of the Red Cross in Iraq said that the Iraqis suffered at least 7,000 dead and 10,000 wounded.[144] But while figures presented by both sides must be treated with caution, it is clear that the Iraqis, Kurds and Arabs alike, paid a heavy price during the fighting. It is also obvious that the casualty figures on both sides were closer to the 60,000 figure given by President Saddam Husain in 1979.


## THE CAUSES OF KURDISH DEFEAT


During the months that followed the collapse of the Kurdish movement, much was written attributing its causes to the agreement between Iran and Iraq. But while the impact of this deal cannot be minimized, it was, nevertheless, a reflection of the difficult circumstances increasingly facing the rebellion. These circumstances stemmed from a number of internal factors which contributed to the strengthening of the government on the one hand and the weakening of the insurgency on the other.

The factors favoring the government included the following:

• The consolidation by the Baath party of its authority inside Arab Iraq and the establishment of a strong political organization capable of implementing leadership decisions.

• The initiation of major programs and policies which gained popular support for the regime for the Kurdish regions under Barzani's control, the nationalization of the oil companies, and the establishment of the National Front, which widened the base of support for the regime while preserving real power in Baathist hands.

• The restructuring of the army and its reorganization along Baathist ideological lines. The politicization of the army was aimed at ending the role which army officers had played in previous years. Anti-Baath officers were removed or isolated and non-Baathists were specifically forbidden from proselytizing in the army and no longer promoted to sensitive or high posts. Political education was initiated at all levels, allowing the regime to use the army as the government's instrument and not as its potential master. The politicization of the army also allowed its members to carry on the most determined and ferocious military campaign the Iraqi army ever waged.

• The furnishing of the army with new and sophisticated weapons and the adoption of rigorous training procedures and new tactics which permitted it to fight in small mobile units and maneuver for victory in Kurdistan's rugged terrain.

• The increase in the government's financial revenues as a result of the nationalization of oil resources and the rise in oil prices.

• The support by large Kurdish sectors of the government's self-rule proposal as a result of the government's careful check on army behavior in the recaptured Kurdish areas.[145] The government's undertaking of major development programs in the areas under its control and the fulfillment of its promises in implementing the March 11 Manifesto.

The Kurdish movement, on the other hand, faced a number of serious defects and problems in spite of the dramatic increase in its financial and military resources.[146] These factors included:

• The failure of the Kurdish leadership to assess their interests vis-a-vis those of their Iranian and American allies whose interests were better served by a prolonged conflict than by a Kurdish victory. Barzani's suspicions of Iran were apparently overcome by American promises.

• The failure of the Kurdish leadership to take into account the increasing power of the Baath government, the changes that took place in Iraq, the capability of the regime, and the degree of international support it received.

• The failure of the KDP leadership to accomplish any of the three conditions necessary to either force the government to change its position or to overthrow it, such as: consistent cooperation with other Iraqi groups and organizations for the formation of united front; gaining of written guarantees to support the Kurds' rights before international organizations; and military success against the government on some fronts while keeping it preoccupied by partisan warfare.[147]

• The adoption of conventional military tactics, at the urging of foreign advisers, and the minimizing of guerrilla warfare, in which the Kurdish forces excelled.

• The initiation of secondary conflicts with Baghdad, such as the refusal to allow agrarian reform to be implemented and the support for the special interests of feudal landlords and others.

• The adoption of two-faced policies toward Baghdad, such as the acceptance of the March Manifesto while opposing some of its main points and emphasizing secondary issues.

• Antagonizing the Iraqi Communist party and the Soviet Union, both of which had previously given strong support to the Kurdish movement.

• Barzani's alienation of important Kurdish leftist and nationalist elements by agreeing not to support the struggle of Turkish or Iranian Kurds and the execution or the handing over of some of their leaders to their governments.[148]

• The prevention of Kurdish intellectuals and high KDP members from participating in the decision-making process.


## AFTERMATH OF THE COLLAPSE


Following the collapse of the Kurdish insurgency, the Iraqi government followed a policy combining leniency with toughness in dealing with the Kurds.

The most controversial aspect of the government's policies involved the deportation and resettlement of thousands of Kurds in areas other than their original places of residence. Close to 210,000 Kurds found refuge in Iran during the fighting and in the first days following the collapse of Barzani's movement.[149] However, by the time the extended amnesty had expired on May 20, 1975, only 140,000 Kurds returned, in two major waves, to Iraq.[150]

After being screened by the government, the majority of these refugees were allowed to resume normal life and return to their villages and towns, but the rest were resettled in the Arab governorates of Diwaniyya, Nasiriyya, and Amara.[151] Those resettled were former members of the Iraqi armed forces who had deserted to join Barzani. Accurate figures about their numbers are difficult to obtain, but while Hashim Aqrawi spoke of "hundreds," anti-government Kurds spoke of 10,000 persons.[152]

There were, however, two other categories of resettlements. The first group included Kurds who came from peripheral areas, such as Khaniqin, Sinjar, and a six to twelve mile zone near Iraq's borders with Iran, Turkey, and Syria where, according to pro-government sources, twenty villages were demolished in order to establish a security belt to prevent smuggling and infiltration.[153] Information Minister Tariq Aziz declared that "some areas have to be totally secure. We're not going to allow people in the rebellion to settle in those areas. We have moved them either to other governorates in the north of Iraq, or to other parts of Iraq, and have settled border guards in their place.[154]

A second category involved the third group of refugees who began to return to Iraq in October 1975. This group was automatically resettled in the Arab areas.[155] The members of this group were considered very hostile to the government since they had decided to remain in Iran past the amnesty deadline. When National Front leader Naim Haddad went to Iran with a delegation to urge this group to return, he was met by demonstrators carrying the Shah's picture and chanting anti-Baath slogans.[156] But when the Iranian government decided to transfer this group to other areas in Iran, away from Iraq's borders and from Kurdish-Iranian areas, they decided to return to Iraq.[157] The Iraqi government allowed this group to return after informing them that they would not be allowed to return to their original homes.[158]

The numbers of people involved in the resettlement schemes are hard to come by but they range from as low as 40,000 to a high of 100,000, depending on the sources.[159] And while pro-government Kurdish leaders have supported the establishment of strategic areas and the transfer of some of the former hard-core insurgents to the south, they have, nevertheless, opposed the resettlement of large numbers of Kurds in the south. ICP leader Mukarram Talibani, KDP leader Aziz Aqrawi, and Executive Council Chairman Pishdari have opposed the resettlement policies and finally succeeded, with the help of Saddam Husain, in putting an end to the resettlement policies.[160]

In a statement published in the Kurdish newspaper, *Al-Iraq,* on July 5, 1976, Saddam Husain admitted that the authorities had "taken several measures such as changing the residences of people of some border villages and strategic areas, as well as changing the residences of some individuals such as civil servants, workers, and others."[161] But Husain declared that the government had decided "to stop such measures completely," because "national unity, stability, and security have been established in the area."[162] He added that such measures may still be necessary in individual cases but that in the future they must be carried out only with the permission of the High Committee for Northern Affairs. Other charges leveled at the government included the accusation that Arabs were being settled in the Kurdish areas, particularly in Kirkuk and the border areas.[163] A pro-government Kurdish leader admitted that there was such a project but that it was a minor one and involved the resettling of approximately one-half of an Arab tribe in Khaniqin and the other half in Sulaymaniyya but that this project had ceased in the early part of 1976.[164] Furthermore, Iraqi leaders and foreign observers say that this policy has been reversed and that most of the resettled Kurds had been allowed to return to new areas in the Kurdish region.[165] The only large group that remained in southern Iraq were several thousand Barzanis (5,000–7,000) who had been resettled in Diwaniyya. In September 1979, the Barzanis were allowed to return to the Kurdish region.[166]

The government, however, has tried to mitigate the impact of the resettlements by paying generous compensation to those who were moved to the new villages in addition to 500 dinars for every family.[167] The government also compensated Kurdish families for all damages to land, trees, orchards, and houses damaged during the fighting.[168] The total number of houses built in these modern villages reached 31,923 in 1979, with 20,649 houses in Sulaimaniyya, 6,529 in Arbil, and 4,700 in Duhok.

In these villages the government established collective farms, small factories for light industries, schools, dispensaries, municipal, and other services. The total cost for the establishment of these villages reached 89,650,000 dinars. The establishment of these villages served a dual function. It allowed the government to establish a "cordon sanitaire" on its borders with Turkey, Iran, and Syria. It also made it easier for the government to push forward its program of economic development in the Kurdish areas as a way of promoting stability by encouraging the Kurds to participate in the economic life of the country. It also made it easier to provide these services to larger and more accessible villages instead of trying to reach smaller villages scattered in the various mountains and valleys of Kurdistan. The estimates on the number of families resettled varies depending on the source, but they fall in the range of some thirty thousand families.

A Swiss group that supported the Kurds presented a list of violations of human rights by the Iraqi government to the United Nations Commission on Human Rights. It claimed that 140 Kurds, either political prisoners or members of the Pesh Merga, have been shot or hanged in Iraq since the end of the fighting.[169] In 1979, Amnesty International noted a report alleging the detention of 760 Kurds and that it has received the names of 200 Kurds who had been executed since the collapse of the movement.[170]

In August 1978 Iraqi President Saddam Husain announced a new amnesty for all Kurdish opponents of the regime remaining outside Iraq, with the exception of Mulla Mustafa, his sons Idris and Massud, and his nephew Khalid Ahmad al-Barzani.[171] While Iraq excluded political prisoners from the 1978 amnesty, in its 1979 amnesty it specifically included about 400 persons associated with Kurdish anti-government activities.

Iraqi leaders admitted that "some executions had taken place but insisted that these were few in number and only involved double agents."[172] But while there were many examples of ill-treatment and "coercive measures" and excesses, interviews with Iraqi leaders and articles published in the *Economist,* the *Observer, The Times,* and the *Swiss Review of World Affairs* paint a picture of generous treatment of the Kurds.[173]

Similar views were presented by other independent observers. Following a tour of the Kurdish region in 1978, Lord Kilbracken of the British-Kurdish society and author of *Kurdistan* said that he found much of the information of Kurdish exiles was not borne out by the facts.[174]

Fred Evans, a member of the British House of Commons, reported following a visit to the Kurdish autonomous region in 1979 that the rehabilitation task was difficult, and went on to add, "But the efforts of the Iraqi government, providing housing, a proper educational system, opportunities for employment in localized industries, the massive financial help which the Iraqi government is prepared to extend to see a proper development in the area; all of these have communicated themselves to the people of the autonomous area, who are quite obviously feeling much happier with the situation."[175]

The autonomy promises, according to these articles and to statements by Kurdish and Iraqi leaders, were being realized in many respects, and the autonomous institutions have been functioning within the framework of the law. Moreover, the government has followed an ambitious development program in the Kurdish areas; close to $1.5 billion was spent between 1970 and 1975 in the construction of factories, the initiation of irrigation projects, the building of schools, and the distribution of 451,000 dunums of land to 7,000 peasants.[176]

Following the collapse of the Kurdish revolt, the government allocated 336,862 million dinars (about $1.15 billion) for the development of

the Kurdish areas. Most of this amount went to transportation and communications, the industrial sector, services and construction, and other
projects. In addition, the government has already begun the implementation of the following projects: the building of homes and new villages for
victims of the fighting; the opening of many hospitals, nursing schools,
medical centers, public clinics, schools and anti-illiteracy centers; the construction of bridges, roads and telecommunications systems; and the construction of tourist hotels and other summer resort projects.[177]

In the industrial sector, the government has established carpet-
weaving centers, a dairy factory, a carpentry factory, a sugar mill, a cement factory, a tobacco blending factory, poultry farms, a wool textile
mill, and a canning factory. The government passed law No. 90 in 1975
which limited land ownership in the autonomous area and about 2,747,937
dunums of land were distributed to 91,433 landless Kurdish peasant
families, and 378 cooperative farms were established in the area, in addition to over 400 agricultural cooperative associations.

The student enrollment jumped from 112,731 in 1974–75 to 332,549 in
the 1978–79 academic year, while the number of schools rose from 474
primary schools in 1968 to 1582 in 1977, and the number of secondary
schools from 38 in 1968 to 141 in 1977.[178] The allocations for investment in
the Kurdish area rose similarly, from 3.5 million dinars ($11.5 million) to
364 million dinars in 1979. The percentage of funds allocated for investment in the Kurdish area also rose from 3.1 percent in 1967 to 12 percent in
1979. The annual allocation for the agricultural sector rose from 579,000
dinars in 1967 to 46 million in 1979, with the percentage of total allocations rising from 1.9 percent in 1967 to 9.3 percent in 1979. The industrial
sector's share rose from 675,000 dinars in 1967 to 79 million in 1979, with
the proportion of total allocations rising from 1.8 percent in 1967 to 6.3
percent in 1979. In the construction and services sector, allocations
showed the same steep increases, from 1.2 million dinars in 1967 to 68 million dinars in 1979, raising the percentage of total allocations from 5.6
percent in 1967 to 13.8 percent in 1979. The area of medical services also
witnessed a dramatic change. The number of doctors rose from 91 in 1967
to 216 in 1977, and hospitals were built in several areas, including Arbil,
Ruwanduz, Koianjaq, Salahal-din and Sulaymaniyya.[179]

Special interest was also accorded for strategic as well as development purposes, to transport and communications. A wide network of
roads has been built to cover the region, linking the principal and secondary towns, the outlying villages and tourist areas. During 1977–78 1,400
kms. of new roads were opened in this region. The 1978 plan allocated
102,695,000 dinars for the transport and communication sectors. The re-

gion's tourist potential has also attracted governmental attention. Many hotels, summer camps, tourist markets, and places of entertainment have been built to absorb the large number of summer visitors.[180]

In the 1977 annual development plan, $2.4 billion was allocated for the region, and in 1978, it was increased by 20 percent.[181] In 1979, the region was allocated about $3.1 billion, while in 1980, it was about $3.04 billion out of a total budget of $46.2 billion. The geographic distribution of the development projects by the central government and the autonomous administration indicate that the "per capita share of the projects in the area is higher than the national per capita share."[182]


## THE NEW KURDISH OPPOSITION


Following the collapse of his movement, Mulla Mustafa went into exile in Iran and then to the United States in June 1976, where he underwent treatment for lung cancer. He died less than three years later on March 1, 1979, and with his death a unique chapter in Kurdish history was closed. Barzani's last years revealed the tragic end of a man who became a myth in his own lifetime. He refused to write his memoirs because he felt he had not succeeded in achieving his goal. He told a friend, "If I had succeeded, it would have been different; if I had accomplished something for my people it would have been different. But I am a failure."[183] A similar perception was revealed when he told an interviewer his view of his life: "Looking back, I suppose most men have some regret on what they might have done or what they should not have done, or what they left unaccomplished. I am one of these men."[184] However, Barzani told the present writer that the Kurdish nationalist movement "does not die because I am finished" and added that one's actions are determined by what appears to be the right thing at a certain time and place.

Barzani's departure and the extent of the defeat created a vacuum among Kurdish opponents of the Iraqi government. The KDP broke into several factions. One faction headed by Habib Muhammad Karim and Dara Tawfiq returned to Baghdad. Another faction led by Mahmud Uthman has broken with Barzani and formed the KDP Preparatory Committee, which criticized both the Baath and the Barzani leadership. A third faction remained loyal to Barzani's sons Idris and Massud, who were surrounded by a small number of intellectuals led by Muhammad Mahmud Abd al-Rahman. This faction established the KDP's Provisional Command (KDPPC) in November 1975 but did not begin any operations until May 26, 1976. This group says that it began its "armed struggle" in response to the government's policy of "deportation and Arabization." In August 1976 it held its conference and called for "partisan warfare" to be waged in Iraq and insisted that its activities must reach the cities, including Baghdad.[185]

The activities of this group, however, were limited by the small number of Kurds remaining in Iran under its leadership (around 30,000) Iranian restrictions, and disillusionment of a number of Kurds with their leadership and its connections with the Shah, Israel, and the CIA. This group advocated recognition of the Kurdish right to self-determination but stressed that the defined solution is autonomy within Iraq and cooperation with a united progressive front, and calls for an end to all past ties.

A fourth group, the Patriotic Union of Kurdistan (PUK) was also formed in November 1975. This group was the first to put Kurdish partisans into the field. It received the backing of Ali al-Askari, who was widely respected as one of the Pesh Mergas bravest and most able commanders. This group vigorously opposed the Iraqi government's policies and published reports of guerrilla activities against it. The PUK advocates Marxist principles and dubs the Iraqi regime as "fascist." It further condemns the Barzani leadership as "reactionary," and calls for a "genuinely democratic government" in Iraq which would grant true autonomy.[186] The Kurdish movement is viewed as a part of the overall anti-imperialist and anti-Zionist movement. The PUK claims to have about a thousand men in the mountains of Iraq and is believed to be backed by Syria.[187]

A small number of spontaneous anti-government incidents began to occur in the summer of 1975 and 1976, involving people who "had escaped to the mountains", or who "oppose forced relocation."[188] The organized military operations are believed to have occurred in 1977 and were reportedly financed by Syria (PUK) and Iran (KDPPC).[189]

The PUK, however, initiated contacts with the Iraqi government in April 1977 through Ali al-Askari who presented a working paper to the government through Saddam Husain's brother Barzan to reach a solution to the problem in the wake of U.S. backed attempts to reach a Middle East settlement.[190] The points for negotiation were to include the issues of the future status of Kirkuk, an end to deportation and Arabization, and an elected legislative council for Kurdistan. The note declared that the conflict between the Arab and Kurdish nationalist movements was "a conflict among brothers and allies" and therefore the solution must be reached through "constructive dialogue, criticism and self-criticism" and in the avoidance of "sharp contradictions." It went on to ask the government to show its confidence in the "progressive Kurdish forces" and to grant them the right to administer the autonomous area and to protect the borders by patriotic units "opposed to imperialism and reaction" and in Arab-Kurdish brotherhood.

These efforts led nowhere, and the PUK sought to increase its attacks on Iraqi targets. The most serious clashes, however, appear to have occurred between the Barzani-led KDP faction and the PUK. Mulla Mustafa's view of Talibani was that he was an "agent for everybody,"[191] and this view appears to have been shared by his children.

In July 1976 a PUK statement charged that Mulla Mustafa's supporters in Turkish Kurdistan had attacked and killed several of their men.[192] Clashes between the two sides, near the Iraqi-Turkish borders led, in the Fall of 1978 to the killing of a number of Kurdish fighters including two prominent PUK leaders, Ali al-Askari and Khalid Said.[193] Iraqi leaders admitted that a small number of infiltrations, kidnappings, attacks on isolated police and army posts had taken place but they maintained that these acts were few in number and were primarily committed by infiltrators from across the borders.[194] The government revealed that these incidents were indeed isolated and that the government was in firm control of the region.

The turmoil in Iran and the collapse of the Shah's regime provided a new opportunity for the Iraqi Kurdish leadership, particularly as relations between the secular Arab nationalist government in Baghdad and the Islamic government in Tehran deteriorated sharply. The quarrel between the two regimes was deep and complex and had its roots in historic, territorial, ideological, strategic and political differences.

Talibani's forces near the Turkish-Iranian border began a number of concentrated attacks on isolated Iranian police posts to capture arms and ammunition in late 1978 and early 1979. The KUP was bolstered in the first months of 1979 by the arrival of about a thousand Iraqi communists fleeing a government crackdown following a discovery of ICP cells in the armed forces.[195] The Provisional Command forces also benefited from the collapse of governmental authority in Iran and began to strengthen their ties with the religious forces in Iran and subsequently with the Khumaini regime. Both groups expressed their solidarity and support for the Islamic government in Iran. Talibani addressed telegrams to Khumaini and Bani-Sadr proclaiming that "all of our forces are at the disposal of the Islamic Revolution of Iran."[196]

The Barzanis appear to have formed a stronger relationship with the Khumaini regime than the one established by Talibani. The Iranian government provided the Provisional Command with radio access and is said to have warned Talibani, several times, to "desist from hatching plots in the Uramanat region and to abide by his statement supporting the Islamic Republic."[197] The Provisional Command's support for the Khumaini regime in its attacks against leftist Kurdish forces in Iran and its cooperation with religious opponents of the Iraqi regime (al-Dawah party) helped to cement the ties between the two groups.

Relations with the Talibani faction were less cordial. It is true that Tehran welcomed Talibani's opposition to the Iraqi government, but it was less certain about his ideology, and its close ties to some of the Iranian Marxist groups.

Syria and Iran, while united in their opposition to Iraq, disagreed on the opposition forces they wanted to support. Syria appeared to be backing a loose coalition of Talibani's PUK, Nasirite elements, pro-Syrian Baathists and the ICP. While Tehran backed al-Dawah party led by Hojjat al-Islam Muhammad al-Hakim, an Iraqi Shii religious leader who was Khumaini's choice for leadership in Iraq and the Barzani-led KDPPC. Tehran was reported to have intercepted arms shipments sent by Syria to Talibani.[198]

The two factions continued throughout 1979–80 to charge the other with waging a "fratricidal war" and to attack each other's forces.[199] Nevertheless, the deterioration of Iraqi-Iranian relations allowed the two sides to escalate their activities and infiltration into Iraq. The two groups claim to have engaged in acts of sabotage against oil facilities, kidnapped Polish, Algerian, and Yugoslav engineers, attacked army and police units and assassinated pro-government Kurdish leaders.[290] Reports appearing in the Western media in the summer of 1979 stated that Massud al-Barzani had returned to Iraqi Kurdistan with 5000 of his men to resume the struggle against the government.[201] Although these reports appear to be highly exaggerated, there is little doubt that these groups had intensified their activities.

In a press conference on July 20, 1980, Saddam Husain admitted that "bullets are being fired in the North" but maintained that the number of these bullets was much lower than the ones fired during "tribal struggles" before the Baath came to power. He indicated that they were being fired by persons instigated by Iran or infiltrating across the Turkish borders. He expressed pride in the autonomy formula and insisted that five or ten infiltrations do not pose a problem because the people of the autonomous region are "able to defend themselves and this is the real victory. It is not to have the army control any area of Iraq."[202]

Following Barzani's death and upheaval in Iran, the KDPPC sought a thorough reappraisal of its strategy, leadership, and organization. Consequently, the ninth KDP congress was held in Iran in November 1979.[203] However, instead of ending the schisms existing in the movement, the congress only helped to widen the gaps. The conflict between the tribal elements and the intelligentsia manifested itself again.

The intellectuals, led by many of Mulla Mustafa's closest aides, including Politburo member Muhammad Mahmud Abd al-Rahman, were unwilling to accept the leadership of Idris and Massud as they had accepted that of Mulla Mustafa. Massud is believed to have tried to reach an understanding between this group and the traditionalist elements who backed Idris. There were also unconfirmed reports in the Fall of 1980 of conflicts between Idris and Massud over the latter's close collaboration with the Khumaini government.[204]

In addition to the serious internal rivalries and divisions, the Kurdish organization faces a more serious problem with Iranian Kurds. In the hope of exploiting the renewed Iran-Iraq tension, the KDP leaders say that because of their eighteen years of fighting their cause takes precedence over that of the Iranian Kurds.[205] In response, the Iranian Kurds accused them of being stooges of Khumaini. Serious clashes have erupted between the Barzani forces and those of the Iranian KDP and its leftist allies.

Jalal Talibani's PUK is still no match for the Barzanis despite the fact that it was the first to put Kurdish partisans into the field. The Barzanis remain by far the stronger of the two forces because of tribal connections and military position. Talibani's forces however seem to be much better organized than those of the Barzani. A third group appears to have been formed in 1979 under the leadership of Dr. Mahmud Uthman formerly of the KDP Preparatory Committee. This group is now organized under the title of the United Socialist Party of Kurdistan and appears to have gravitated in the direction of forming a loose alliance with the Barzani led KDP against the PUK.

Whatever the military capabilities of the three groups, it is unlikely that they will pose a serious threat to the Iraqi regime, short of a major upheaval in Iraq or the region. Their reliance on outside forces to support their struggle placed them at a serious disadvantage. These forces seem to have cooperated with the Kurds as long as they serve its interests. Past experiences have taught the Kurds that the future is not likely to be much different from the past.

# conclusion

The defeat of Mulla Mustafa al-Barzani's Kurdish rebellion by the Iraqi Baath government brought to an end the Barzani type of Kurdish struggle for independence in Iraq. The government's victory and the quick collapse of Barzani's movement came as a surprise to many outside observers who held the view that it was impossible for any Iraqi government to survive without reaching a truce with Mulla Mustafa. This assessment has led many to attribute Barzani's defeat solely to the Iran-Iraq agreement reached in Algiers. Such analysis ignores the political and military achievements scored by the Iraqi government which were the major factors that brought about the collapse of the traditional structure of the Barzani regime.

The suppression of the Kurdish nationalist movements by strong central governments in Iran and Turkey during the first half of the twentieth century left only Iraq as the arena for Kurdish nationalistic activities. The weakness of former Iraqi governments, the geographic terrain of Iraqi Kurdistan, and the high percentage of Kurds in the country made it possible for a de facto functional autonomy to exist in some of the Kurdish areas of northern Iraq. This situation, while allowing for the creation of a Kurdish intelligentsia, at the same time preserved the Kurdish tribal-religious feudal structure and retarded modernization.

Mulla Mustafa al-Barzani, exploiting existing conditions, monopolized the leadership of the Kurdish movement. He benefited from the traditional leadership of the Barzani family and from his appeal to powerful tribal allies and some sectors of the urban Kurdish intelligentsia. Nevertheless, the socioeconomic makeup of the Kurdish leadership alienated three important categories among the Kurds who opposed the movement. First, there were the traditional and tribal enemies of the Barzanis, such as the Herkis, Surchis, Zibaris, and Bardosts. Second, there were the educated Kurds who held high government positions or who had done well in business and consequently were hostile or indifferent to the Kurdish movement. Third, there were the leftist intellectuals and Marxists who viewed with suspicion and disfavor the traditional leadership, which they considered backward, oppressive, and reactionary. Despite the challenge of these groups, the traditional leadership, particularly under Barzani, was able to maintain and expand its authority, bolstered by its tribal alliances and its military capability.

Direct confrontation between the Iraqi government and the Kurdish movement became inevitable following the overthrow of the Hashimite monarchy. The new regime emphasized the need to create a strong central government and advocated Arab nationalism to supersede local and parochial feelings. The threat of direct control by Baghdad instilled a sense of unity among the Kurds. The tribal and traditional elements viewed the central authority as a threat to their way of life, and the secular nationalists saw it as a threat to their goal of establishing an autonomous or separate Kurdish entity.

The instability of the Iraqi regime since 1958, the strong and able leadership of Barzani, and the support given to the Kurdish leadership by various foreign countries antagonistic to the regime allowed the Kurdish fighters to withstand attempts to subdue them. The failure of the central government to defeat the Kurdish revolt became a major source of instability and contributed in no small measure to the overthrow of three Iraqi governments since 1958.

However, the situation began to change with the return of the Baath party to power in 1968. Advocating what is considered to be perhaps the most attractive ideology in the Middle East, the Baath combined the appealing principles of Arab unity and socialism. The Baath leaders learned a lesson from their short experiences in power in 1963. Tough, pragmatic and secular in outlook, they were convinced of the righteousness of their cause and determined to make Iraq both a model, if not a leader of a modern state in the Arab world. Beset with social, political, and economic difficulties, the Baath party realized that the establishment of a stable regime had to be ensured before its ideology could be transformed into a reality.

Guided by their socialist and Arab nationalist ideology, the Baathists decided to pursue a strategy which would create the necessary prerequisite for stability. They implemented measures to ward off threats to the regime, put an end to inter-party factionalism, offered to cooperate with the Iraqi Communist party, and made generous and far-reaching proposals to the Kurdish, Turkoman, and Assyrian minorities. They also maintained that an ideology consisting of socialist and secular principles might help to resolve the problem of minorities within the country.

The Baathist leadership, from the very start realized that a solution had to be found to the Kurdish problem which weakened Iraq both internally and externally. The proposals to the Kurds, as expressed in the Manifesto of March 11, 1970, and in the Autonomy Law of March 11, 1974, acknowledged the existence of the Kurdish people as a distinct national group within Iraq possessing their own language and culture. It further recognized the existence of a "Kurdish area," which by virtue of the majority of its population gave it the designation of Iraqi Kurdistan. The Autonomy Law also granted a number of national rights to the Kurds and offered them the opportunity to run their own affairs locally through autonomous government organs.

At the same time, however, this Autonomy Law limited Kurdish control over natural resources and placed the security apparatus of the autonomous area under central control. The law made it clear that the Iraqi government considered the Kurdistan area and its people to be an indivisible part of Iraq.

Misled by promises of aid from external sources, Mulla Mustafa, in his drive for an independent Kurdish state or in the establishment of a Kurdish-Arab confederation in Iraq, was overly ambitious in his expectations of government reception to his demands. He insisted that the Kurdistan region should include Kirkuk and its oil resources and that the Kurds have the authority to maintain their own army and conduct their own foreign relations. The government rejected these proposals and the subsequent fighting culminated in the defeat of his movement.

After the collapse of the Barzani movement, the Iraqi government followed a policy that combined severity with leniency in dealing with the Kurds. Tough security measures were adopted in which thousands of Kurds were deported and resettled in Arab areas, leading to the creation of a strategic border zone cleared of all Kurds.

At the same time, aware that the solution to the Kurdish problem lies beyond the achievement of military and political victory, the Baathist leadership has tried to win the support and loyalty of the Kurds through a peaceful process of social and economic reconstruction. Baathist leader Zayd Haydar stated that the "final and peaceful solution to the Kurdish question lies in bringing development to the farthest Kurdish villages and in making sure that the benefits of the socialist revolution reach all the people and giving the Kurds a stake in the economy."[1] This social and political integration is seen by the Iraqi leaders as the only means to resolve the Kurdish problem.

The government has implemented major economic development pro-

grams designed to appease the Kurds by transforming the economic structure of the Kurdish area and improving their conditions. This would be
achieved by agrarian reform and the establishment of cooperative and
collective farms. New school and housing projects have already been initiated, and public works projects expanded.[2]

The government kept its promise of granting autonomy. During his
visit to the North in 1976, Saddam Husain declared:

> When the political leadership decided to establish autonomy in the
> northern area, its decision was not incidental or circumstantial. We, the
> Iraqis, have to prove to the Arab nation and the whole world that our
> faith in autonomy is deep rooted in our conscience and that development
> of the autonomous region should be in keeping with the development of
> the rest of Iraq.[3]

As *al-Thawra al-Arabiyya* put it, the regime is determined:

> • to draw as much and as fast as possible from the Kurdish tide mov-
> ing in the direction of the government following the disillusionment with
> the Barzani leadership;
> • to strengthen the ties to the masses;
> • to erase from our minds the fact that we have accomplished what
> has been accomplished for our Kurdish people under the pressure of spe-
> cial circumstances;
> • to entrench and activate the self-rule institutions, through the real-
> ization of development programs in the North, the welcoming of Kurd-
> ish returnees and the creation of a tourist environment in the North in
> order to get the Kurdish citizen to support order and stability.[4]

Saddam Husain has continued his efforts to rally Kurdish support
for the autonomy process in the Kurdish areas. During several tours of
the Kurdish areas in March and August 1979 he said that the Baath party
was open to all Iraqis without discrimination.[5] In August 1979, following
his elevation to the presidency, he offered a special amnesty to Kurdish
militants outside the country, urging them to lay down their arms and return to Iraq. Many Kurds, especially those in Iran, responded favorably,
and some 10,000 Kurds, including members of the Jaf tribes, returned in
the fall of 1979. The returnees included five prominent Kurdish leaders
who were closely associated with Mulla Mustafa and who were appointed
as counselors to the Kurdish affairs bureau of the RCC. These were Mulla
Mustafa's son Sabir and his cousin Shaikh Uthman Shaikh Ahmad al-
Barzani, former KDP Central Committee member, Abdallah al-Pishdari,
former KDP Politburo member, Muhammad Jamil Rozbayani, two former key military and political leaders, Abd al-Wahhab al-Atrushi and

Rashid al-Sindi, and Haidar Ali who was responsible for student affairs.

On January 1, 1980, the RCC expanded the authority of the chairmen of the legislative and executive councils of the Kurdish region by granting them ministerial powers. Shortly afterward, the government ratified the laws for the election of a National Assembly for Iraq and a Legislative Council for the Kurdish region. The elections for the National Assembly were held in June 1980 with a membership of 250 for four years. Twenty-nine Kurds were elected from the autonomous region and several others were elected from outside it.[6]

In August 1980, during a tour of the Kurdish region, Saddam Husain reiterated earlier promises to continue and deepen the autonomous rule in Kurdistan. On September 20, 1980, elections were held for the Legislative Council where 701,000 voters elected fifty deputies from among 194 candidates. The majority of the deputies came from occupational groups such as teachers, lawyers, engineers, and farmers. The elections, the first to be held in Iraq since the fall of the monarchy, were part of the government's plans for internal reconstruction of the country.

The fall of Mulla Mustafa has ended the costliest war in Iraq's modern history. The government now felt freer to pursue its objectives at home and abroad. Externally, the end of the war meant that Iraq is able to play a more effective role in regional affairs, especially in the Gulf region and in the nonaligned movement. Iraq has also embarked on major programs for industrial and agricultural development and for improving the standard of living of its people. It has also embarked on modernizing and strengthening its armed forces by purchasing weapons from European countries while continuing to purchase Soviet weapons. Iraq's policy of cooperation with Arab neighbors and the expansion of relations with the Third World and with European and Latin American countries has revealed its growing role as a regional power and active member of the nonaligned movement. This is demonstrated in Iraq's decision to host the Baghdad summit conference, using it as a forum to explain its Arab and regional policies, and in the decision to hold the non-aligned summit conference in Baghdad in 1982.

The granting of autonomy to the Kurds and ambitious development schemes have strengthened Iraq's hand in its confrontation with the new regime in Iran. The conflict over the Shatt al-Arab and the land border areas was sharpened by ideological differences between an Arab nationalist and socialist regime in Baghdad and a fundamentalist Islamic regime in Tehran. The Iranian leadership made no secret of its intention to export its Islamic revolution to Iraq and has supported some Kurdish and religious opponents to the Iraqi regime. Iran has accused Iraq of supporting

Arab, Kurdish, Baluchi, and Persian opponents to the Khumaini regime. Iraq has also been able to take advantage of Iran's rejection of Kurdish demands for autonomy in Iran to improve its standing with its Kurds and counteract Barzani and Talibani propaganda by pointing to their ties with the Khumaini regime.

Broadly speaking, Iraq has proved in practice to recognize Kurdish national rights to a greater extent than either Turkey or Iran. However, the Iraqi resort to force to resolve the Kurdish question has aroused suspicion in Kurdish nationalist circles.

The Iraqi experience has shown that a separatist movement cannot possibly win in a landlocked country if it faces a strong central government. To survive, such a movement must have strong foreign support, cooperation with Kurds in the neighboring countries, and allies from within the country. However, the experiences of the Kurds in Iran, Iraq, and Turkey have shown that the Kurds cannot expect massive external support and have to rely primarily on themselves. This reality was reflected poignantly in former Secretary of State Henry Kissinger's response to a Congressional Committee seeking information on his role in the Kurdish movement. He stated that "Covert action should not be confused with missionary work." Kissinger encouraged the Kurdish leadership to escalate its demands against the Baath government with promises of American military and financial aid with a commitment not to abandon the Kurds or to allow Iran to do so. Kissinger's actions in this episode appear to have been motivated by his "strategic" design in destabilizing the Baathist regime, in strengthening the Shah's role as a United States surrogate in the Gulf region and in protecting Israel's interests rather than by any concern for the fate of the Kurdish people.[7] External forces may be willing to help the Kurds to weaken or undermine an undesirable regime, but will not support them to gain independence.

History has also shown that cooperation among the Kurds of all neighboring countries is even more difficult to achieve than cooperation of Kurdish factions within one country. Iranian KDP leader Qasimlu has rightly pointed out in his study on Iranian Kurdistan that while similar social, political and economic conditions establish certain "common characteristics" among the Kurds in various parts of Kurdistan, the importance of these similarities should not be exaggerated.[8] He went on to say that it is not only the borders which separate the Kurds but also the complex influences to which they have been subjected after living so long in those countries.

The current situation where Kurdish opponents to the Iranian regime supported by Iraq and Kurdish opponents of the Iraqi regime supported by Iran reveals the complexities and difficulties confronting Kurdish nationalism. Attempts to carry the struggle in one country while hoping to gain the support or at least the neutrality of neighboring countries has not been successful in the past and is unlikely to succeed in the future.

There is indeed little reason to entertain the idea that the states of the region or the superpowers might be tempted to use the Kurds again to serve their own purposes, if the need should arise. In any case, the success of such a venture would be unlikely due to the security measures at the disposal of the Iraqi government to prevent the reoccurrence of a Kurdish uprising, and the hesitancy of regional powers to become involved in aiding a Kurdish nationalist movement which is likely to promote separatist instability in their own countries. Thus the Kurds are unlikely to engage in another serious attempt to achieve independence by violence. Today most Kurds seem to have opted for integration with Iraq. This will at least assure them the enjoyment of a national and cultural identity and the opportunity to achieve social and economic progress. The long-term success of the autonomy process will depend to a large extent on the ability of Kurdish nationalists to come to terms with the Iraqi state and autonomous institutions. This may well eventually take place, since the government has assured the Kurds of maintaining and strengthening the autonomy process — and provided they are satisfied with their participation in the socioeconomic and political life of the country.

# ΝΟΤΕS

## CHAPTER 1 — ORIGINS OF THE KURDISH QUESTION IN IRAQ

1. For the text of the memorandum, see Abd al-Razzaq al-Hassani, *Tarikh al-Wazarat al-Iraqiyya* (History of Iraqi Cabinets) (Beirut: Dar al-Kutub Press, 1974), 3, pp. 323-30.

2. For details on this debate, see Majid Khadduri, *Republican Iraq* (London: Oxford University Press, 1969), pp. 1-10.

3. C. J. Edmonds, *Kurds, Turks and Arabs* (London: Oxford University Press, 1957), p. 3. See also Shakir Khasbak, *Al-Kurd wa al-Masalah al-Kurdiyya* (The Kurds and the Kurdish Question) (Baghdad: Al-Thaqafa Press), pp. 14-15. Extreme Kurdish nationalists also include as part of Kurdistan Liwa al-Iskandaraun in Turkey, al-Jazira in Syria, parts of the Arab-Persian Gulf, and parts of Armenia. See Jemal Nebez, *About the Kurdish Problem* (National Union of Kurdish Students in Europe, 1969), p. 1.

4. Edmund Ghareeb, *Al-Haraka al-Qawmiyya al-Kurdiyya* (The Kurdish Nationalist Movement) (Beirut: Dar al-Nahar, 1973), p. 10.

5. Muhammad Amin Zaki, *Tarikh al-Kurd wa Kurdistan* (History of the Kurds and Kurdistan), trans. by Muhammad Awni (Cairo: Al-Saada Press, 1939), pp. 23-25. Abd al-Rahman Qasimlu, *Kurdistan wa al-Akrad* (Kurdistan and the Kurds) (Beirut: Lebanese Foundation for Publications, 1970), p. 25. Jalal Talibani, *Kurdistan wa al-Haraka al-Qawmiyya al-Kurdiyya* (Kurdistan and the Kurdish Nationalist Movement), 2nd ed. (Beirut: Dar al-Talia, 1971), pp. 40-41.

6. The mullas have played an important role in leading the Kurdish uprisings and movements since the late 19th century. For further information on the social structure of the Kurds see Ghareeb, *Al-Haraka*, pp. 13-15.

7. Hassan Arfa, *The Kurds: An Historical and Political Study* (London: Oxford University Press, 1966), p. 24.

8. Derek Kinnane, *The Kurds and Kurdistan* (London: Oxford University Press, 1924), p. 14.

9. Mukarram Talibani, Minister of Irrigation and Social Planning in Iraq and a member of the Iraqi Communist party, considered this a major factor because of the many

Kurds who worked in Ottoman consulates and embassies abroad (the writer's interview, Baghdad, November 20, 1976). Talibani lost his post in the spring of 1979, following a government crackdown on the Iraqi Communist party. See also Arshak Safrastian, *Kurds and Kurdistan* (London: Harvill Press, 1948), pp. 49–50; Basil Nikitine, *Al-Akrad* (The Kurds) (Beirut: Dar al-Rawi, 1958), p. 47; J. Talibani, *Kurdistan,* pp. 67–84.

10. Interview with Mukarram Talibani, November 20, 1976.

11. J. Talibani, *Kurdistan,* pp. 95–97.

12. Safrastian, *Kurds,* p. 77.

13. Arfa, *The Kurds,* pp. 29–30.

14. Qasimlu, *Kurdistan wa al-Akrad,* p. 64.

15. Thomas Bois, *al-Akrad* (The Kurds) (Beirut: Khayats, 1966), p. 147.

16. Joyce Blau, *Le Probleme Kurde: Essai sociologique et historique* (Brussels: Centre pour l'Etude des Problemes du Monde Musulman Contemporain, 1963), p. 38.

17. For a full discussion of this phase of the Kurdish movement in Turkey, see Chris Kutschera, *Le Mouvement National Kurde* (Paris: Flammarion, 1979), pp. 339–42.

18. *Ibid.,* p. 342.

19. Edmund Ghareeb, "The Growing Leftist Forces in Turkey," *Daily Star* (Beirut), May 19, 1971. Some of the guerrilla acts included the kidnappings of the Israeli consul-general, wealthy Turks, and U.S. servicemen; bank robberies and bombings of several local and foreign businesses; and the attempted kidnappings of an American AID official and the local president of Coca-Cola.

20. David Hirst, "Turkey Plays Waiting Game to Counter Premature Revolt," *The Guardian,* December 6, 1979.

21. Voice of the Turkish Communist party (clandestine radio, VOTCP), Foreign Broadcast Information Service (FBIS), September 19, 1978; February 14, 1979; February 17, 1979.

22. *8 Days* (London), September 22, 1979.

23. VOTCP, FBIS, August 31, 1979.

24. *Washington Post,* January 3, 1980.

25. *New York Times,* June 11, 1980.

26. Georgie Anne Geyer, "Turks Caught in Classic Ideological Struggle," *Columbia Missourian,* May 22, 1980.

27. Kinnane, *The Kurds and Kurdistan,* p. 32.

28. Arfa, *The Kurds,* p. 78.

29. William Eagleton, *The Kurdish Republic of 1946* (London: Oxford University Press, 1963), p. 14.

30. Kutschera, *Le Mouvement National Kurde,* p. 240.

31. *Ibid.,* pp. 344–47. A pro-Jalal Talibani Kurdish leader whom I interviewed in Washington, March 1976, also charged Barzani with arresting and executing not only some of the leaders of the IKDP, but also Dr. Chwan of the Turkish KDP. Barzani apparently believed that the Kurds needed an outside ally and could not fight on two or three fronts at the same time. As a result, his struggle took precedence over the others.

32. The writer's interview with an Iraqi Kurdish official, Baghdad, July 1974.

33. Kutschera, *Le Mouvement National Kurde,* p. 348.

34. The writer's interview with a pro-J. Talibani Kurdish leader, Washington, March 1976; see also *8 Days,* September 15, 1979.

35. See the "Constitution of the Islamic Republic of Iran," *Middle East Journal* 34 (Spring 1980): 184–204.

36. *Al-Hawadith* (London), January 26, 1979.

37. *Al-Majallah* (London), May 24, 1980.

38. *Events,* March 9, 1979; see also FBIS, January 8, 1979.

39. *Middle East International* (London), March 2, 1979.

40. *Washington Post,* March 2, 1979.

41. Al-Majallah, May 24, 1980.

42. *Washington Post,* March 2, 1979.

43. "What is Happening in Kurdistan?" statement by Komeleh, August 25, 1979.

44. Tehran Radio, FBIS, March 20, 1979.

45. The events described here and below can be traced in the chronology of the *Middle East Journal* (Summer 1979).

46. *The Washington Star,* September 16, 1979.

47. See FBIS, July and August 1980.

48. "For a Peaceful Solution to the Kurdish Question in Iran," published in *Al-Hurriyya* (Beirut), September 3, 1979, pp. 48–49.

49. Chronology of *Middle East Journal* 38, no. 4.

50. *Al-Nahar/Arab Report and Memo,* September 3, 1979. Hereafter, *Al-Nahar.*

51. Chronology of *Middle East Journal,* 38, no. 4.

52. *Al-Nahar,* September 3, 1979.

53. *Washington Star,* September 16, 1979.

54. *Le Monde,* October 7–8, 1979.

55. Interview with Defense Minister Mustafa Chamran in *Jomhuriye Eslami,* FBIS, October 12, 1979.

56. Tehran Radio, FBIS, October 12, 1979.

57. *Ibid.*

58. FBIS, October 29, 1979.

59. Agence France Presse, October 27, 1979.

60. *Al-Nahar,* November 3, 1979.

61. *Washington Post,* November 23, 1979.

62. This and the account of Qasimlu's reaction that follows appeared in *Le Monde,* November 22, 1979.

63. FBIS, November 26, 1979.

64. *Al-Khalij Times,* November 30, 1979.

65. *Le Monde,* December 18, 1979.

66. FBIS, January 2, 1980.

67. *Washington Star,* January 7, 1980.

68. *Al-Nahar,* January 17, 1980.

69. *Al-Sharq al-Awsat,* January 13, 1980; see also *Le Monde,* December 18, 1979.

70. *Christian Science Monitor,* April 1, 1980.

71. *Tehran Times,* March 3, 1980.

72. For this account of the rejection of the KDP "autonomy plan" see FBIS, March 7, 1980.

73. *Washington Post,* May 5, 1980; see also *Christian Science Monitor,* April 1, 1980.

74. BBC broadcast, May 15, 1980.

75. FBIS, May 29, 1980.

76. NVOI radio broadcast, September 15, 1979. See also FBIS, September 19, 1979.

77. *Al-Thawra,* April 3, 1980. See also FBIS, April 7, 1980.

78. The writer's interview with a high-ranking U.S. State Department official, Washington, D.C., July 1980.

79. The Daily Telegraph, October 1, 1979. See also statements by Iranian Deputy Prime Minister Sadeq Tabatabai, FBIS, October 10, 1980, and September 4, 1980. See also *Tariq al-Shab,* February 7, 1980.

80. FBIS, February 5, 1980.

81. *L'Espresso* (Rome), December 23, 1979.

82. FBIS, February 5, 1980.

## CHAPTER 2 – THE IRAQI KURDISH QUESTION
## BEFORE THE ACCESSION OF THE BAATH PARTY

1. See Philip W. Ireland, *Iraq: A Study in Political Development* (London: Jonathan Cape, 1937), pp. 63–73.

2. For an account of the revolt, see Abd al-Razzaq al-Hasani, *Tarikh al-Iraq al-Siyassi al-Hadith* (Political History of Modern Iraq), 2nd ed. (Beirut: Dar al-Kutub Press, 1975), pp. 88–158.

3. Mahmud Durra, *Al-Qadiyya al-Kurdiyya* (The Kurdish Case) (Beirut: Dar al-Talia, 1966), pp. 113 and 147.

4. According to al-Hasani, the British government pressured the Iraqi government to give the Mosul oil concession to the Turkish Petroleum Company, later known as the Iraq Oil Company, under the threat of separating Mosul from Iraq. See al-Hasani, *Tarikh al-Iraq,* 1, p. 30.

5. C. J. Edmonds, *Kurds, Turks and Arabs* (London: Oxford University Press, 1957), p. 398.

6. Nikitine, *Al-Akrad,* p. 218.

7. Al-Hasani, *Tarikh al-Iraq,* 1, pp. 262–63.

8. Durra, *Al-Qadiyya al-Kurdiyya,* p. 146.

9. See a statement by Nuri al-Said accompanying his letter of resignation (April 19, 1944) in al-Hasani, *Tarikh al-Wazarat,* 5, p. 311.

10. Al-Hasani, *Tarikh al-Iraq,* 3, p. 267.

11. Stephen Longrigg, *Iraq 1900–1950: A Political, Social and Economic History* (London: Oxford University Press, 1953), pp. 193 and 196.

12. According to some Iraqis, Shaikh Mahmud was encouraged to revolt by the British. See Durra, *Al-Qadiyya al-Kurdiyya,* p. 157.

13. Qasimlu, *Kurdistan wa al-Akrad,* p. 95.

14. J. Talibani, *Kurdistan,* pp. 112–14.

15. Kinnane, *The Kurds,* p. 40.

16. Durra, *Al-Qadiyya al-Kurdiyya,* p. 163.

17. The writer's interview with Ubaidullah al-Barzani, Mulla Mustafa's eldest son, Baghdad, April 1979. Ubaidullah, who is a minister in the Iraqi cabinet and was recently elected to the Iraqi parliament, began to oppose his father's policies in the mid-1960s.

18. Ubaidullah al-Barzani told the writer that Shaikh Ahmad had intended to cooperate with the government because he did not want to oppose an Islamic government head by a Hashimite. Ahmad's initial willingness to cooperate with Faisal's government was reflected in his refusal to respond to requests for aid from Shaikh Mahmud because the government was "Arab and Muslim" and it was his "Islamic duty to obey it." See also the interview with Kurdish leader Nuri Shawis, cited in Kutschera, *Le Mouvement National Kurde,* p. 111.

19. Longrigg, *Iraq 1900–1950,* p. 194.

20. The writer's interview with M. Talibani, November 20, 1976.

21. Ghareeb, *Al-Haraka,* pp. 35–37.

22. See al-Hasani, *Tarikh al-Wazarat,* 6, p. 213.

23. *The Times* (London), "Unrest in Kurdistan," April 11, 1946.

24. Longrigg, *Iraq 1900–1950,* p. 327. For details on the Barzanis' recurring conflicts with other Kurdish tribes such as the Rikanis, the Zibaris, the Shirwanis, and the Baradosts, see Ghareeb, *Al-Haraka,* pp. 25–28.

25. William Eagleton, *The Kurdish Republic,* pp. 77, 112. Eagleton quotes Barzani as saying, "It wasn't the Kurds who were defeated by Iran, but the Soviets who were defeated by the British and the Americans." See also Archibald Roosevelt, "The Kurdish Republic of Mahabad," *Middle East Journal* (July 1947) 1:225.

26. Longrigg, *Iraq 1900–1950,* pp. 234–36; Maruf Jiyawuk, *Masat Barzan al-Mazlumah* (Baghdad: Al-Arabiyya Press, 1954).

27. J. Talibani, *Kurdistan,* p. 121; and *Min Wathaiq Al-Hizb al-Thawri al-Kurdistani* (From the Documents of the Kurdistan Revolutionary Party) (Beirut: 1970), p. 30.

28. J. Talibani, *Kurdistan,* p. 146.

29. *Ibid.;* see also *Min Wathaiq,* pp. 32–34.

30. J. Talibani, *Kurdistan,* pp. 151–52; see also *Min Wathaiq,* p. 35.

31. Interview with M. Talibani, November 20, 1976.

32. Bochard Prentiss, as quoted in J. Talibani, *Kurdistan,* pp. 151–52.

33. Longrigg, *Iraq 1900–1950,* p. 353.

34. The writer's interview with Mulla Mustafa's son Massud al-Barzani, September 28, 1976.

35. Khadduri, *Republican Iraq,* p. 2.

36. "The Kurdish Revolution after Eight Years," *Kurdish Journal* 4, no. 3 (September 1969): 87. See Blau, *Le Probleme Kurde,* p. 55.

37. Durra, *Al-Qadiyya al-Kurdiyya,* pp. 282, 286.

38. Ghareeb, *Al-Haraka,* pp. 43–45.

39. Arfa, *The Kurds,* pp. 134–35.

40. For more details, see Ghareeb, *Al-Haraka.*

41. David Adamson, *The Kurdish War* (New York: Praeger, 1965), p. 109.

42. Durra, *Al-Qadiyya al-Kurdiyya,* p. 354.

43. See Durra, *Al-Qadiyya al-Kurdiyya,* p. 357.

44. Luqa Zodo, *The Kurdish Question and Racial Minorities in Mesopotamia* (Beirut: 1969), p. 119.

45. Wathaiq, *Al-Hizb,* p. 51.

46. Durra, *Al-Qadiyya al-Kurdiyya,* pp. 360–71.

47. *Al-Jumhuriyya* (Baghdad), June 30, 1966. See also Khadduri, *Republican Iraq,* p. 276.

48. Ghareeb, *Al-Haraka,* p. 94.

49. The writer's interview with M. Talibani. See also Qasimlu, *Kurdistan,* p. 192. I was told that the man who suggested writing the letter noticed the presence of a man whom he suspected of being a British agent, and then belatedly added, "that is, if the British agree."

50. Lettie M. Wenner, "Arab-Kurdish Rivalries in Iraq," *Middle East Journal* (Winter-Spring 1963) 17: 79–80.

51. Jabbar Ali, "The Current Situation in Iraq," *World Marxist Review* 6, no. 11 (November 1963): 36.

52. The writer's interview with M. Talibani, November 20, 1976.

53. Durra, *Al-Qadiyya al-Kurdiyya,* p. 382.

54. Wenner, *Arab-Kurdish Rivalries,* p. 125.

55. *Ibid.,* p. 76.

56. *Al-Manar* (Baghdad), January 19, 1966.

57. Durra, *Al-Qadiyya al-Kurdiyya,* p. 388.

58. The writer's interview with Aziz Aqrawi, a minister without portfolio in the Iraqi cabinet, Summer 1974. Prior to his break with Barzani in 1973, Aqrawi was a member of the KDP Politburo and chief of staff of the Kurdish rebel forces.

59. The writer's interview with an anti-Barzani, anti-Baath Kurdish leader, March 16, 1976.

60. Wenner, *Arab-Kurdish Rivalries,* p. 78.

61. From the interview with anti-Barzani, anti-Baath Kurdish leader, March 16, 1976.

62. Dana Adams Schmidt, "The Kurdish Insurgency," *Strategic Review* 2 (Summer 1974): 54.

CHAPTER 3 – THE BAATH PARTY FROM ITS ORIGINS THROUGH 1963

1. For background on the Baath party, see Kamel S. Abu Jaber, *The Arab Ba'th Socialist Party* (Syracuse: Syracuse University Press, 1966); John Devlin, *The Baath Party* (Stanford: Hoover Institution Press, 1976); Majid Khadduri, *Socialist Iraq* (Washington,

D.C.: The Middle East Institute, 1978); Majid Khadduri, *Arab Contemporaries* (Washington, D.C.: Johns Hopkins University Press, 1973); Gordon Torrey, "The Baath Ideology and Practice," *Middle East Journal* 23 (Autumn 1969): 445-70.

2. Abu Jaber, *The Arab Ba'th,* p. 19.

3. Devlin, *The Ba'th Party,* p. 4.

4. Michel Aflaq, *Maarakat al-Masir al-Wahid* (The Battle For One Destiny) (Beirut: Dar al-Ilm lil-Malayin, 1958), p. 18. See also Shibli al-Aysami, *Hizb al-Ba'th al-Arabi al-Ishtiraki,* June 1974, p. 21; *Nidal al-Ba'th* (The Struggle of the Baath) (Beirut: Dar al-Taliah, 1965) 1:104-105.

5. Al-Aysami, *Hizb,* p. 21.

6. Sylvia Haim, *Arab Nationalism: An Anthology* (Berkeley: University of California Press, 1964), p. 19.

7. Torrey, *The Ba'th,* p. 445.

8. Elias Farah, *Tatawur al-Idiulugiyya al-Arabiyya al-Thawriyya* (Evolution of the Arab Revolutionary Ideology) (Beirut: Al-Mussassa al-Arabiyya lil-dirasat wa al-Nashr, 1975), p. 5.

9. Aflaq, *Maarakat,* p. 50.

10. Michel Aflaq, *Fi Sabil al-Ba'th* (On the Path of al-Baath) (Beirut: Dar al-Talia, 1974), p. 198.

11. Haim, *Arab Nationalism,* p. 244.

12. *Nidal al-Ba'th,* 1, p. 175.

13. *Nidal al-Ba'th,* 9, p. 14.

14. *Lamahat min Tarikh Hizb al-Ba'th al-Arabi al-Ishtiraki* (Glances at the History of the Arab Baath Socialist Party) (N.P.W.D.), p. 17.

15. Devlin, *The Ba'th Party,* p. 107.

16. For an account of these early years of the Baath party in Iraq, see *Nidal al-Ba'th,* 1, pp. 34-36.

17. *Nidal al-Ba'th,* 5, p. 9.

18. *Lamahat,* pp. 55-56.

19. *Nidal al-Ba'th,* 9, pp. 34-40.

20. *Lamahat,* p. 59.

21. Devlin, *The Ba'th Party,* p. 108.

22. *Nidal al-Ba'th,* 7, p. 15.

23. Devlin, *The Ba'th Party,* p. 120.

24. *Nidal al-Ba'th,* 7, p. 40.

25. Devlin, *The Ba'th Party,* p. 149.

26. *Lamahat,* p. 71.

27. Devlin, *The Ba'th Party,* p. 175.

28. *Ibid.,* p. 191.

29. See the party circulars distributed on February 19, 1961; May 1, 1961; late July, 1961; and early October 1961, all quoted in *Nidal al-Ba'th,* 7, pp. 116-72.

30. *Nidal al-Ba'th,* pp. 170-72.

31. *Ibid.,* 7, p. 7.

32. Devlin, *The Ba'th Party,* pp. 194–95.

33. Khadduri, *Republican Iraq,* p. 189.

34. Devlin, *The Ba'th Party,* p. 195.

35. Khadduri, *Republican Iraq,* pp. 189–90. See also Devlin, *The Ba'th Party,* p. 233.

36. *Al-Jamahir* (Baghdad), February 12, 1963.

37. The writer's interview with Zayd Haydar, Baghdad, November 1976.

38. Aflaq's complete statement during this meeting can be found in Aflaq, *Fi Sabil,* pp. 168–78.

39. *Ibid.,* p. 181.

40. Haim, *Arab Nationalism,* p. 236.

41. Nadim Al-Yasin, *Al-Masala al-Kurdiyya* (The Kurdish Question) (Baghdad: Ministry of Information, 1975), p. 9.

42. *Al-Jumhuriyya* (Baghdad), January 8, 1958.

43. The writer's interview with a Kurdish leader who wishes to remain unidentified, March 1976. However, this was not confirmed by other sources.

44. Al-Yasin, *Al-Masala,* p. 10.

45. *Nidal al-Ba'th,* 7, p. 146.

46. Al-Yasin, *Al-Masala,* p. 11.

47. *fibid.,* p. 13.

48. Cited in *Nidal al-Ba'th,* 7, p. 146.

49. *Ibid.,* p. 221.

50. Dana Adams Schmidt, *Journey among Brave Men* (Boston: Little, Brown, 1964), p. 248.

51. The writer's interview with a Kurdish leader, March 1976.

52. Uriel Dann, *Iraq Under Kassem: A Political History, 1885–1963* (New York: Praeger, 1969), pp. 344–45.

53. Devlin, *The Ba'th Party,* p. 278.

54. The writer's interview with an Iraqi leader familiar with the 1962–63 negotiations, Beirut, 1972.

55. Al-Yasin, *Al-Masala,* p. 14.

56. Khadduri, *Republican Iraq,* p. 269.

57. Clare Hollingsworth, "The Ba'thist Revolution in Iraq," *World Affairs* (London: Oxford University Press, May 1963), p. 229.

58. Al-Yasin, *Al-Masala,* p. 15.

59. Durra, *Al-Qadiyya al-Kurdiyya,* p. 308.

60. The writer's interview with a pro-Talibani Kurdish leader, March 1976.

61. The delegation also included Faiq al-Samurrai, former vice-president of the al-Istiqlal party; Husain Jamil, one of the leaders of the National Democratic party; Faysal Khayzaran, a leading Baathist; Dr. Aziz al-Duri, dean of Baghdad University; and Zayd Ahmad Uthman, a leading Kurdish figure.

62. Al-Yasin, *Al-Masala,* p. 14.

63. The writer's interview, July 10, 1974, with an Iraqi familiar with the negotiations.

64. See text of NRCC statement in Al-Yasin, *Al-Masala,* p. 34.

65. Ismet Sharif Vanly, *Revolution of Iraqi Kurdistan,* Committee for the Defense of the Kurdish People's Rights, April 1965. See also Devlin, *The Ba'th Party,* p. 206.

66. Durra, *Al-Qadiyya al-Kurdiyya,* p. 313.

67. Al-Yasin, *Al-Masala,* p. 15.

68. The writer's interview with a pro-Talibani Kurdish leader, March 1976. See also Ghareeb, *Al-Haraka,* p. 72.

69. Vanly, *Revolution of Iraqi Kurdistan;* see also Khadduri, *Socialist Iraq,* p. 27.

70. Khadduri, *Republican Iraq,* p. 27. The leading members in addition to Talibani included some tribal leaders as well as some of the more progressive elements of the KDP. Khadduri mentions KDP Secretary-General Ibrahim Ahmad as being a member of the committee, but one Kurdish source told this writer that Ahmad was not a member. Some of the other members included were Salih al-Yusufi, Muhammad Khaffaf, Rashid Arif, Mustafa Aziz, Habib Muhammad Karim, Hashim Aqrawi, and Shakha Dan Namiq.

71. J. Talibani, *Kurdistan,* pp. 339–40.

72. J. Talibani, Kurdistan, pp. 321–23. Also see Durra, *Al-Qadiyya al-Kurdiyya,* pp. 316–17.

73. KDP circular distributed on April 10, 1963.

74. For the full text of this proposal see Durra, *Al-Qadiyya al-Kurdiyya,* pp. 318–24.

75. For detailed information on the negotiations see Durra, *Al-Qadiyya al-Kurdiyya,* pp. 314–25; Khadduri, *Republican Iraq,* pp. 268–71; and Schmidt, *Journey among Brave Men,* pp. 244–65.

76. For full text of the plan see *Al-Jamahir* (Baghdad), June 11, 1963.

77. The writer's interview with a Baathist official, Baghdad, July 1974.

78. *Ibid.*

79. *Arab Political Documents: 1963–65* (Beirut: AUB Press), pp. 285–88.

80. Interview with a high-ranking Iraqi officer who took part in the operation; July 10, 1974.

81. *Arab Political Documents,* pp. 288–90.

82. The writer's interview with high-ranking Iraqi officer who took part in the operation, July 10, 1974.

83. The Kurds were able to get some anti-aircraft guns and reportedly brought down some Iraqi planes. Interview with anti-government Kurdish leader, Beirut, June 1971.

84. Durra, *Al-Qadiyya al-Kurdiyya,* p. 344.

85. Vanly, *Revolution of Iraqi Kurdistan,* p. 45.

86. *Le Monde,* October 29, 1963, quoted in Vanly, p. 46.

87. *Arab Political Documents,* pp. 288–90.

88. Quoted in *New York Times,* June 19, 1963.

89. *Al-Ahram,* October 18, 1963.

90. *New York Times,* May 7, 1963.

91. Vanly, *Revolution of Iraqi Kurdistan,* p. 38.

92. *New York Times,* July 12, 1963.

93. James Kinsman, "The Changing Face of Kurdish Nationalism," *The New Middle East* 20 (May 1970):21.

94. Arfa, *The Kurds,* p. 143.

95. *Kurdish Facts,* pp. 2–3.

96. Kinsman, "The Changing Face," pp. 21–22.

97. Gebran Majdalani, "The Ba'th Experience in Iraq," *Middle East Forum* 41 (Autumn 1965):41–48.

98. *Ibid.*; see also Aflaq's speech in *Nidal al-Ba'th,* 10, pp. 90–92.

99. *Nidal al-Ba'th,* 9, p. 5.


## CHAPTER 4 — THE BAATH AND THE KURDISH QUESTION, 1968-70

1. Aziz al-Hajj, *L'Irak Nouveau et le Probleme Kurde* (Paris: Khayat, 1977), p. 115.

2. Devlin, *The Ba'th Party,* pp. 274–75. See also *Thawrat 17 Tammuz: al-Tajriba wa al-Afaq; al-Taqrir al-Siayssi al-Sadir an al-Mutamar al-Qutri al-Thamin li-Hizb al-Ba'th al-Arabi al-Ishtiraki, al-Qutr al-Iraqi* (Political Report of the Baath party's Eighth Regional Conference) (Baghdad: 1974), pp. 11–12.

3. The Iraqi Baath party accused the Syrian Baathists, whom it describes as "February deserters," of cooperating with the Arif regime and providing it with information about the Iraqi Baath. It further accused the Syrian regime of backing some of the "schismatic" Iraqi Baathists against them. See *Thawrat,* pp. 12–13.

4. "Historical Background and Ideological Foundations of the ABSP," *Iraq Today* (Baghdad), March 16–31, 1977, p. 2–7.

5. *Thawrat,* pp. 17, 22–23.

6. *Ibid.,* p. 29.

7. "Historical Background and Ideological Foundations of the ABSP," p. 7. See also al-Hajj, *L'Irak Nouveau,* pp. 116–117; and *Thawrat,* pp. 19–131.

8. C. J. Edmonds, "The Kurdish War in Iraq," *World Today* 24 (London: December 1968): 520. See also al-Yasin, *Al-Masala,* p. 12.

9. Al-Yasin, *Al-Masala,* p. 18.

10. *Al-Hizb al-Thawri al-Kurdistani,* p. 18. See also al-Hajj, *L'Irak Nouveau,* p. 116.

11. On December 10, 1964, Arif announced that negotiations with the Kurdish movement included: "The recognition of the national rights of our Kurdish brothers within the Iraqi people, in one national and fraternal unity, and the confirmation of this in the Provisional Constitution." The statement then enumerated certain measures to free political prisoners, lift the economic embargo on the north, restore local administration, reconstruct the north, and other minor measures.

In a response to Arif's statement, Barzani declared his acceptance of Arif's offer "because we have become convinced of the goodwill of the government" and concluded that "everyone should know that the sovereignty of the law, security and order in the area, are apt to resolve every problem regardless of how difficult it may be." Barzani further declared that he trusted Arif because he was a religious man and "the believer is believable" — a dig at the Baathists, who were accused of being atheists by their conservative opponents. Barzani went on to declare his support for "the abolition of the [political] parties as long as this measure realizes the interests of the country and its national objectives."

The statement concerning the abolition of parties also angered some of the leaders of the KDP. See *Al-Hizb al-Thawri al-Kurdistani,* pp. 45–47, and al-Yasin, *Al-Masala,* p. 22.

12. The writer's second interview with Mulla Mustafa al-Barzani, Washington, D.C., September 28, 1976.

13. *Al-Nur* (Baghdad), November 19, 1968.

14. *Ibid.,* December 5, 1968.

15. *Ibid.,* November 9, 1968.

16. "Statement by the Executive Bureau Regarding the Recent Announcement by the Agency for the Affairs of the North," *Kurdish Journal,* 4, no. 1 (1969): 34–36.

17. The writer's interview with Zayd Haydar, formerly a Baathist National Command member and head of the party's foreign relations bureau, November 1976.

18. *Al-Nur* (Baghdad), November 19, 1968.

19. *Ibid.,* December 5, 1968.

20. *Ibid.,* September 9, 1968.

21. *Khibat* 506 (October 1968), trans. in the *Kurdish Journal* 6 (March

22. Chronology, *Middle East Journal* 23, no. 2 (Summer 1969): 310.

23. "Memorandum on the Kurdish Question," *Kurdish Journal* 6, no. 1 (March 1969): 37–40.

24. *Daily Telegraph* (London), March 10, 1969.

25. *Kurdish Affairs Bulletin* 1 (April 28, 1969): 1–2.

26. *Min Wathaiq Al-Hizb al-Thawri al-Kurdistani,* p. 52.

27. The writer's interview with Mukarram al-Talibani, November 20, 1976.

28. The writer's interview with Babakr Mahmud al-Pishdari, chairman of the legislative council of the Autonomous Kurdish Region, Arbil, November 17, 1976. Pishdari, who broke away from the Barzani KDP in 1970, was a leading figure in the Kurdish movement. He later became minister of labor and social affairs.

29. Al-Hajj, *L'Irak Nouveau,* p. 116.

30. *Ibid.,* p. 114. Also interview with M. Talibani, November 1976.

31. James Kinsman, "Kurds and Iran: Iraq's Changing Balance of Power," *New Middle East* 22 (July 1970): 26.

32. Chronology, *Middle East Journal* 23, no. 3 (Autumn 1969): 512.

33. Mustafa al-Barzani, "Memorandum," *Kurdish Journal* 4, no. 2 (1969): 80–82.

34. Chronology, *Middle East Journal* 23, no. 3 (Autumn 1969): 513.

35. Al-Hajj, *L'Irak Nouveau,* p. 118.

36. The writer's interview with Tariq Aziz, November 25, 1976. At the time of the interview, in addition to holding a post as information minister, Aziz was a candidate member of the Regional Command of the party. See also al-Hajj, *L'Irak Nouveau,* p. 119.

37. Interview with Tariq Aziz.

38. Interview with M. Talibani, November 20, 1976.

39. *Al-Thawra* (Baghdad), February 2, 1969.

40. Michel Aflaq, *Nuqtat al-Bidayah* (Starting Point) (Beirut: al-Muassassa al-Arabiyya lil-dirasat wa al-Nashr, 1971), pp. 105–108.

41. *Al-Jumhuriyya* (Baghdad), July 18, 1969.

42. *Al-Thawra* (Baghdad), December 17, 1969.

43. *Hawl al-Masala al-Kurdiyya* (Baghdad), 1971, pp. 18–21.

44. *Thawrat,* p. 69.

45. Kinsman, *Kurds and Iran,* p. 27.

46. See Abbas Abbas, *Azamat Shatt al-Arab* (The Shatt al-Arab Crises) (Beirut: Al-Muassassa al-Arabiyya Lil-Dirasat wa al-Nashr, 1973).

47. Kinsman, *Kurds and Iran,* p. 27.

48. *Baghdad Observer,* July 30, 1969.

49. Saddam Husain, *Ahadith fi al-Qadaya al-Rahina* (Statements on Current Issues) (Baghdad, 1971), p. 33.

50. *Ibid.,* p. 25.

51. Interview with Tariq Aziz, November 25, 1976. Also see Husain, *Ahadith,* p. 33.

52. "Muthakarat Hizb al-Ba'th al-Arabi al-Ishtiraki ila al-Hizb al-Dimukrati al-Kurdistani," (Memorandums from the Baath party to the KDP) cited in *Likay Yusan al-Salam Watatazaz al-Wihda al-Wataniyya* (Baghdad, 1973), p. 158.

53. Interview with Mustafa al-Barzani, September 13, 1976.

54. "Muthakarat," in *Likay Yusan,* p. 159.

55. Interview with Mustafa al-Barzani, September 13, 1976.


CHAPTER 5 – THE MARCH 1970 MANIFESTO


1. Mahmud Bakali, "A New Page in the History of Iraq," *Review of International Affairs* 21 (Belgrade, Yugoslavia: May 5, 1970): 23–25.

2. March 11 Manifesto as quoted in FBIS, Middle East and North Africa, March 12, 1970.

3. *Al-Nahar* (Beirut), March 12, 1970. See also *New York Times,* March 12, 1970.

4. "Memorandum on the Kurdish Question," p. 25.

5. Kinsman, *Kurds and Iran,* p. 25.

6. Interview with al-Pishdari, November 17, 1976.

7. Nebez, *About the Kurdish Problem,* pp. 50–56. These parties called for an Aryan confederation among Kurds, Persians, Afghans, Indians, Pakistanis, and Armenians in order "to withstand the aggressive designs of those, who in the name of Arab unity, from the Gulf to the Ocean want to colonize Kurdistan, and annex the islands of the Persian Gulf, oil-rich Kurdistan, and other parts of the Aryan homeland."

8. *Tanfith Bayan 11 Athar* (Baghdad: Ministry of Information, n.d.), pp. 68–107.

9. "Iraqi Communist Party Calls for Autonomy for Kurds," *World Marxist Review* 11, no. 4 (April 1968): 82.

10. As quoted in *Tanfith,* pp. 83–87.

11. *Al-Taakhi* (Baghdad), January 14, 1971.

12. *Tanfith,* p. 88.

13. *Al-Taakhi,* July 4, 1970.

14. *Tanfith,* p. 80.

15. *Al-Shararah* 6 (March 1970).

16. *Christian Science Monitor,* July 15, 1970.

17. *Ibid.*

18. *Al-Nahar,* March 12, 1970.

19. Aziz Jasim, *Al-Qadiya al-Kurdiyya* (The Kurdish Case) (Baghdad: Dar al-Hurriyya, 1973) pp. 27–42.

20. Interview with Tariq Aziz, November 25, 1976.

21. *Al-Jumhuriyya* (Baghdad), March 19, 1970. See also al-Hajj, *L'Irak Nouveau,* pp. 127–28.

22. The article is reprinted in *Hawl al-Masala al-Kurdiyya* (Baghdad), 1971. Quotations in this section from the article can be found in that document on pp. 1–36. According to Dr. Elias Farah, Baath theoretician and National Command member, the party contained some chauvinist elements who opposed concessions to the Kurds. Consequently, the party began through a series of articles in its internal literature a campaign to educate its members on the question of Kurdish national rights. These articles began to appear in 1969 and continued throughout the early seventies. From the writer's interview with Elias Farah, Washington, D.C., August 1977.

23. Interview with Tariq Aziz, November 25, 1976.

24. *Al-Hayat* (Beirut), November 24, 1971. See also *Tanfith,* p. 127.

25. *Tanfith,* pp. 108, 129.

26. *Al-Hayat,* November 24, 1971.

27. "The July Revolution in Two Years" (Baghdad: Ministry of Culture and Information, 1970), pp. 8–9. See also *Tanfith,* p. 23.

28. *Tanfith.*

29. *Ibid.,* p. 127.

30. *Ibid.,* pp. 129–30.

31. For details concerning the development projects, see *ibid.,* pp. 40–58.

32. "The July Revolution" (Baghdad: Ministry of Culture and Information, 1970), pp. 8–9.

33. For details see *Tanfith,* pp. 131–39.

34. Chronology, *Middle East Journal* 24, no. 3 (Summer 1970): 362.

35. Kinsman, "Kurds and Iran," p. 22.

36. The writer's interview with an anti-Barzani, pro-Talibani Kurdish leader, Washington, D.C., March 1976.

37. *Al-Amal* (Beirut), May 22, 1970.

38. Iraqi News Agency (Baghdad), July 16, 1970.

39. "Text of the Provisional Constitution," cited in Iraqi News Agency's "Special Supplement to Bulletin No. 195" (Baghdad), July 16, 1970.

40. *Christian Science Monitor,* July 15, 1970.

41. The writer's interview with Amir Kamuran Badr-Khan, Washington, D.C., December 11, 1970.

42. *Al-Nahar,* December 27, 1970.

43. *Ibid.,* July 7, 1970.

44. *Al-Thawra,* December 27, 1970.

45. *Al-Nahar,* December 29, 1970.

46. *Al-Thawra,* October 18, 1972.

47. *New York Times,* December 31, 1970.

48. *Al-Nahar,* December 25, 1970.

49. Cited in *Washington Post,* December 13, 1970.

50. *New York Times,* December 21, 1970.


## CHAPTER 6 – DETERIORATION OF RELATIONS
## BETWEEN THE BAATH AND THE KDP


1. Interview with Mustafa al-Barzani, September 13, 1976.

2. Interview with Tariq Aziz, November 25, 1976.

3. Interview with Mustafa al-Barzani, September 13, 1976.

4. *Al-Thawra,* March 11, 1971.

5. *Al-Jumhuriyya,* March 11, 1971.

6. *Ibid.,* May 20, 1971.

7. *Al-Hawadith* (Beirut), June 18, 1971, p. 18.

8. *Le Jour* (Beirut), May 25, 1971.

9. *Ibid.*

10. *Al-Jumhuriyya,* May 20, 1971.

11. *Arab World Report,* April 29, 1971.

12. *Roz-al-Yusif* (Cairo), May 25, 1971.

13. *Ibid.*

14. *Al-Hayat,* November 24, 1971.

15. *Ibid.*

16. *Ibid.*

17. *Daily Star* (Beirut), October 10, 1971.

18. Iraqi News Agency, October 2, 1971.

19. *Ibid.,* October 6, 8, 1971.

20. Interview with Mustafa al-Barzani, September 13, 1976.

21. *Al-Nahar,* December 23, 1970.

22. Eric Rouleau, "Aftermath of a Tyrant's Downfall," *The Guardian,* August 11, 1973.

23. *Al-Thawra,* November 25, 1971.

24. *Al-Taakhi,* November 24, 1971.

25. *Al-Thawra,* November 25, 1971.

26. Iraqi News Agency, November 15, 1971.

27. *Al-Taakhi,* November 16, 1971.

28. *Al-Nahar,* November 20, 1971.

29. Interview with Mukarram Talibani, November 20, 1976.

30. *Al-Nahar,* November 20, 1971.

31. *Ibid.*

32. Iraqi News Agency, November 25, 1971.

33. *Al-Nahar,* April 14, 1972.

34. *Ibid.,* July 12, 1972.

35. *Ibid.*

36. *Ibid.*

37. *Ibid.*

38. *Ibid.*

39. *Ibid.*

40. *Al-Taakhi,* as quoted in *Al-Nahar,* October 23, 1972.

41. *Al-Thawra,* October 22, 1972.

42. Baath Party Memorandum to the KDP, "Settlement of the Kurdish Problem" (Baghdad: Al-Thawra Publications, n.d.), p. 123. Further quotations in this section are taken from this publication, pp. 133–63, *passim.*

43. Quotations in this section from the KDP memorandum may be found in George Hajjar's *Al-Masala al-Kurdiyya* (Beirut: Dar, al-Quds, 1975), pp. 77–109, *passim.*

44. *Al-Thawra,* October 18, 1972.

45. *Ibid.,* October 31, 1972.

46. *Al-Nahar,* November 23, 1972.

47. *Ibid.,* November 2, 1972.

48. *Al-Thawra,* November 5, 1972.

49. *Ibid.,* November 13, 1972.

50. *Min Wathaiq,* pp. 37–46.

51. *Al-Nahar,* February 11, 1972.

52. Interview with Mustafa al-Barzani, September 13, 1976.

53. Interview with M. Talibani, November 20, 1976.

54. *Christian Science Monitor,* June 3, 1973.

55. *Ibid.*

56. *Washington Post,* June 23, 1973.

57. The writer's interview with Baath officials who do not wish to be named.

58. For details see Khadduri, *Socialist Iraq,* pp. 63–67. See also Rouleau, "Aftermath of a Tyrant's Downfall," *The Guardian,* August 11, 1973.

59. See also *Al-Nahar Arab Report,* March 25, 1974.

60. Interview with Mustafa al-Barzani, September 13, 1976.

61. *Al-Jabha fi Marhalat al-Milad* (Baghdad: Al-Thawra Press, n.d.), pp. 7, 34.

62. *Al-Taakhi,* August 19, 1973.

## CHAPTER 7 – FOREIGN INTERFERENCE

1. The writer's interview with Hashim Aqrawi, a member of the KDP's Central Committee, who broke with Barzani in December 1973. Baghdad, July 15, 1974. Aqrawi is currently a minister of state in the Iraqi government.

2. The writer's interview with Aziz Aqrawi, commander of Kurdish forces until December 1973. This was confirmed also by Kurdish opponents of Barzani and of the government. They believe, however, that the CIA contributed to the formation of Parastin as well. Baghdad, July 18, 1973.

3. Aron Latham, *What Kissinger Was Afraid of in the Pike Papers* (New York: October 4, 1976), p. 59.

4. The *Village Voice* (New York), February 11, 1976, p. 85.

5. Iraqi Information Minister Tariq Aziz said that he and other officials were unable to go to the Kurdish areas without prior permission from the Kurdish forces. Interview with Tariq Aziz, November 25, 1976.

6. *Al-Thawra,* November 6, 1972.

7. *Al-Kadir* 14–15 (July/August 1972), as quoted in *Al-Thawra,* October 10, 1972.

8. Interview with Mustafa al-Barzani, September 28, 1976.

9. Interview with Tariq Aziz, November 25, 1976.

10. Abd al-Nafi Mahmud, "Nazarat fi al-Khilaf al-Irani al-Iraqi" (Perspective on the Iraq-Iran Dispute), *Al-Thawra,* August 6, 1974.

11. *Ibid.*

12. Blau, *Le Probleme Kurde,* p. 38.

13. Abd al-Nafi Mahmud, "Nazarat fi," *Al-Thawra,* August 6, 1974.

14. For Iran's foreign policy, see Ruhollah Ramazani, *The Persian Gulf: Iran's Role* (Charlottesville: University Press of Virginia, 1972); and Sharam Shubain and Sepehr Zabih, *The Foreign Relations of Iran* (Berkeley: University of California Press, 1974).

15. See Abd al-Nafi Mahmud, "Nazarat fi," *Al-Thawra,* August 6, 1974.

16. Interview with a pro-Talibani Kurdish leader, March 1976. Other Kurdish sources say such an agreement was reached in 1966 and that Barzani helped to suppress the Kurdish movement in Iran in 1967–68.

17. Interview with Mustafa al-Barzani, September 13, 1976.

18. Gerard de Viellier, *The Imperial Shah* (Boston: Little, Brown, 1976), pp. 245–47.

19. *Baghdad Observer,* July 30, 1969.

20. David Adamson, *The Kurdish War,* p. 94. See also Dana Adams Schmidt, "The Kurdish Insurgency," *Strategic Review* (Summer 1974): 56; and *Washington Post,* December 13, 1970.

21. Lee Dinsmore, "The Forgotten Kurds," *The Progressive* (April 1977): 39.

22. *Al-Ahad* (Beirut), August 10, 1969. The information supplied by *Al-Ahad,* a pro-Iraqi magazine, was denied by a high U.S. State Department official, who claimed that no such agreement was ever reached between Barzani and the U.S. government. Interview Washington, D.C., July 19, 1978.

23. *Al-Ahad* (Beirut), August 10, 1969.

24. *Ibid.*

25. As quoted in *The Village Voice,* February 11, 1976.

26. *Ibid.*

27. *Ibid.*

28. *New York Times,* November 2, 1975.

29. Interview with Tariq Aziz, November 25, 1976.

30. Interview with Mustafa al-Barzani, September 13, 1976.

31. *The Village Voice,* February 11, 1976.

32. *Ibid.*

33. Latham, *What Kissinger Was Afraid Of,* p. 59.

34. *New York Times,* March 13, 1975.

35. Latham, *What Kissinger Was Afraid Of,* p. 60.

36. Saddam Husain, *On Current Affairs* (Baghdad: Al-Thawra Publications, n.d.), pp. 14–17.

37. *The Village Voice,* February 11, 1976.

38. *Ibid.*

39. The writer's interview with a high-ranking U.S. State Department official. March 1976. See also *Christian Science Monitor,* May 1, 1974.

40. Interview with Aziz Aqrawi, July 18, 1974.

41. *Al-Manar* (London), May 20, 1980.

42. *Christian Science Monitor,* October 6, 1980. See also Associated Press, September 30, 1980.

43. Interviews with Mukarram Talibani, November 20, 1976, and a pro-Jalal Talibani Kurdish leader, March 1976.

44. *Al-Ahad* (Beirut), August 10, 1969.

45. *Ibid.*

46. *Washington Post,* September 17, 1972.

47. Interview with Mustafa Al-Barzani, September 13, 1976.

48. Interview with Zayd Haydar, November 1976.

49. *Ibid.*

50. Rouleau, "Aftermath of a Tyrant's Downfall." *The Guardian,* August 11, 1973.

51. Dinsmore, "The Forgotten Kurds," *The Progressive* (April 1977): 39.

52. *The Village Voice,* February 11, 1976.

53. *Ibid.*

54. Latham, "What Kissinger Was Afraid Of," p. 61.

55. Interview with Mustafa al-Barzani, September 13, 1976.

56. Latham, "What Kissinger Was Afraid Of."

57. William Safire in *New York Times,* February 12, 1976.

58. Interview with Mukarram Talibani, November 20, 1976.

59. Interview with Tariq Aziz, November 25, 1976.

60. Interview with Mustafa al-Barzani, September 28, 1976.

61. *Ibid.*

62. *Ibid.*

63. *Al-Nahar,* July 23, 1973.

64. *Pravda,* March 14, 1974, as quoted in *Current Digest of the Soviet Press* 26, no. 11 (April 10, 1974): 21.

65. *New York Times,* April 27, 1974.


## CHAPTER 8 – AUTONOMY AND THE RESUMPTION OF FIGHTING

1. *Al-Nahar,* September 9, 1973.

2. *Taqyim Masirat al-Thawra al-Kurdiyya* (Assessment of the March of the Kurdish Revolution), KDP Preparatory Committee, pp. 41–42.

3. *Taqyim Masirat*; this report was also confirmed in an interview with a pro-Jalal Talibani Kurdish leader, March 1976.

4. *Taqyim Masirat,* p. 42.

5. *The Village Voice,* February 11, 1976.

6. *Taqyim Masirat,* p. 21.

7. Al-Hajj, *L'Irak Nouveau,* p. 149.

8. *Ibid.*

9. *Al-Balagh* (Beirut), March 25, 1972, p. 29.

10. *Ibid.*

11. *Ibid.*

12. Al-Hajj, *L'Irak Nouveau,* p. 159.

13. *Ibid.,* pp. 153–56.

14. *Ibid.,* p. 157–58.

15. *Ibid.*

16. *Ibid.,* p. 160.

17. *Al-Balagh,* March 25, 1972, p. 29.

18. *Ibid.*

19. *Ibid.*

20. Saddam Husain, *On Current Affairs,* p. 23.

21. *Al-Nahar,* September 7, 1973.

22. *Baghdad Observer,* March 3, 1975.

23. Al-Hajj, *L'Irak Nouveau,* p. 141.

24. *Baghdad Observer,* March 3, 1975.

25. Saddam Husain, *On Current Affairs,* p. 25.

26. See *Thawrat 17 Tammuz-Taqrir al-Mutamar al-Qutri al-Thamin.*

27. Husain, *On Current Affairs,* p. 42.

28. *Revolutionary Iraq* (Baghdad), January 1974, pp. 102–103.

29. Husain, *On Current Affairs,* p. 38. The account of the conference which follows is from that publication. Documentation for statements made here may be found on pp. 38–63, *passim.*

30. Interviews with Hashim and Aziz Aqrawi, Baghdad, July 1974. Aziz Aqrawi also stated that they had sent two other letters to Barzani on December 16 and December 28, 1973, urging him to change his policies, but that he had responded by expelling them from the KDP.

31. *Al-Nahar,* March 25, 1974.

32. Interview with Aziz Aqrawi, July 1974.

33. *Ibid.*

34. Interview with Ubaidullah al-Barzani, Baghdad, July 19, 1974.

35. *Ibid.*

36. *Al-Nahar,* March 25, 1974.

37. *Ibid.*

38. *Al-Thawra,* March 12, 1974.

39. Autonomy Law as cited in "The Kurdish Problem in Iraq" (Baghdad: Al-Thawra Press, 1974), pp. 185–98.

40. *The Times,* March 15, 1974; *Financial Times,* March 15, 1974.

41. *The Times,* March 15, 1974.

42. *Financial Times,* March 15, 1974.

43. *Al-Nahar,* March 13, 1974.

44. *Ibid.*, March 18, 1974.

45. Interview with Mukarram Talibani, November 20, 1976.

46. *Al-Nahar,* March 25, 1974.

47. *Financial Times,* March 28, 1974.

48. Latham, "What Kissinger Was Afraid Of," p. 68.

49. *Ibid.*

50. Interview with Mustafa al-Barzani, September 13, 1976.

51. Barzani's letter to President Carter, February 9, 1977.

52. Dinsmore, "The Forgotten Kurds," p. 5.

53. Latham, "What Kissinger Was Afraid Of," p. 62.

54. Interview with a pro-Jalal Talibani Kurdish leader, March 1976.

55. Jamal al-Ghitani, *Hurras al-Bawwaba al-Sharqiyya* (Guardians of The Eastern Gate) (Beirut: Dar al-Talia, 1975), p. 63.

56. *Christian Science Monitor,* December 12, 1974.

57. *Ibid.* See also *Financial Times,* May 1, 1974.

58. *Sunday Times,* April 14, 1974.

59. *Financial Times,* May 1, 1974.

60. *Al-Balagh,* April 15, 1974.

61. *The Guardian,* April 22, 1974.

62. *Ibid.*, April 19, 1974.

63. *The Guardian,* April 23, 1974.

64. *Financial Times,* May 1, 1974.

65. *The Guardian,* May 9, 1974.

66. Smith Hempstone, *Free Trade Union News,* April 1977, p. 3.

67. *Ibid.*

68. Interview with a pro-Jalal Talibani Kurdish leader, March 1976.

69. *The Guardian,* May 9, 1974.

70. *Ibid.*

71. *Ibid.*

72. *Sunday Times,* April 14, 1972.

73. Ghitani, *Hurras al-Bawwaba,* p. 64.

74. *Ibid.*

75. *Ibid.*

76. *Ibid.*

77. *Ibid.,* p. 82.

78. *Christian Science Monitor,* August 18, 1974.

79. *International Herald Tribune,* September 28–29, 1974.

80. *Ibid.*

81. Interview with Mustafa al-Barzani, September 13, 1976.

82. Ghitani, *Hurras al-Bawwaba,* p. 81.

83. *Financial Times,* August 29, 1974.

84. *Christian Science Monitor,* September 10, 1974.

85. *Financial Times,* September 12, 1974.

86. *The Guardian,* October 15, 1974.

87. Interview with a high-ranking Iraqi official, Baghdad, November 1976.

88. *Financial Times,* October 3, 1974.

89. *Al-Nahar,* October 6, 1974. See also *The Guardian,* October 15, 1974.

90. *Al-Nahar,* October 6, 1974.

91. Interview with Zayd Haydar, November 1976.

92. *Al-Nahar,* October 11, 1974.

93. *Christian Science Monitor,* September 10, 1974.

94. *Al-Nahar,* October 11, 1974.

95. *Ibid.*

96. *Ibid.,* December 2, 1974.

97. *Washington Post,* February 2, 1975.

98. *Al-Thawra,* July 31, 1974.

99. *Ibid.,* August 25, 1974.

100. *Ibid.,* September 25–26, 1974.

101. Ghitani, *Hurras al-Bawwaba,* pp. 71–74.

102. Also substantiated in an interview with a high-ranking Iraqi official, March 1979.

103. *Al-Thawra,* September 1, 1974; also interview with Hashim Aqrawi, November 1976.

104. *Al-Nahar,* July 23, 1974.

105. Husain, *On Current Affairs,* pp. 141–42.

106. *International Herald Tribune,* January 22, 1975.

107. *The Times,* January 8, 1975.

108. *The Observer* (London), March 30, 1975. See also *Washington Post,* December 17, 1974.

109. *International Herald Tribune,* January 22, 1975.

110. *Washington Post,* January 21, 1975.

111. *Al-Thawra,* December 16, 1975.

112. *Al-Jumhuriyya,* February 3, 1975.

113. *Ibid.,* January 1, 1975.

114. *Financial Times,* February 4, 1975.

115. *Al-Nahar,* September 3, 1974.

116. *Washington Post,* January 21, 1975.

117. *Financial Times,* February 4, 1975; *Al-Thawra,* February 3, 1975.

118. *Al-Jumhuriyya,* January 1, 1975.

119. *Al-Thawra,* February 16, 1975.

120. Interview with a high-ranking U.S. State Department official, March 15, 1977.

121. Interviews with Mustafa al-Barzani and Tariq Aziz; September 13, 1976, and November 1976.

122. Interview with Zayd Haydar, November 1976. He also said that Saddam Husain had offered to settle the Shatt al-Arab issue in a "peaceful and positive manner" but the Shah refused.

123. *New York Times,* March 13, 1975.

124. Interview with a high-ranking U.S. State Department official, March 15, 1977.

125. Interview with Zayd Haydar, November 1976.

126. *Ibid.* and *Al-Jumhuriyya,* February 3, 1975.

127. Interview with Zayd Haydar, November 1976. See also *The Guardian,* April 1, 1975.

128. *The Guardian,* October 24, 1975.

129. *The Observer,* March 30, 1975.

130. *Times,* March 17, 1975.

131. *Al-Thawra,* March 14, 1975.

132. Gwynne Roberts, "The Harsh Realities," *Middle East International* (May 1975): 15.

133. *Al-Thawra,* March 20, 1975.

134. *Ibid.* See also *The Daily Telegraph* (London), March 20, 1975.

135. *The Guardian,* April 1, 1975.

136. *Ibid.,* October 24, 1975. See also *Washington Post,* March 31, 1975.

137. *Washington Post,* March 31, 1975.

138. *Ibid.,* March 23, 1975. See also Hempstone, *Free Trade Union News,* April 1977.

139. *New York Times,* April 1, 1975. See also *Al-Thawra,* March 22 to April 4, 1975.

140. Interview with Zayd Haydar, November 1976.

141. Interview with Mukarram Talibani, November 1976.

142. Interview with al-Pishdari, November 1976.

143. *Washington Post,* March 23, 1975.

144. Jon Kimche, "Selling out the Kurds," *The New Republic* (April 19, 1975): 20–21.

145. Interviews with Talibani, Pishdari, and Haydar, November 1976.

146. The Preparatory Committee of the KDP, led by Mahmud Uthman, who broke with Barzani following the defeat, estimated that the Kurdish movement's budget reached 48 million Iraqi dinars (more than $100 million) between 1970 and 1975. See *Taqyim,* p. 63.

147. *Ibid.,* pp. 34–38.

148. *Ibid.,* pp. 50–51. Also interview with pro-Jalal Talibani Kurdish leader, March 1976.

149. *The Guardian,* October 24, 1975.

150. *Ibid.,* and interviews with Talibani and Pishdari, November 1976.

151. *The Times,* May 1, 1975.

152. *The Guardian,* October 24, 1975.

153. Interviews with Pishdari, Haydar, and Talibani, November 1976.

154. *The Times,* November 28, 1975.

155. *The Guardian,* October 24, 1975.

156. Interview with Mukarram Talibani, November 1976.

157. Interview with a high-ranking U.S. State Department official, March 15, 1977.

158. Interview with Mukarram Talibani, November 1976.

159. Pishdari estimated them at 40,000; Talibani said there were around 50,000 to 70,000, while anti-government Kurds estimated the number to be close to 150,000 persons.

160. Interviews with Talibani and Pishdari, November 1976, and with Mustafa al-Barzani, September 28, 1976.

161. *The Times,* July 27, 1976.

162. *Ibid.*

163. Memorandum to the United Nations on the situation of the Kurdish people in Kurdistan, Patriotic Union of Kurdistan, March 1977, p. 7.

164. Interview with Pishdari, November 1976.

165. *Ibid.* Also, interview with Hashim Aqrawi, April 1979. See also *The Economist* (London), November 26, 1976.

166. *Iraq Today,* March 16–31, 1979, p. 13.

167. *Ibid.*

168. Interview with Ahmad abd al-Qadir and Muhammad Amin, Chairmen of the Executive Council and Legislative Council for Kurdistan, April 1979.

169. *The Guardian,* February 4, 1976.

170. See *Country Reports on Human Rights Practices for 1979,* U.S. State Department Report submitted to Congressional Committees on February 4, 1980, p. 750.

171. *Al-Ittihad,* July 22, 1978.

172. *International Herald Tribune,* March 24, 1976.

173. See *The Economist,* November 26, 1976; Arnold Hollinger, *Swiss Review of World Affairs,* July 1975; *The Observer,* April 6, 1975; *The Times,* November 28, 1975; *New York Times,* March 26, 1975.

174. *The Voice* (London), April 15, 1979.

175. *Iraq Today,* March 1–15, 1979, p. 15.

176. *Al-Jumhuriyya,* March 3, 1977.

177. *Iraq Today* (Baghdad), March 1–15, 1978, p. 5.

178. Interviews with Ahmad Abd al-Qadir and Muhammad Ali-Amin; See also *Alif-Ba,* May 2, 1979.

179. Interviews with Ahmad Abd al-Qadir and Muhammad Ali-Amin.

180. Interview with Ministry of Planning official, April 1979.

181. *Iraq Today,*

182. Iraqi News Agency, February 16, 1980.

183. *Washington Star,* April 18, 1978.

184. *Washington Post,* March 3, 1979.

185. *Al-Ghad* (London), November 1978.

186. Interview with a pro-Jalal Talibani Kurdish leader, March 1976.

187. *Christian Science Monitor,* February 9, 1976.

188. Interview with Mustafa al-Barzani, September 28, 1976.

189. Interview with Professor Kamal Majid, an independent Kurdish figure, published in *Al-Ghad,* June 1978, pp. 22–23.

190. Interview with pro-Jalal Talibani Kurdish leader, March 1976. See also *Ila al-Amam* (Beirut), January 6, 1980.

191. Interview with Mustafa al-Barzani, September 28, 1976.

192. *Al-Sharara,* September 1976.

193. *Al-Liwa* (Beirut), December 3, 1978.

194. The writer's interviews with Baathist leaders in the Kurdish region, April 1979.

195. *Al-Ittihad* (Abd Dhabi), August 1, 1979.

196. FBIS, May 7, 1980.

197. *Ibid.,* May 30, 1980.

198. *Le Monde* October 20, 1980.

199. See FBIS, May 30, 1980 and June 4, 1980.

200. See *ibid.,* January 2, 1980; February 7, 1980; March 11, 1980; May 7, 1980; and October 23, 1980.

201. See *Middle East International,* August 3, 1979, and *Washington Post,* July 31, 1979.

202. *Al-Thawra,* July 21, 1980.

203. Foreign Broadcast Information Service, May 30, 1980. See also *The Guardian,* December 5, 1979.

204. *Al-Hawadith,* September 19, 1980.

205. *The Guardian,* December 5, 1979.

## CONCLUSION

1. Interview with Zayd Haydar, November 1976.

2. *Le Monde,* September 14, 1976, quoted in al-Hajj, *L'Irak Nouveau,* pp. 165–66.

3. *Iraq Today,* July 15, 1976, p. 7.

4. *Al-Thawra Al-Arabiyya* (4): 23.

5. *Al-Thawra,* March 23, 1979, and *Al-Nahar,* September 3, 1979.

6. One of the aftermaths of the election for the National Assembly was the defeat of Minister of State Aziz Aqrawi, who subsequently defected to Syria and is believed to have joined Jalal Talibani forces.

7. After the collapse of the Shah's regime, Kissinger explained the decision to back the Shah as a response to the growing Soviet influence in Iraq and the need to fill the "vacuum" created by British withdrawal from the Gulf region. He states that "Iran seemed to us a factor of extraordinary importance at the time. Then in 1973, during the Middle East war, Iran was the only country that did not join the oil embargo, that continued to supply our friends with oil and that did not permit overflights of Soviet airplanes. And all these elements colored our perceptions." See "Lesson of Iran" in *Washington Post Parade Magazine,* May 25, 1980, p. 16.

8. Cited in Kutschera, *Le Mouvement,* p. 354.

# index

**THE KURDISH QUESTION IN IRAQ**

was composed in 10-point Compugraphic Times Roman and leaded two points
by Metricomp Studio,
with display type in Typositor Thor by Partners Composition;
printed on 55-pound acid-free Glatfelter Offset Vellum,
Smythe-sewn and bound over boards in Joanna Arrestox C,
by Maple-Vail Book Manufacturing Group, Inc.;
and published by

SYRACUSE UNIVERSITY PRESS
SYRACUSE, NEW YORK 13210